A Field Guide to the
WILDLIFE OF THE
FALKLAND ISLANDS
AND SOUTH GEORGIA

A Field Guide to the

WILDLIFE OF THE FALKLAND ISLANDS

AND SOUTH GEORGIA

Written and illustrated
by Ian J. Strange

HarperCollins*Publishers*

HarperCollins*Publishers*
London · Glasgow · Sydney · Auckland
Toronto · Johannesburg

For Maria
and in memory of Crispin Fisher

First published 1992

ISBN 0-00-219839-8

© Ian J. Strange 1992

Printed and Bound by Butler and Tanner Ltd., Frome

Contents

5

Illustrations

Foreword

During a visit to the South Atlantic in 1990, I was fortunate enough to see for myself something of the spectacular wildlife of these remote but very beautiful islands, and to meet Ian Strange, who, having devoted more than a quarter of a century to the study of the flora and fauna of the Falkland Islands, has established himself as perhaps the leading authority on the natural history of this archipelago.

The islands have suffered more than their share of past depredation, from uncontrolled burning and grazing to the commercial exploitation of seals, sea lions and penguins, and as an active conservationist and owner of one of the largest private nature reserves in the islands, Mr Strange has done a great deal to promote an awareness of the sensitivity of the environment and of the need to safeguard it from similar excesses in the future. His advice, too, has enabled British Forces in the islands to ensure that disturbance caused to the wildlife by the increased level of military activity in the area since 1982 has been kept to a minimum.

Although the conflict brought South Georgia and the Falkland Islands briefly to the centre of the international stage, they remain one of the few unspoiled areas of the world in which the wildlife is still at ease with man. It is only by improving our knowledge and awareness of the finely balanced ecosystem of the islands that we can ensure their unique character is preserved, and this field guide makes an important contribution to the advancement of that understanding. I commend it to all those who share an interest in the islands and to visitors alike.

The Rt. Hon. Tom King M.P.

Preface

When I first set eyes on the Falkland Islands, on Christmas Eve, 1959, I instinctively knew that I had found a very special part of this earth and that I was going to make it my home. I had a passion for nature and wilderness and the islands were to develop that even more, for nature here is quite unique. It is also very vulnerable and I was very concerned that if false moves were made irrevocable problems could result. Therefore I decided to dedicate my time to learning as much as I could about the islands' environment and their nature and to make plans for conserving at least a small part of that life.

We often hear from our critics that the Falkland Islands are behind the times. In my view, as a conservationist, this gave the islands a tremendous advantage: with a little forethought and planning, could we not sidestep the mistakes made elsewhere? I also felt that, although we have a strong moral obligation to conserve, if conservation was to work in these islands, it had in part to be commercially viable. Around these basic concepts, I embarked on a modest attempt at building up some form of conservation plan for the islands. Each aspect of my work as a field naturalist, wildlife artist, stamp designer and author plays its part in supporting this plan and I hope this field guide will do the same.

One of my most ambitious projects was centred around my belief that for conservation to be effective it had to be financially self-supporting and that one way in which this could be achieved was through wildlife tourism. In 1972, with the backing of a partner and ally, Roddy Napier, a project was started with the purchase of New Island (later to be divided as New Island North and New Island South), which lies in the extreme south west corner of the archipelago and is one of the most scenic areas and one of the best wildlife sites in the Falklands. The project which developed was a practical demonstration of how specialised wildlife tourism had potential for the islands as a whole and, more importantly, illustrated that it could also assist conservation: the simple concept being that wildlife tourism placed new values on wildlife.

New Island became a base for studies in the management and control of wildlife tourism and a site for scientific studies. Much of the information, inspiration and support for this field guide is the direct result of the New Island project and its aims. It is therefore fitting that this book should be the platform for announcing the establishment of the New Island Conservation Trust and affiliated organisation in the USA, the New Island Wildlife Conservation Foundation. Both organisations have as their aim the continuation of my original project and the preservation in perpetuity of New Island South, owned by the author, as a wildlife reserve.

I. J. Strange, Falkland Islands

Acknowledgements

So closely linked is the New Island Project to this field guide, it would be incorrect not to acknowledge in these pages those who have given so much support and encouragement to both. I owe thanks to a great number, but one of my greatest debts, aside from that to my wife Maria, is to Bill and Margaret Betchart, of Betchart Expeditions Inc., Cupertino, California, who through their interest in conservation were so keen to sponsor this book and assisted greatly in the practicalities of writing the manuscript. Also, for their very special support, I owe thanks to Barbara and Don Carlson, Norm Singer, Edgar Wadley, Rob Woolford, Wilf Vevers, Mrs Nan West, Mrs Gansser, Diane Prescott and Sheila Pankhurst.

For supporting the actual publication I am most grateful to the Ministry of Defence. Their view that this work would educate and encourage members of H.M. Forces stationed in these islands to take interest in and help preserve this delicate environment, is in itself a very valuable contribution to conservation. I am especially indebted to General Sir Peter de la Billiere, to The Rt. Hon. Michael Heseltine M.P., to the late Crispin Fisher of Collins Publishers who supported the project in its early stages and last but not least to Richard Fitter who persuaded me to present my idea of a field guide to Collins.

A very large number of individuals both in the Falkland Islands and elsewhere have contributed in varying ways to my work generally and therefore in turn to this book. To name all would be outside the scope of these pages, however I do feel I owe a special debt to a number who over the years have repeatedly sent information or given assistance. The following islanders are no longer with us but are remembered: Tom Aldridge, Cecil Bertrand, Ian Campbell, Griff Evans, Fred Newman, Muzzie Napier, Ted Robson, Jack Sollis, Mr and Mrs George Short, Frank Smith and George Stewart.

The late Dr. Robert Cushman Murphy is also remembered with affection, for he, along with Dr. Dean Amadon, gave me a great deal of encouragement during my early years in the islands. The same gratitude is extended to Dr. George Lindsay and Dr. Robert Orr of the California Academy of Sciences and to the late Dr. F. C. Fraser of the British Museum of Natural History.

Special thanks also go to the following: Eddie Andersen, Kitty Bertrand, Sturdee Betts, Sally and Tim Blake, Tony Blake, Nigel Bonner, Stuart Booth, Bill Bourne, John Croxall, Annie and Tony Chater, Albert Davis, Tony Felton, Bob Ferguson, Ronnie Larsen, Dick Laws, Sydney Miller, Rob McGill, David, Shona, Bobby and Janet McLeod, Roddy Napier, David and Bill Pole Evans, Robin Pitaluga, Peter Prince, John Reid, Osmond Smith, Kate Thompson, Dan Hale, John Reid and Sally Poncet.

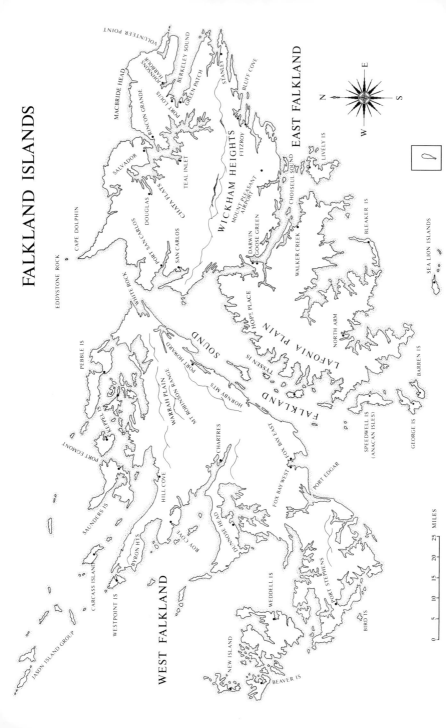

Introduction

General notes on the use of the guide

In this field guide the main emphasis is on the birds and mammals found in and about the Falkland Island Archipelago, although the work is also designed to assist identification of species found in South Georgia and extended to cover certain fish, invertebrates and plants, largely selected for their relation to birds and mammals.

The introductory section places considerable emphasis on the inter-relationship between species and the environment and in particular the marine environment and the important part it plays in the general ecology of the islands' fauna and flora. Habitats are discussed in some detail, not only as a feature of the species' ecology, but also as an aid to the identification of different animals and plants and where they may be seen. In addition the Falkland climate is described, largely in the context of the influence it has on the distribution of certain birds in the islands and on the introduction of vagrant species from the continent of South America.

As inhabitants of a relatively small and vulnerable archipelago, Falkland species are very susceptible to the impact of human exploitation and a section on the history of depredation identifies some of the changes that have taken place. A section on conservation demonstrates what is being done to prevent further damaging changes.

The field guide section is divided into five separate parts, covering birds, mammals, fish, invertebrates and plants. The bird and mammal sections open with a checklist and all divisions are then made up of individual species texts and illustrated with integrated line drawings and a colour plate section, cross referenced to the text, at the centre of the guide. Some mammals and invertebrates are also illustrated in four black and white plates which follow the colour section.

Throughout the guide the species are named as follows: where there are several common names used for a single species, the more commonly used or logically acceptable name taken from the scientific name is given first. Scientific names are based on the latest revisionary work. In the case of more recently recorded breeding species, for example the Royal Penguin, the sub-specific name is taken, although taxonomists may at some stage define the Falkland population as distinct from that of Macquarie Island.

Each species entry includes identification notes. Where size is important for identification, comparisons are drawn with a familiar species and measurements given in both metric and imperial for the length and standing height of the bird or animal. Most Falkland Island species of bird and seal can be identified by sound alone; however, as the phonetic alphabet can be variously interpreted and thus misleading, voice is described only where there can be no mistake.

The bird section describes all birds known to have occurred in the Falkland Islands as regular breeders and annual visitors, together with some of the more common vagrants. The checklist includes all species known to have occurred in the islands as breeders, annual visitors and vagrants and is ordered accordingly. South Georgia breeding species are listed separately. Following an introduction to the topography of a typical species, a total 151 species are individually described.

The section on mammals opens with the topography of a typical cetacean and goes on to include all known breeding species, land and marine, introduced and indigenous. For seals and whales the species list is extended to cover those found in South Georgia and the Antarctic Peninsula, all of which are possible vagrants to the Falkland Islands.

The fish and invertebrates included in their respective sections are largely listed on the strength of their being important prey of birds and mammals. Although a small number of the more unusual fish recorded in Falkland waters are also included and the invertebrate section also covers the more common marine forms and the main forms of insect life, with notes on some spiders.

Finally, the plant life section includes marine algae (seaweeds and kelps), vascular flora, ferns and flowering plants. There are some 164 species of flowering plant and vascular cryptogam native to the Falkland Islands and a further 92 introduced or alien species. For this guide, 45 species have been selected either for their importance as habitat plants or, in the case of some berried shrubs (for example, Diddle-dee and Teaberry), as vital feed sources for certain species of goose and finch. A number of the more typical and interesting plant forms are also described. The more commonly found marine algae which form important feeding habitats or, as in the case of some seaweeds, are grazed by birds such as the Kelp Goose are covered.

This section opens with a diagrammatic representation of a Tussock Grass plant as an ecosystem, with particular reference to the importance of the plant as a nesting site for different species of birds. Diagrams are given of a typical tussock island and of a mainland area showing the position of the major habitat forms and plant associations.

Information on feeding, breeding, distribution and habitat is based on the author's own observations and studies over a number of years and perhaps one of the most significant points that has arisen from this work is that there are more exceptions than there are rules in these particular aspects of avian and mammalian ecology. In formulating such information on each species an *average* has been attempted, but the observer should always be prepared for the exception.

Notes on codes and symbols in the text

The species headings may be followed by certain symbols. Where a figure in metres is shown alongside the $\oplus$ symbol, observers are reminded that, during the breeding months given in the text, the species are more vulnerable to disturbance and breeding sites should be avoided altogether or at least by the distance quoted. In the case of the $+$ symbol, observers are reminded that it is preferable to keep a low profile and the use of binoculars is recommended for the observation of species. However, care should be taken at all times towards all species.

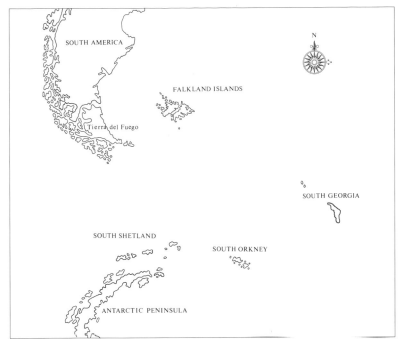

Fig. 1 The Falkland Islands and South Georgia in relation to South America and the Antarctic peninsula

Geography

The Falkland Islands, an archipelago composed of some 420 islands, are situated in the South Atlantic between latitudes 51° and 53° south and longitudes 57° and 62° west. In relation to South America, they lie approximately 280 miles (450 km) north-east of Tierra del Fuego and about 373 miles (600 km) due east of Patagonia. South Georgia lies about 900 miles (1450 km) to the east, and the nearest point of the Antarctic Peninsula is approximately 745 miles (1200 km) away.

In extent the archipelago covers a distance of around 160 miles (257 km) from west to east and approximately 85 miles (136 km) from north to south. The total land area is over 4700 square miles, approximately 12,000 square km. Much of the islands' land mass is made up of two main islands, East Falkland and West Falkland, which are separated by the Falkland Sound.

The islands owe their existence to the folding movements of sedimentary rocks in the Palaeozoic and Mesozoic eras. This folding gave rise to three principal mountain ranges: the Wickham Heights, which forms a slightly curved range from east to west on the northern section of East Falkland and includes Mount Usborne, the highest elevation in the islands, rising to 2312 ft (705 m); the Byron Heights on West Falkland which extends across the northern limits on an east-west axis; and the Hornby Mountains, also on West Falkland, which run almost at right angles to the other two. Mount Adam, part of the Hornby Range, is the second highest elevation, reaching 2297 ft (700 m) . The Wickham Heights comprise the more formidable terrain, much of the region being broken by high standing rocky ridges and rock debris, while on West Falkland the hill ranges are predominantly dome shaped.

West Falkland and the adjacent islands, together with the northern section of East Falkland, are predominantly composed of Palaeozoic sedimentary rocks, quartzites, sandstones and shales. The southern section of East Falkland, known as Lafonia, and its adjacent islands are composed of younger Mesozoic rocks, represented by sandstones and mudstones. Lafonia is the only large area which qualifies as a plain, a gently rolling landscape which rarely rises more than 196 ft (60 m) above sea level.

Although there is no evidence that the Falkland Islands supported permanent glaciers, those areas rising over 2000 ft (600 m) show evidence of localised glaciation and ice dome formation. In the region of Mount Usborne on East Falkland and of Mount Adam, Mount Robinson and Mount Maria on West Falkland, pronounced corries, or hollows, with small glacial lakes are evident, indicating glacial action, while other areas of the islands appear to have experienced only peri-glacial conditions.

A period of freeze-thaw weathering in peri-glacial or sub-glacial conditions is believed to have resulted in the formation of 'stone runs', the most controversial feature in the geology of the islands. These accumulations of rock debris, which may be several miles in extent, are made up of huge blocks of stone, and generally lead from the remnants of peaks. What is not fully understood is how the rock debris was transported to form these rivers of stone. The generally accepted theory is that mud, derived from the breaking down of the softer rocks, acted as a vehicle for the transport of the harder blocks of quartzite through a process known as solifluction (the movement of wet soil or mud down a slope). There are variations to this theory: one is that as ice domes and glaciers receded on the higher elevations, the higher rock peaks or towers would have been gradually exposed, protruding out of a mantle of ice which, like a cape, would have surrounded the shoulders and slopes of the mountains. With the freeze-thaw conditions, the process of breaking down the rocky peaks would have begun and solifluction followed, but on the surface of an ice sheet. In this way rock debris could have been transported over a much larger area until, as the underlying ice sheet melted, the debris settled to form the stone runs where we find them today.

The coastlines of the Falklands are deeply indented, forming many sheltered harbours. Large sandy beaches are a common feature, and numbers of 'barrier' beaches cut off lagoons and lakes which were formerly seaways. Estuaries are common, but generally not extensive having been formed by the islands' relatively small rivers. Much of the coastline surrounding the southern section of East Falkland and some of the inland seaways, such as Port Salvador, to the north of this island, are low-lying and rocky but with gently sloping shorelines. Elsewhere on this island the coast is more formidable, featuring rocky headlands, low cliffs and boulder beaches. On West Falkland, the coastlines to the south, south-west and north-west are dominated by rugged cliffs which, in parts, rise vertically to some 700 ft (213 m). On those coasts with a south-west aspect, stacks and bluffs are a feature.

There are several thousand ponds and lakes in the Falkland Islands. The majority are shallow, appearing to have formed in the eroded or subsided areas of peat which dominate the surface soils of the islands.

Climate

The Falklands have a generally cool, oceanic climate, dominated by westerly winds, a high percentage from the north west. Lying on the northern edge of the depression belt which passes through the Drake Passage, the islands experience fairly continuous variations in weather, caused by the air masses and fronts which pass across. Although modified by the nearly 250 miles (400 km) of relatively cold water that separate the islands from the South American mainland, they experience some of the warming and drying effects of this continent. The dominant westerly winds play a significant part in the introduction of vagrant species to the islands and in several instances these arrivals have coincided with periods of exceptional winds.

The Falklands climate has a narrow temperature range. At Stanley, on the extreme east, the mean monthly temperature during the summer months of January and February is 10°C, (although significantly higher on the west side of the islands) and 7°C during the winter months of June and July. The average wind speed is about 16 knots, long periods of calm being unusual except in the winter months.

Fog is comparatively rare, generally occurring only on hills and in some coastal areas. Because the islands' weather is dominated by westerlies there is a noticeable difference between conditions on the western side of the archipelago and those in the east. Although there are few days when the entire archipelago is cloudless, such conditions are not uncommon on islands in the extreme west, and as a result sunshine levels are generally higher and precipitation lower in these areas.

Stanley and Port Howard (West Falkland) are two of the wetter places in the islands, with an annual precipitation of about 25 in (630 mm) and 26 in (650 mm) respectively. West Point Island, lying to the north west of West Falkland, has an annual rainfall of 17 in (431 mm), and there is evidence that some islands lying further west and to the south west have even lower levels. Vegetation, especially Tussock Grass, growing in such areas does not exhibit the vigour of plants growing in areas of higher rainfall and this modifies the tussock community as a habitat for certain species.

Contrary to general belief, accumulations of snow are rare and although statistics show that snow flurries can occur in many months of the year, they are generally brief and localised. Although long term weather records only exist for Stanley, local variations in weather and climate do exist with quite substantial differences between one area and another. Such variations may influence those

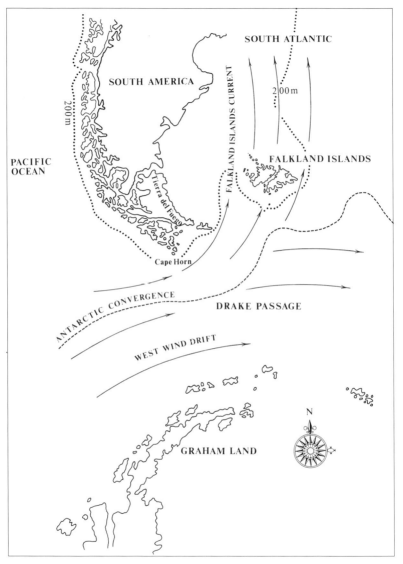

Fig. 2 The Falkland Current

species which perform local migrations, or those which migrate out of the archipelago in some winters but remain in others.

Marine environment

The Falklands lie almost on the edge of an extension of the Patagonian Continental Shelf. Between 60 and 110 miles (96 and 177 km) to the north of the islands lies the 656 ft (200 m) deep contour which denotes the edge of this shelf. To the east, the shelf edge lies approximately 10–20 miles (16–32 km) from the coast and to the south 20–30 miles (32–48 km) away. A feature of continental shelves generally, and of this one in particular, are their richness in demersal and pelagic species of fish and other marine life.

The Falkland Islands provide breeding grounds for large numbers of birds and mammals, but it is upon this rich marine resource and its ready availability that they ultimately depend for survival. A particularly important factor affecting the availability of this food is the Falkland Current, a current which owes its existence to larger circumpolar zonal movements of water further south.

The southernmost parts of the Atlantic, Indian and Pacific oceans form a continuous circumpolar movement around Antarctica, from west to east. For most of its course this vast current (known as the West Wind Drift) is unrestricted in its movement. However, between the tip of South America and Antarctica's Graham Land Peninsula, the current's great width is restricted, its waters being forced through the Drake Passage, a comparatively narrow channel about 650 miles (1050 km) wide. After passing through this passage, the drift again widens greatly, its northern tip forming the Cape Horn Current. Rounding the tip of the South American Continent it divides: the larger branch passes eastwards to South Georgia and the smaller loops northwards to form the Falkland Current.

The Falkland Current is strongest along the outer edge of the Patagonian coastal shelf on which the archipelago is situated, with a general flow northwards of some two knots. When it reaches the islands the flow is split, one stream going to the west of the group and the other to the east. The archipelago itself, with its many offshore islands, submerged ridges and plateaux, creates a barrier to the current. The effect is a modified upwelling as the water is forced up and over underwater ridges, or squeezed between the many passes to form tide rips. This movement is particularly noticeable in the north west where the Jason Island group protrudes out into the main flow of the current, producing tide races of considerable strength. Birds are noticeably prolific in these areas, as marine life is effectively funnelled to the surface and becomes more readily available as feed.

Much has yet to be learnt about the precise movements and effects of the Falkland Current around and about the archipelago, although fisheries research is revealing interesting comparisons with what is known about the general movement of some bird and animal life. Research shows that there is a particularly rich zone of marine life to the north of the islands. Large catches of squid, *Illex argentinus* and *Martialia hyadesi* species, on which some penguins, albatross and Fur Seal feed, are being found in this area at a time which corresponds with the late breeding season of some birds and mammals (when species require maximum food intake), or, in other cases, with the beginning of a general migration northwards.

The presence of this rich zone suggests an upwelling of water, rich in phosphates, on the edge of the continental shelf to the east side of the islands. With the Falkland Current's northerly set, such an upwelling, deflected by the islands' land mass, may then curve back on the islands' northern side. This could result in a concentration of diatoms in an area of comparatively still water, and consequently in a build up of food chains of importance to the squid.

To the southeast of the Falkland group lies Beauchêne Island, the most remote of the offshore islands and the site of one of the largest concentrations of breeding seabirds. The island is situated almost on the edge of the 656 ft (200 m) deep contour, close to a shallow plateau exceptionally rich in marine life, and in particular in the species of squid *Loligo gahi*. The huge seabird population owes its existence to this rich feeding ground, which must in turn be supported by lower food chains and a rich supply of nutrients from some upwelling.

The Falklands lie in a zone of Subantarctic Surface Water with a colder zone of Antarctic Surface Water just south of the islands. The low average temperature of the Antarctic Surface Water ($1-2°C$ in winter and $3-5°C$ in summer) is due to the melting of Antarctic ice. This meltwater also lowers the salinity of the water in this zone, allowing it to float on the surface of an intermediate layer of water with a higher salinity. The intermediate layer has a southerly flow towards the Antarctic continent, while the surface layer generally moves northwards. At its northern extent the Antarctic Surface Water meets and sinks below the warmer Subantarctic Surface Water. The area at which this sinking occurs is known as the Antarctic Convergence, one of the most striking oceanic features in the world, and also one of immense ecological importance. Although the Subantarctic waters are relatively rich in marine life, they do not have the mineral-rich and therefore highly fertile qualities of the Antarctic Surface Waters. The exceptionally rich marine resource close to Beauchêne Island may well denote an area where the convergence occurs, perhaps only as a narrow extension of its main front but sufficient to influence that area and render it highly fertile.

Species of euphausiaceans, collectively known as 'krill', are probably the most important food source for southern species of seabird and for marine mammals. Certain species of euphausiaceans are restricted to either the Subantarctic or Antarctic water zones, as are some species of birds. On Beauchêne Island there is a large breeding population of Fairy Prions which are not found elsewhere in the archipelago, which leads to the interesting possibility that there may be some relationship between the proximity of the Antarctic Surface Water zone, and its euphausiacean population, to this island and the isolated presence of these species on it.

Studies of Rockhopper Penguins found that at a certain point in their breeding season, the food they brought ashore changed from euphausiaceans to squid. This change was often quite dramatic and occurred at the same time each season. Similar food changes were also noted in the feeding patterns of Gentoo Penguins and Fur Seal. It is possible that both birds and seals are selective feeders, taking specific forms of marine life, studies of Rockhopper Penguins during the early stages of chick feeding seemed to indicate that this was the case. However, there is more evidence to support the theory that different forms of feed move into specific zones at different times of year and that the positioning of breeding sites, especially those of penguins, are related to these zones or 'food fields'. The shallow shoal or plateau off Beauchêne Island is one example.

During the latter part of the breeding season, when Rockhopper Penguin chicks are being fed daily by both parents, adults are restricted in the distance they may travel for food. Observations revealed that they were rarely away from their colonies for more than eight hours. Often birds were observed heading out to sea in the same direction, both observations suggesting that specific areas are used for foraging. In the Falkland Islands there are some 33 colonies of Rockhopper Penguin, all situated on the western and eastern perimeters of the archipelago, but widely distributed. These same colonies have been in use for thousands of years (see *Rockhopper: Species Account*) and this is a further indication that feeding zone and breeding ground may be related. A similar pattern is thought to exist for the Falkland Fur Seal, for their breeding sites have also remained the same for many thousands of years.

A striking feature of the Falkland Islands sublittorals is the kelp beds. Kelps are found growing in two main zones, an offshore zone and the sublittoral fringe. In the first, Giant Kelp may grow in depths of between 13–198 ft (4–30 m) and extend in beds over several hundred square metres out from the coast. The sublittoral fringe zone lies below the extreme low water level where two other large forms of kelp, *Durvillea antarctica* and Tree Kelp, are generally found growing. Beds of these two species may extend along a coast for several miles, depending on the type of shoreline, but rarely extend out more than 65 or 98 ft (20 or 30 m). Those plants growing on the upper fringe tend to become exposed in part at low tide.

In the middle and lower shore zones, in an intertidal area, with upper boundaries set by the average high tide level and lower by extreme low water levels, another important group of seaweeds and kelps is found growing. Two of these, Sea Lettuce *Ulva* sp., a green form of seaweed, and *Iridea* sp., a small brown seaweed, form meadows on which Kelp Geese graze. This intertidal area, the sublittoral fringe and offshore zones, are rich in marine life and form very important feeding zones for a number of bird species and some mammals.

Land environment and habitats

A wide diversity of habitats exists in different areas of the archipelago. Variations may be due to the influence of climatic conditions, the geological make-up and changes wrought in habitat vegetation by stocking the islands with ruminants. This last situation is particularly evident on the two main islands, East Falkland and West Falkland, and on other larger offshore islands which have been settled and used for sheep ranching.

Of particular note is the difference between these larger islands and those smaller offshore islands, which are largely untouched by the sheep farming industry and therefore still covered with Tussock Grass. These tussock islands present a unique habitat of immense importance to many species and accordingly are described separately from the main islands below.

The main islands

In general the soils covering the main islands are rather cold and acidic, tending towards a very peaty nature and low fertility. These peat soils vary from shallow, rather hard, dry forms overlying quartzite ridges, to soft black humus-type peat in lower, damper regions. The two types are often referred to as hard and soft 'camp', a corruption of *campo,* the Spanish word for 'countryside'. Accumulations of peat are widespread and vary from a few centimetres to several metres in depth, depending on rainfall and local drainage. However, unlike other parts of the world there are no large areas of 'blanket' or 'bog' peat, as accumulations are frequently interposed with other ground cover. On higher elevations of 1640 ft (500 m) or more, peat layers may give way to stony or clay soils supporting *feldmark* formations, cushion forming plants, while peat accumulations on lower slopes are frequently interspersed with stone runs. In the lower valleys and in many coastal areas, peat accumulations are replaced by peaty soils of higher fertility, supporting 'greens', areas of fine grasses and sedges.

Large areas of the two main islands are covered by oceanic heath formations. On soils with poor drainage, these are dominated by White Grass (the plain of Lafonia is typical of this formation), and on the drier, better drained soils, by dwarf shrubs. Diddle-dee is the most common, but Mountain Berry and Christmas Bush are also widespread. However, within these two formations a complex variety of other plants may appear, depending on the composition of the subsoil and topographical conditions. In the moister areas of White Grass heath, Brown Swamp Rush forms almost pure stands which are used by a variety of ground nesting birds. Within the dwarf shrub heath, Tall Fern and the small fern *Blechnum penna marina* may form pure communities or be co-dominant with Diddle-dee, growing on well drained slopes or in soils overlying stone runs. These 'fern beds', form another nesting habitat for some ground nesting species, especially in coastal areas.

In general terms the predominant oceanic heath formations which cover the higher elevations in the interior regions of the main islands support little fauna, especially birds. However, where this heath meets or integrates with other formations and habitats there is a noticeable increase in bird life.

The many streams that cross the heath lowlands at the base of small valleys are often bordered by rich green swards dominated by the small rush *Juncus scheuzerioides,* annual grasses and Cinnamon Grass. These green valleys, which are often quite narrow, form a very small percentage of the total heath area. However, their sheltered greens attract a number of species, in particular Upland and Ruddy-headed Geese, which play an important part in the build-up of such areas by grazing and continuous manuring with their droppings. Before the introduction of stock, many of these valleys supported Fachine Bush, one of the two shrubs native to the Falklands. Today, extensive thickets of this species, which grows

I   Interior region of main island showing stone run or river of stone. These accumulations of rock debris, often several miles in extent, originate from one time peaks. Today these peaks exist as quartzite ridges shown here on the background hills.

II   Typical settlement habitat. The establishment of wind-breaks, made up of introduced species such as Gorse, coniferous trees and many other shrubs and plants planted around settlements, has created a niche for many species of bird.

III Offshore tussock island with dense Tussock Grass cover shown in the background. In the foreground the grass is 'open' – of low to medium height – and forms a habitat for species of gull, tern and, in this example, for Giant Petrels.

IV A coastal fringe of Tussock Grass pushed back by a colony of Black-browed Albatross and Rockhopper Penguins. The living crown of the grass and the dead leaf skirt has been reduced by the action of the birds, revealing the fibrous pedestal. The Striated Caracara has a nest to the right.

between 3 ft 2 in and 6 ft 4 in (1 and 2 m) high, are rare, but where it does survive, populations of passerine birds are often noticeably higher. Where the lowland valleys open onto low-lying coasts, the greens are generally more extensive and frequently dotted with shallow freshwater ponds. Although ponds are common to most areas, coastal ponds are generally more fertile, more prolific in aquatic vegetation and attract large numbers of duck and grebe.

Oceanic heath, with its main plant associations, is still dominant in these areas, although extensive stands of Brown Swamp Rush, Tall Rush and the small rush *Juncus scheuzerioides* frequently form a transition point between the heath and these coastal greens. Most low-lying coastal greens are associated with extensive sandy areas, shingle or sand beaches. Except for bunches of Sea Cabbage and the *Juncus scheuzerioides* rush, vegetation is often sparse. However, such areas found in association with coastal greens are the most prolific in birds on the main islands. Such areas are influenced greatly by the marine environment. Marine algae, in particular the larger kelps, thrown ashore by high seas, accumulate to form extensive mats of decaying vegetation which become habitats for amphipods and insect life on which several species of bird feed. By direct and indirect means, nutrients from this vegetation are carried ashore. Gentoo and Magellan Penguins, which frequently inhabit these low lying coastal areas, supply rich nutrients in the form of excreta. This is also true, although to a lesser extent, of gulls, terns, oystercatchers and some marine duck which feed at sea, but breed in these areas.

Before the introduction of stock to the main islands, Tussock Grass was an important habitat formation on the coasts (see *History of depredation*). If it is to flourish, the grass requires highly fertile soils and a moist, salt-laden air environment. Therefore the most extensive communities existed on exposed points and in low coastal areas where bird and animal life was more abundant. Today these areas are generally characterised by eroded coast lines, by coastal heath meadows dotted with small hillocks marking former tussock pedestals, and by coastal greens. Wildlife is still relatively prolific in these highly fertile coastal green areas and in some areas species such as the Magellan Penguin, which used tussock as a nesting habitat, have adapted to a new habitat of open heath or stands of rush. However, one has only to compare these areas with offshore tussock islands to appreciate how many species and populations have been greatly affected on the main islands by the loss of this giant grass.

Offshore tussock islands

There are some 272 islands, islets and stacks which hold some form of Tussock Grass community (*Tussock Island Survey,* Strange 1987). These vary in size from as little as 0·5 to 800 acres (0·2 to 324 hectares). Islands may lie less than 323 ft (100 m) off a mainland coast while Beauchêne Island, the most remote outlier, lies almost 50 miles (80 km) from the nearest mainland shore. Most offshore islands have similar geological characteristics to those mainland areas lying closest to them and they may also exhibit the same variations and types of coast (sand, shingle, boulder and rocky beaches, or sheer cliff), although generally speaking such features are likely to be more pronounced. However, in other respects these islands present a marked difference to the mainlands, the most outstanding feature being the dominant vegetative cover of Tussock Grass. As its common name suggests, the plant forms a tussock, the base of which is a fibrous pedestal from which a mass of green leaf is produced. Individual leaves may grow 6 ft 6 in (2 m) in length, forming a canopy above the pedestal, while the whole plant may grow over 10 ft (3 m) in height. Individual plants, generally spaced some 2 ft – 3 ft 2 in (60 cm – 1 m) apart, form stands which may entirely cover an island with an almost impenetrable growth.

The Tussock Grass habitat offers an ideal nesting habitat for a variety of birds, early voyagers to the islands referred to it as Penguin Grass. It is also rich in invertebrate fauna, and thus provides a feeding niche for insect-eating birds, while tussock panicles are eaten by seed-eating species such as Siskins and Black-throated Finches. Of the 62 or so regular breeding bird species in the Falklands, 46 use tussock either as a nesting or feeding habitat. Of the three breeding species of seal found in the islands, two commonly use the tussock environment as a shelter for breeding or as a hauling-up ground.

Tussock thrives in a maritime environment where it is subjected to sea spray and a moisture-laden atmosphere with a high salt content. Whether the plant benefits nutritionally in a direct manner from this salt-laden air is not clear, but its tolerance to such an environment plays an important part in reducing competition from other plants. In old, well-established tussock communities, where large plants over 10 ft (3 m) high produce a dense canopy, often excluding light from the ground, the ground flora is almost non-existent; thus a Tussock Grass community may be considered monospecific. The area between the individual pedestals is covered instead with dead leaf litter from the tussock skirts.

Alongside tolerance to salt, other factors play an important part in the development of a tussock community. The plants receive nutrients directly from the excrement of birds passing through the stands and from the seepage from nesting sites on the ground. Ground-burrowing species, such as petrels, shearwaters and Magellan Penguins, nesting in tussock stands, deposit excrement straight into the pedestals of the plants. Seal excrement also supplies nutrients.

On some sites, where large seabird colonies are annexed to, but not always integrated with tussock communities, the stands receive amounts of volatilised nitrogen from these colonies. This is particularly evident when the guano-rich ground of a colony, dampened by precipitation or sea spray, is warmed by the sun. In such conditions, volatilised nitrogenous compounds rise as visible vapour and in this form nutrients may be dispersed over considerable areas, explaining the vigorous growth of tussock on some higher elevations.

The extent to which dispersed, volatilised nutrients and sea spray are carried inland is probably a major factor in determining the width of coastal tussock communities. Although there are exceptions, tussock stands are generally restricted to a coastal belt which rarely exceeds 1000 ft (about 300 m) in width. Outside this limit the tussock plants diminish noticeably both in size and vigour and at this point the monospecific community tends to be taken over by peripheral species such as Wild Celery and Sword Grass. Outside this narrow peripheral zone, the ground flora may then be taken over by grassland or dwarf shrub associations according to the soil layers, altitude and climatic conditions. So it can be said that most offshore islands have an inter-coastline extent of about 2625 ft (800 m), with an interposing plain composed of other flora (see *Tussock island heath formation*). Smaller islands are generally entirely covered with tussock.

While mainland soils are generally not very fertile, tussock peat has high concentrations of total and available nitrogen and phosphorus. The rather specialised environment in which tussock grows and its inter-relationship with bird and animal life are important factors in established tussock communities. However, the development of the supporting structure, the continuing high build-up of a tussock stand and the biomass of most tussock islands have to be principally the result of the original ground layers having high concentrations of elements initially laid down by seabirds and mammals.

One of the most important factors of the habitat is the insulating quality of the tussock. The thatch-like form of the skirt offers insulation to both the underlying pedestal and to the area between the tussock plants. The generally dense nature and deflexed form of the skirt serves as a waterproof mat to the interior, while at the same time assisting the retention of moisture in the fibrous pedestal. The surface ground debris of loosely compacted leaf matter can also form a base insulation. On the upper surfaces, where the plant's growing point produces a dense canopy of leaf, wind is deflected, effectively producing an area of still air between the pedestals below. Thus the whole 'forest' produces an exceptional and very favourable thermal environment, where ground and air temperatures are typically higher than those registered externally. Evaporation of the ground layers is also reduced, thus in an environment subjected to drying winds and where evaporation levels are high, tussock is capable of maintaining optimum moisture levels in the substrata. Such an environment, in islands where other forms of vegetative cover are not prolific, has an exceptionally high value not only as a nesting and feeding habitat but as an important shelter zone.

Settlement habitats

In establishing settlements and holdings (there are 80 situated about the islands) man has created a niche for a number of bird species. Trees, bushes and other plants were introduced for ornamental purposes and for shelter. Planted as shelter belts or as hedges around gardens, Gorse *Ulex europaeus, Cupressus macrocarpa* and *Veronica* sp. attract both breeding and vagrant species.

Native Boxwood, a native shrub growing up to 10 ft (3 m) in height, is also quite common in some settlements, although in its wild state it is now only found on some unstocked offshore islands and in a few inaccessible coastal locations on West Falkland. Before the introduction of sheep and cattle the species was locally common in many coastal areas of this island. Its disappearance from its original localities has probably influenced the movement of a number of passerine species into settlement localities.

History of depredation

When the small French expedition led by de Bougainville landed at the Falkland Islands in February 1764 to establish the first settlement, they brought with them cattle, pigs, goats, sheep and horses. These were the first herbivores to be introduced to the islands and their introduction signalled the start of a slow but continuous spoliation of much of the natural vegetation.

Dom Pernetty, botanist to the expedition, wrote the first descriptions of the vegetation found on East Falkland. In his chronicles and those of de Bougainville, there are references to Tussock Grass – "All the sea coast and islands are covered". There is also specific mention of what Pernetty describes as a 'Cornflag' being commonly found growing in the coastal areas. While in his descriptions of tussock, de Bougainville mentions that this grass had been "erroneously termed a Cornflag", a reference to Pernetty's chronicles. In this case, Pernetty was almost certainly describing Sword Grass and this suggests that this plant grew commonly on the periphery of Tussock Grass communities before the introduction of herbivores.

Shortly after de Bougainville's expedition landed at Port Louis on the main island of East Falkland, he recorded that some of the party had set fire to a tussock island, whereby some two hundred penguins perished. Loss of vegetation, in particular tussock, by this means was to be quite significant, but by far the greatest losses were due to grazing. In 1785, during Spanish occupation of the islands, Ramon Clairac recorded that domestic animals, mainly cattle, numbered 7774 head. By 1838, when East Falkland was surveyed by Mackinnon, first officer of HMS Arrow, some 30,000 head of cattle roamed the island. Between 1840 and 1847 various estimates were given for the cattle herds on East Falkland, with figures as high as 80,000 but it is probable that the exact figure was never known.

In 1842 Governor Moody wrote of the 'avidity' with which cattle, horses and pigs fed upon the tussock communities. Hooker, writing at the same time, described how pigs rooted into the pedestal of the tussock in order to get at the succulent growing point, with the result that the plant died. In 1853 it was recorded that tussock on East Falkland could only be found growing in situations inaccessible to the wild cattle and horses. Taking into account the confusion between Tussock Grass and Sword Grass, this reference is probably to both species.

In 1840 the first proper attempt at sheep raising was made on East Falkland. In 1859 there were some 8000 sheep on East Falkland, by which time tussock appears to have all but disappeared from this island, for the sheep appear to have been able to reach tussock in those areas inaccessible to cattle and horses and as young seedlings were also grazed, regeneration was prevented.

On the main island of West Falkland the history of the depletion of vegetation, especially Tussock Grass, is slightly different. Except for the possible destruction of some vegetation by burning, the island was to remain free of stock until 1839, when 66 cattle were introduced. These cattle were left as feral animals to roam and breed unattended, but were not to multiply and survive for as long a period as they had on East Falkland. Following the complete settlement of East Falkland by sheep farmers, West Falkland was also opened to settlers in 1867. By 1868

V   Low coast with typical sand beach backed by coastal 'green'. Such areas are often rich in bird life and inhabited by large numbers of geese and Magellan Penguins. The stand of Brown Swamp Rush in the foreground forms an important nesting habitat for geese and other species.

VI   High cliff coastline, more typical of the west and south-west of the archipelago, generally used by species such as Rockhopper Penguins, Black-browed Albatross, King Cormorants and some smaller species of ground-burrowing petrels. Note generally exposed position of Tussock Grass on lower cliff slopes.

VII   Typical open soft 'camp' on the main island of East Falkland. Much of the vegetation is composed of White Grass, with patches of *Astelia pumila* forming dense mats around the small ponds or stands of fresh water. The darker region on the mid-horizon is largely composed of Diddle-dee, 'Red Crowberry', which forms hard 'camp'. Both facies integrate to form Oceanic Heath formation.

VIII   Oceanic Heath formation composed largely of Diddle-dee, a dominant species of evergreen heath-like shrub which commonly grows on drier well-drained soils, or what is commonly referred to as hard 'camp'. Here Gentoo Penguins have cleared the shrub and used it to build nests. Note the fairly high elevation and distance inland of the colony.

all available land had been taken up for sheep farming. In the thirty years between the introduction of cattle to West Falkland and their replacement by sheep, cattle probably did deplete some of the tussock communities, but there is little doubt that sheep were the main cause of the disappearance of this grass on the island.

With the leasing of the West Falkland mainland complete, attention was focussed on the larger offshore tussock islands, with sheep farming spreading to islands such as Pebble, Saunders, Carcass, West Point, Weddell, Beaver, Keppel and New Island. Some of these islands had already suffered some spoliation by whalers and sealers, but sheep farming practices from the mid 1860s to the present day bear greatest responsibility for the loss of Tussock Grass in the archipelago as a whole. Whether or not it existed in the whole littoral of the archipelago is the subject of some debate, but a recent survey of present day stocks and studies of the plant's early distribution (Strange, 1987), indicates that 81% of the Falklands' original stocks have been lost since settlement; of the original estimated 54,788 acres (22,181 ha) of tussock, only 10,272 acres (4159 ha) now remain. Of this remaining tussock, 9388 acres (3801 ha) is confined to smaller offshore islands largely left alone by the sheep farming industry.

Shortly after Louis de Bougainville had established his little colony in the islands, he is recorded as having shipped whale oil back to France. At the same time Pernetty records that on one occasion between 800 and 900 seals had been killed in one day, suggesting that seals were also being exploited, probably for their oil. By 1774 whaling vessels were sailing out of North American ports for the Falkland Islands. The West Falklands became the principal whaling region, with Sperm Whale and the Southern Right Whale as the main quarry, while Elephant Seal oil was taken to supplement cargoes.

How prolific whales were in the waters about the Falklands in these early periods is not recorded. Available records give little detail of populations, but they do suggest they were comparatively small compared with those further south and in the Pacific. This early period of whaling around the Falklands was to continue until the 1850s, but the principal interest of the whalers in the islands was as a base and place of replenishment. The archipelago, especially those islands on the west, offered excellent harbours, fresh water, an abundance of game and the eggs of penguins and albatross. Islands such as West Point, Beaver and New Island became the adopted homes of American whaling fleets. The name New Island reflects the New England origins of the whalers.

Pigs, goats and, in some instances, rabbits were placed on some islands as a source of fresh meat. It became a practice of whalers and sealers to release pigs on tussock islands where they bred and fared well, feeding not only on tussock, but also on ground nesting petrels. However, although tussock was important for the ultimate survival of the pigs placed on such islands, it was a hindrance to the whalers when they came to hunt these animals. Hunting was carried out using dogs brought specifically for this purpose, and in many cases the grass was deliberately fired in order to drive pigs from their cover, a method also used by sealers to drive seals. For a period during Spanish occupation of the islands, large areas of tussock were also deliberately fired to deter seal herds from settling and in turn discourage American and English sealers from establishing bases.

Feral pigs and goats introduced during this early whaling and sealing period were not to survive, although rabbits remain on some islands. In some areas, particularly in the Beaver and New Island group, islands exhibit signs of past burning and in some cases are documented as having been burnt by whalers for the purpose of driving pigs. Such islands are now badly eroded with thin soil layers and little or poor Tussock Grass cover (see *Land environment*). A number of these islands have populations of rats, probably introduced inadvertently by whalers.

Sealing for skins as distinct from sealing for oil (the latter was often referred to as 'elephanting'), was probably first conducted on a large scale in the Falkland Islands some years after Captain Cook's publication of his discovery of Fur Seals at South Georgia in 1775. The first recorded cargo of Fur Seal skins, numbering some 13,000, was taken from the islands by an American vessel in 1784. There are records of other cargoes of seal skins being taken from the Falklands during this period, but none quite as large. Edmund Fanning, one of the most successful sealers of this period, who made several trips to the islands, left records that indicate that seals were quite numerous on some of the outer islands in 1792, but less so by 1798. How extensive fur sealing was in the Falkland Islands is not recorded, but it is probable that, as in the case of whaling, the islands were used to supplement the much larger cargoes being obtained in places like South Georgia, South Shetlands and Masafuera Island off the Chilean coast.

Fur Seal hunting was to continue in the islands for a further century, the only protection being afforded by the unprofitability of hunting when population numbers fell. Only in 1881 did the Falkland Islands Government attempt to protect the remaining stocks by declaring a closed season. Not until 1921 was complete protection given to the species.

Knowledge of present day Fur Seal colonies, type of breeding ground and evidence of old sites does support the belief that, although a number of Fur Seal colonies were exterminated at sites such as Beauchêne Island, Sea Dog Island and Tea Island, the Falkland population survived because it was comparatively small, forming isolated pockets in generally inaccessible areas.

Elephant Seal hunting for oil followed a very similar pattern, in that animals were probably taken in the Falklands to supplement larger cargoes being obtained further south or to make up cargoes of whale oil. No records exist to indicate how large the original Sea Elephant populations were, but by about 1871 the species had vanished from the islands, only to reappear as a fairly rare sight in the early 1900s.

The early history of the exploitation of sea lions in the Falkland Islands is not clear. When Captain Byron first arrived at the new found harbour of Port Egmont on Saunders Island in 1765, he reported that the beaches were crowded with 'Fur Seals', however, these were almost certainly in fact sea lions. Early references to the species as distinct from the Fur Seal are few, probably because the two were often confused, but early accounts often described locations which leave little doubt that the species being referred to were sea lions, a species widely distributed and common at the time of early settlement. This early confusion between the two species probably led to a considerable depletion of the sea lion population, assisted by its generally more accessible breeding grounds (see *Mammals*). Sea Lions were also to be exploited by 'oilers', supplementing the stocks of oil obtainable from the Elephant Seal as the population of the latter declined.

Between 1855 and 1860, with the Fur Seal populations depleted and Elephant Seal almost extinct in the islands, there was renewed interest in the sea lion and both skins and oil were taken. No restrictions were imposed and only when numbers of seal were so low that it became unprofitable did this operation stop. Three more sealing operations involving the exploitation of sea lion were to be carried out in the islands before the animal was finally protected. The first operation ran for seven years between 1928 and 1940 and took a total of 39,696 seals. In 1949 a new operation started, but, due to a shortage of seals, stopped in 1952. This operation accounted for only 3045 sea lions. The last operation commenced in 1964, even though initial surveys were to show that populations were low (see *Conservation*). The operation was a failure, less than 400 skins were obtained.

Exactly when the first attempt was made at taking penguin oil in the Falklands is not clear. The American schooner *General Knox* is thought to have taken such oil while lying at West Point Island during a visit there in 1820, but it is possible that the penguins were only being taken to use as fuel for firing the vessel's try-pots. There are records of penguin skins being used for this purpose by elephant oilers in South Georgia before this date, so this could also apply to the Falklands.

The first locally recorded penguin oil industry was started in 1862–1863 in response to the scarcity of seals. The industry reached its height in 1864, when seven locally registered vessels were in operation. The Rockhopper Penguin is recorded as having been the main quarry, and there is evidence of birds having been taken from Steeple Jason Island, New Island, Bird Island, Arch Islands, Speedwell Island and Pebble Island.

Between 1864 and 1866 some 63,000 gallons of penguin oil were trans-shipped through Port Stanley. The actual number of birds taken is not recorded, but it was generally accepted by the oilers that eight Rockhoppers produced one gallon of oil. The larger Gentoo Penguin is not recorded as having been hunted, but is almost certainly the species exploited on Speedwell Island, and, allowing for the size difference between the two species, it is estimated that over half a million birds were killed during this period. In 1871 the industry declined and then revived again between 1876 and 1880, when a total of 39,776 gallons of oil was exported, a figure which probably amounts to the destruction of some 320,000 penguins. Although it is possible that many of the more inaccessible rookeries were untouched, several were decimated and never recovered. Some of these old sites are still marked by the low stone wall corrals into which penguins were herded and deep banks of penguin bones at the sites of the try-pots.

Exactly how many birds were destroyed during the 16 years of the industry's life is not recorded, but the oil obtained during this period required the deaths of around 1·5 million birds, although in practice the rough methods used probably resulted in well over 2 million penguins being killed, the majority of which would have been Rockhoppers.

The collecting of wild birds' eggs, especially penguin and albatross eggs, for food was first documented by the early whalers in the late 1700s, and developed into a tradition which still continues today. Several accounts by early whalers describe how large numbers of Black-browed Albatross and Rockhopper Penguin eggs were collected from rookeries on New Island. In 1798 Fanning describes how the eggs of Rockhoppers, if immersed in seal oil and then packed in casks with dry sand, would keep for around nine months, and how they were preferred by his crew to those of the 'common hen'. How many eggs were collected annually is not known, but some colonies must have been exploited to their near limits, for it

Fig. 3 Try-pot, for extracting oil, and sealing lances

became the practice of some whaling fleets to establish depot ships at places like New Island for holding stores of eggs which were sold to other vessels. Until the late 1960s and early 1970s, the collecting of penguin and albatross eggs was, for a few islanders, a part-time business. Such operations have now died out, although in a few instances the annual tradition of collecting, carried out under licence, continues (see below).

Conservation

Changes in the islands' fauna

Few records exist today which give a full and accurate picture of what species of fauna and flora were to be found in the islands at the time of the first settlement in 1764. The status of several species of plant, bird and mammal has certainly changed, usually with a decline in numbers (see *History of depredation*), but only one species known to have existed at this period, the Falkland Wolf or Warrah *Dusicyon antarcticus,* has become extinct.

This wolf-like fox was the only quadruped found when man first landed; but was it indigenous? If it was, why were there no other indigenous and less exotic forms, such as rodents? Few records are available on populations of the Warrah, but it does not appear to have been common. It is also curious that the population should have been restricted to the two main islands of East and West Falkland. Both these islands, with their plentiful sources of food and formidable terrain, offered excellent opportunities for a well established species such as this to survive man's persecution, yet the creature was exterminated in a short space of time.

If, as the author believes, this wolf-like fox was a late introduction and was still establishing itself in the islands at the time of the first settlement, how and where did it originate? Closely related to the Falkland Wolf is the Culpeo or South American Fox or Jackal *Dusicyon culpaeolus,* at one time a species common to the southern regions of Chile and the Magellan Straits. These animals were partially domesticated by the Yaghan Indians for use as hunting dogs. The Yaghans were canoe Indians and commonly carried their dogs on these craft. Although our wolf-like fox could have arrived in the Falklands aboard one of these canoes by itself, there are records of such canoes being discovered on Falkland shores, it is more plausible that lone groups of Yaghans, together with these animals, were at some time driven out of the protection of the Straits and carried to the islands on the prevailing currents that sweep up from that region.

Certain birds may have disappeared from the islands as breeding species. When Darwin visited the Falkland Islands in 1833 and 1834 he recorded the Cinereous Harrier *Circus cinereus.* In 1860, C.C. Abbott also made references to this species, which suggests that it may have been a breeding species at this time, however, it is now only recorded as a rare vagrant species. The King Penguin, still a relatively uncommon breeding species in the islands, is mentioned by some present day authors as having been numerous before the penguin oiling industry exterminated populations. However, the evidence is against this, as references to this species by early voyagers and naturalists mention it as scarce, being found only amongst larger numbers of other penguins, probably Gentoo Penguins with which it often associates. If numerous and large colonies of such a large and colourful species had existed it is curious that no accounts of these have been made.

Conservation measures

The history of depredation gives a rather depressing picture of the Falkland Islands as a group whose natural resources have been exploited by man with no thought to the claims of conservation. However, in the last 25 years some considerable strides have been made although, in view of the more recent fisheries development, it would be wrong to be complacent. Fisheries of the type the islands are now experiencing could represent the most serious threat yet and there is a need for new conservation initiatives.

It would be incorrect to say that no moves were made to preserve the islands' natural life in earlier times. A number of the early settlers followed certain conservation measures, the results of which can still be seen on certain farms today, but on an official, national scale, efforts were generally perfunctory. The first Wild Animals and Birds Protection Ordinance was not enacted until 1913 and only gave protection to a very small number of species. In 1921 the almost depleted Fur Seal colonies were given complete protection, but an ordinance to provide for the establishment and control of Nature Reserves was not introduced until 1964. In that same year the original Birds Protection Ordinance was radically revised.

The enactment of the Nature Reserves Ordinance was the first major step towards effective conservation, recognising the importance of conserving not just species but also habitats. Probably the greatest single ecological disaster to have occurred in the islands has been the destruction of natural vegetation due to burning and the introduction of stock, the destruction of Tussock Grass was particularly significant, resulting in the loss of a major habitat.

The Nature Reserves Ordinance offered, for the first time, an opportunity to conserve these valuable island habitats. Briefly interpreted, the legislation made provision for areas to be preserved for both fauna and flora, and therefore they could not be stocked or despoiled in any way. An amendment to the Birds Protection Ordinance also made provision for sanctuaries, areas where the fauna is protected from man's direct assault, shooting, trapping etc., but where, under certain provisions, stocking with ruminants is not prohibited. Depending on these provisions, this ordinance therefore presents an opportunity for land owners to give some protection to their wildlife while allowing the land to be stocked, while under other provisions of the same ordinance a sanctuary can offer as much protection as a reserve.

In 1970 two islands, Grand and Steeple Jason Islands, with a total acreage of 5360 acres (2170 ha) were acquired privately as wildlife reserves. They remain valuable refuges today. In 1971 New Island was purchased for the purpose of wildlife preservation and the New Island Preservation Company (now the New Island South Conservation Trust) was formed with the objective of illustrating a new concept in conservation. Although run as a wildlife reserve, New Island retained a small sheep farm, a centre for wildlife tourism was established and scientists and students are encouraged to visit and work on the reserve; thus demonstrating that conservation can be self-supporting and thus a viable operation. The success of this practical demonstration was sufficiently encouraging for plans for wildlife tourism to be incorporated into a Falkland Islands development programme. More significantly, however, it has placed a different value on the island's wildlife with the result that there is a more enlightened view towards conservation.

In 1972 the Society for the Promotion of Nature Conservation extended its interest in offshore islands by acquiring nine small islands as wildlife reserves. In 1980 a new conservation body, the Falkland Islands Foundation, was created with offices in England. This body also recognised the importance of offshore tussock islands as reserves and made a number of acquisitions.

It is of great concern to the Foundation that many offshore tussock islands are still under threat. The present policy of dividing up many of the larger sheep farms into smaller sub-divisions has not helped matters. There is evidence that new sub-division owners are turning their attention to small offshore tussock islands, which, prior to the break up of some larger estates, were deemed to be too remote. However, the division and selling of some estates has been in some respects advantageous and a number of freehold offshore islands have been purchased by private individuals for the purpose of putting them aside as reserves.

At the end of 1987, 53 islands and islets could be listed as wildlife reserves, either officially under the Falkland Islands Government Ordinance of 1964, or as private reserves owned by individuals and organisations such as the Falkland

Islands Foundation, the Royal Society for Nature Conservation and the New Island South Conservation Trust. The total acreage at that time amounted to 17,936 acres, with tussock coverage of some 5804 acres. A very large majority of these reserves lie to the west of West Falkland (see map and reserves list). Thus one of the richest areas for wildlife in the archipelago now has the largest refuge area.

Laws and the country code

Notes on legal protection

The Falkland Islands have three ordinances for the protection of wild animals, birds and their habitats. However, at the time this field guide was being prepared for publication, the laws governing such matters were under review with radical changes being proposed.

At the present time The Wild Animals and Birds Protection Ordinance enacted in 1964 gives general protection to most species, although two categories of birds, game birds and a small number of birds considered to be pests, are excluded or partly excluded. This ordinance also allows for the establishment of wild animal or bird sanctuaries. Such sanctuaries may by Order provide protection for animals and birds, but depending on omissions or inclusions in an Order for the establishment of a particular sanctuary, it may not be unlawful to stock a sanctuary with domestic animals such as sheep, cattle or horses. In a few cases where virgin tussock islands have been declared sanctuaries and then stocked, the ordinance is anomalous.

In the same year, a Nature Reserves Ordinance became law. This makes provision for the establishment of Nature Reserves, land being reserved for the purpose of protecting both the flora and fauna. Such reserves also provide, under suitable conditions and control, for the study and research of the islands' fauna and flora. Entry into and activities within such reserves are restricted, including the burning and cutting of vegetation.

A third ordinance known as the Seal Fishery Ordinance was originally brought in for the control of sealing. Sealing is no longer carried out in the islands, although the ordinance still provides protection for a number of Seal Reserves. These reserves cover a number of the major breeding grounds of the Falkland Island Fur Seal. Some maps of the Falkland Islands show these Seal Reserves, it should be noted that these are distinct from Nature Reserves.

Private reserves and sanctuaries

An island or area of private land can be declared and termed a wildlife reserve by the owner without being made an 'official' nature reserve or sanctuary under the former two ordinances. A number of private reserves exist under such organisations as The Falkland Islands Foundation, The New Island Conservation Trust, The Royal Society for the Promotion of Nature Conservation and private individuals. However, protection of these is the responsibility of their owners and they cannot receive protection under ordinances.

Equally, by consent of an owner and by Order by the Governor in Council, private land can become an official nature reserve or sanctuary and receive protection of the law as provided in the respective ordinances. Following is a list of private wildlife reserves, and private land with official sanctuary status (shown in italics). This is followed by a list of areas owned by the Crown, which are official Government Nature Reserves or Sanctuaries.

Falkland Islands Protected Areas

Private Reserves
(Land privately owned)

Steeple Jason Island   1952 acres
Grand Jason Island   3408
The Twins (2)   57
Gibraltar Rock Island   49
Split Island   543
Low Island *sanctuary*   185
Dunbar Island *sanctuary*   556
Third Passage Island   198
Fourth Passage Island   370
Middle Island *sanctuary*   383
Gid's Island *sanctuary*   *74*
North Island   185
Saddle Island   86
Ship Island   22
Beef Island   25
Landsend Bluff   17
Cliff Knob Island   5

Coffin Island   111
New Island (South) *sanctuary*   2841
Penn Island   382
Low Island   185
Barclay Island   272
Fox Island   198
Quaker Island   482
Hill Island   123
Rookery Island   6
Inner North West Island   86
Outer North West Island   161
Brandy Island   62
Brandy Islet   32
Sea Lion Easterly Island   210
Cape Dolphin *sanctuary*   2200
Volunteer Point *sanctuary*
Bleaker Island (North) *sanctuary*

Official Government Nature Reserves and Sanctuaries
(Land owned by the Crown)

Jason West Cay   54
Jason East Cay   49
The Fridays   52
Flat Jason Island   926
Seal Rocks   54
North Fur Island   185
Elephant Jason Island   642
South Jason Island   926
South Fur Island   62
Sea Dog Island   74
Bird Island   296

Clump Island   7
Pyramid Rock   2
Tussock Island   22
Natural Arch Island   217
Peat Island   74
Arch Island East   494
Albemarle Rock   15
Cochon Island   20
Kidney Island   79
Beauchêne Island   420

TOTAL: 21 4,670 acres

South Georgia legislation

The Falkland Islands Dependencies Conservation Ordinance came into force in 1975 and in many respects it has greater control than the Falkland Islands Wild Animal and Bird Protection Ordinance. There is more control over the collecting and destruction of both animals and plants and the ordinance makes provision for the establishment of three classes of 'reserve' as follows:

Specially Protected Areas

A representative example of a major land, freshwater, or coastal marine ecological system. An area with a unique complex of species, or only known habitat of any native plant or invertebrate species. Areas which should be kept inviolate so that in the future they may be used for comparison with localities that have been disturbed by man.

Sites of Special Scientific Interest

Areas maintained exclusively for scientific investigations in localities where such investigations may be jeopardised by accidental or wilful disturbance.

Areas of Special Tourist Interest

Areas representative of wildlife and scenic beauty which are open for tourism and recreation.

Administration

Responsibility for Government Reserves and Sanctuaries in the Falkland Islands lies with the Senior Assistant Secretary, Secretariat, Stanley, Falkland Islands. Enquiries regarding access to reserves and sanctuaries and details of existing laws should be directed to the Senior Assistant Secretary. In the case of similar information regarding South Georgia, enquiries should be directed to the Governor's Office, Government House, Stanley, Falkland Islands.

It should, however, be noted that apart from areas of 'common land' in the area of Stanley, all land on the main islands of West Falkland and East Falkland, together with all offshore islands, is either privately owned, Crown land or in some cases owned by the Ministry of Defence. As rules and conditions of entry may vary from one property to another, owners should be contacted for advice and permission before entering.

Military personnel stationed in the Falkland Islands should refer to *Notes on Conservation British Forces Falkland Islands 5608 G3TRG* and *Falkland Islands Training and Conservation Aide Mémoire,* obtainable from the BFFI Conservation Officer.

BIRDS

Falkland Islands Breeding Species

King Penguin *Aptenodytes p. patagonica*
Gentoo Penguin *Pygoscelis papua*
Rockhopper Penguin *Eudyptes chrysocome*
Macaroni Penguin *Eudyptes chrysolophus*
Royal Penguin *Eudyptes chrysolophus schlegeli*
Magellanic Penguin *Spheniscus magellanicus*

White-tufted Grebe *Podiceps rolland rolland*
Silvery Grebe *Podiceps occipitalis*
Black-browed Albatross *Diomedea melanophris*

Northern Giant Petrel *Macronectes halli*
Southern Giant Petrel *Macronectes giganteus*
Slender-billed Prion *Pachyptila belcheri*
Fairy Prion *Pachyptila turtur*
White-chinned Petrel *Procellaria aequinoctialis*
Greater Shearwater *Puffinus gravis*
Sooty Shearwater *Puffinus griseus*

Wilson's Storm Petrel *Oceanites oceanicus*
Grey-backed Storm Petrel *Garrodia nereis*
Black-bellied Storm Petrel *Fregetta tropica*
Falkland Diving Petrel *Pelecanoides urinatrix berard*

Rock Shag *Phalacrocorax magellanicus*
Imperial or King Cormorant *Phalacrocorax atriceps albiventer*

Black-crowned Night Heron *Nycticorax n. cyanocephalus*

Black-necked Swan *Cygnus melancoryphus*

Ruddy-headed Goose *Chloephaga rubidiceps*
Ashy-headed Goose *Chloephaga poliocephala*
Upland Goose *Chloephaga picta leucoptera*
Kelp Goose *Chloephaga hybrida malvinarum*
Patagonian Crested Duck *Lophonetta s. specularioides*
Falkland Flightless Steamer Duck *Tachyeres brachypterus*
Flying Steamer Duck *Tachyeres patachonicus*
Yellow-billed Teal *Anas flavirostris*
Chiloë Wigeon *Anas sibilatrix*
Brown Pintail *Anas georgica spinicauda*
Silver Teal *Anas versicolor fretensis*

Turkey Vulture *Cathartes aura falklandica*

Red-backed Buzzard *Buteo polyosoma*

Striated Caracara *Phalcoboenus australis*
Crested Caracara *Polyborus p. plancus*
Peregrine (Cassin's) Falcon *Falco peregrinus cassini*

Pied or Magellanic Oystercatcher *Haematopus leucopodus*
Black Oystercatcher *Haematopus ater*
Two-banded Plover *Charadrius falklandicus*
Rufous-chested Dotterel *Charadrius modestus*

Common Snipe *Gallinago gallinago*
Magellan Snipe or Paraguayan Snipe *Gallinago paraguaiae*

Falkland Skua *Catharacta skua antarctica*

Dolphin Gull   *Larus scoresbii*
Dominican Gull   *Larus dominicanus*
Pink-breasted (Brown-hooded) Gull
   Larus maculipennis
South American Tern   *Sterna
   hirundinacea*

Barn Owl   *Tyto alba*
Short-eared Owl   *Asio flammeus sanfordi*

Tussock Bird   *Cinclodes antarcticus
   antarcticus*

Dark-faced Ground Tyrant
   Muscisaxicola macloviana macloviana

Grass or Marsh Wren   *Cistothorus
   platensis falklandicus*
Cobb's Wren   *Troglodytes aëdon cobbi*

Falkland Thrush   *Turdus falcklandii
   falcklandii*

Falkland Pipit   *Anthus correndera grayi*

Long-tailed Meadowlark   *Sturnella
   loyca falklandica*

Black-throated Finch   *Melanodera m.
   melanodera*
Black-chinned Siskin   *Carduelis
   barbata*

House Sparrow   *Passer domesticus*

Annual Visitors

(* Probably breed in small numbers)
Wandering Albatross   *Diomedea exulans*
Royal Albatross   *Diomedea epomophora*
Grey-headed Albatross   *Diomedea
   chrysostoma*

Silver-grey Fulmar   *Fulmarus
   glacialoides*
Cape Pigeon   *Daption capense*
* Blue Petrel   *Halobaena caerulea*
* Dove Prion   *Pachyptila desolata*

Buff-necked Ibis   *Theristicus caudatus
   melanopis*

Cattle Egret   *Bubulcus ibis*

* Coscoroba Swan   *Coscoroba
   coscoroba*
* Cinnamon Teal   *Anas cyanoptera*
Red Shoveler   *Anas platalea*

Southern Lapwing   *Vanellus chilensis*
White-rumped Sandpiper   *Calidris
   fuscicollis*
Sanderling   *Calidris alba*
Whimbrel   *Numenius phaeopus
   hudsonicus*

Snowy Sheathbill   *Chionis alba*

Arctic Tern   *Sterna paradisaea*

Violet-eared Dove   *Zenaida auriculata*

* Barn Owl   *Tyto alba*

Chilean Swallow   *Tachycineta
   leucopyga*
Barn Swallow   *Hirundo rustica
   erythrogaster*

Rufous-collared Sparrow (Chingolo)
   Zonotrichia capensis

Vagrant Species

Emperor Penguin   *Aptenodytes forsteri*
Adelie Penguin   *Pygoscelis adeliae*
Chinstrap Penguin   *Pygoscelis
   antarctica*
Erect-crested Penguin   *Eudyptes sclateri*
Yellow-eyed Penguin   *Megadyptes
   antipodes*

Great Grebe   *Podiceps major*

Yellow-nosed Albatross   *Diomedea
   chlororhynchos*
Sooty Albatross   *Phoebetria fusca*
Light-mantled Sooty Albatross
   Phoebetria palpebrata

Antarctic Petrel   *Thalassoica antarctica*
Snow Petrel   *Pagodroma nivea*
Kerguelen Petrel   *Pterodroma
   brevirostris*

White-headed Petrel   *Pterodroma macroptera*

Soft-plumaged Petrel   *Pterodroma mollis mollis*

Broad-billed Prion   *Pachyptila vittata*

Magellan Diving Petrel   *Pelecanoides magellani*

Georgian Diving Petrel   *Pelecanoides georgicus*

Common Diving Petrel   *Pelecanoides urinatrix*

Red-legged Cormorant   *Phalacrocorax gaimardi*

Blue-eyed Cormorant   *Phalacrocorax atriceps*

Cocoi Heron   *Ardea cocoi*

Common Egret   *Egretta alba*

Snowy Egret   *Egretta thula*

Green-backed Heron   *Butorides striatus*

Roseate Spoonbill   *Ajaia ajaja*

Chilean Flamingo   *Phoenicopterus chilensis*

South Georgia Pintail   *Anas georgica*

Rosy-billed Pochard   *Netta peposaca*

Sharp-shinned Hawk   *Accipiter striatus*

Cinereous Harrier   *Circus cinereus*

Chimango Caracara   *Milvago chimango*

American Kestrel   *Falco sparverius cinnamominus*

Purple Gallinule   *Porphyrula martinica*

Red-gartered Coot   *Fulica armillata*

White-winged Coot   *Fulica leucoptera*

Red-fronted Coot   *Culica rufifrons*

Speckled Crake   *Coturnicops notata*

Tawny-throated Dotterel   *Eudromias ruficollis*

Magellanic Plover   *Pulvianellus socialis*

Golden Plover   *Pluvialis apricaria*

Lesser Yellowlegs   *Tringa flavipes*

Baird's Sandpiper   *Calidris bairdii*

Pectoral Sandpiper   *Calidris melanotos*

Upland Plover   *Bartramia longicauda*

Hudsonian Godwit   *Limosa haemastica*

Cordilleran Snipe   *Gallinago stricklandii*

Wilson's Phalarope   *Steganopus tricolor*

White-bellied Seedsnipe   *Attagis malouinus*

Least Seedsnipe   *Thinocorus rumicivorus*

Brown Skua   *Catharacta skua lonnbergi*

Chilean Skua   *Catharacta chilensis*

Grey Gull   *Larus modestus*

Olrog's Gull   *Larus atlanticus*

Common Tern   *Sterna hirundo*

Antarctic Tern   *Sterna vittata*

Violet-eared Dove   *Zenaida auriculata*

Chilean Pigeon   *Columba araucana*

Austral Parakeet   *Enicognathus ferrugineus*

Dark-billed Cuckoo   *Coccyzus melanocoryphus*

Burrowing Owl   *Speotyto cunicularia*

Little Nightjar   *Caprimulgus parvulus*

Ashy-tailed Swift   *Chaetura andrei*

Green-backed Firecrown   *Sephanoides sephanoides*

Andean Tapaculo   *Scytalopus magellanicus*

Fire-eyed Diucon   *Pyrope pyrope*

White-browed Ground Tyrant   *Muscisaxicola albilora*

Rufous-backed Negrito   *Lessonia rufa*

Fork-tailed Flycatcher   *Muscivora tyrannus*

White-crested Elaenia   *Elaenia albiceps chilensis*

Great Kiskadee   *Pitangus sulphuratus*

Southern Martin   *Progne modesta*

Purple Martin   *Progne subis*

Rough-winged Swallow   *Stelgidopteryx ruficollis*

Wood Thrush   *Hylocichla mustelina*

South Georgia Pipit   *Anthus antarcticus*

Yellow-bridled Finch   *Melanoderax anthogramma*

Patagonian Sierra Finch   *Phrygilus patagonicus*
Gray-hooded Sierra Finch   *Phrygilus gayi*

Mourning Sierra Finch   *Phrygilus fruticeti*

South Georgia Breeding Species

King Penguin   *Aptenodytes patagonicus*
Gentoo Penguin   *Pygoscelis papua*
Chinstrap Penguin   *Pygoscelis antarctica*
Rockhopper Penguin   *Eudyptes chrysocome*
Macaroni Penguin   *Eudyptes chrysolophus*

Wandering Albatross   *Diomedea exulans*
Black-browed Albatross   *Diomedea melanophris*
Grey-headed Albatross   *Diomedea chrysostoma*
Light-mantled Sooty Albatross   *Phoebetria palpebrata*

Northern Giant Petrel   *Macronectes halli*
Southern Giant Petrel   *Macronectes giganteus*
Cape Pigeon   *Daption capense*
Snow Petrel   *Pagodroma nivea*
Blue Petrel   *Halobaena caerulea*
Dove Prion   *Pachyptila desolata*
Fairy Prion   *Pachyptila turtur*
White-chinned Petrel   *Procellaria aequinoctialis*

Wilson's Storm Petrel   *Oceanites oceanicus*
Black-bellied Storm Petrel   *Fregetta tropica*
Grey-backed Storm Petrel   *Garrodia nereis*

South Georgia Diving Petrel   *Pelecanoides georgicus*
Common Diving Petrel   *Pelecanoides urinatrix exsul*

Blue-eyed Cormorant   *Phalacrocorax atriceps georgianus*

Yellow-billed Teal   *Anas flavirostris*
South Georgia Pintail   *Anas georgica georgica*

Snowy Sheathbill   *Chionis alba*

Brown Skua   *Catharacta skua lonnbergi*

Dominican Gull   *Larus dominicanus*
Antarctic Tern   *Sterna vittata*

South Georgia Pipit   *Anthus antarcticus*

47

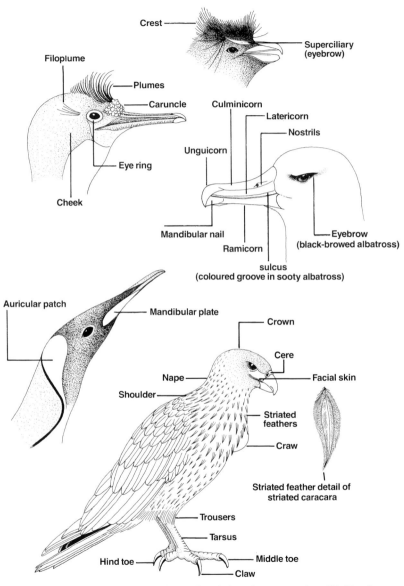

Fig. 4 Topographical terms used in the description of some species of Falkland Islands birds

---

Order **SPHENISCIFORMES** Penguins

Family **SPHENISCIDAE** Penguins

Flightless, aquatic birds with dark upperparts and silver-white underparts. Eleven species have been recorded in the Falkland Islands, six of these breed regularly.

Emperor Penguin *Aptenodytes forsteri* **Pl. 1**

Rare vagrant

Antarctic species. Range at sea may overlap with King Penguin. May wander to Falkland Islands and South Georgia seas, but rarely ashore. Length 42–44 in (106–111 cm) – largest of all penguins. Has broad yellow and white auricular patches which continue down side of head to join silver-yellowish white of breast. Head and throat black. Back light blue-grey, except for darker borders which extend down sides of neck to flanks. In relation to King Penguin, has shorter, decurved bill with narrower orange, coral pink or purple-pink mandibular plate. Immatures display less colourful plumage than adult.

King Penguin *Aptenodytes p. patagonica* **Pl. 1**

Resident: breeding

Circumpolar, breeding on Subantarctic islands. Extensive colonies are to be found at South Georgia, Marion, Crozet, Kerguelen and Macquarie Islands. The Falklands present its most northerly range where it is an uncommon breeding penguin (see *Conservation*). Highly gregarious, which probably accounts for its common association with colonies of Gentoo Penguins.

Length 37 in (94 cm), stands 30 in (76 cm) – largest and most highly coloured of Falkland and South Georgia breeding species. Has very distinct bright golden-orange auricular patches on sides of head which extend down as narrow band of colour across throat to form a deep orange and golden-yellow patch on silver-white upper breast. Nape and shoulders a clear steel-blue, blending to black-grey on back. Leading edges of auricular patches and head a deeper black. Mandibular plate varies from orange to pinkish-orange. Immature birds similar, but not clear, deep colour of adults. Young over 10 days old are covered with dense, deep brown down with purplish tints. Fully grown young often appear much larger than attending adults.

Unique breeding cycle: incubation of the one egg lasts for 54–55 days and chick rearing 11–12 months. As the complete breeding cycle takes about 14 months (South Georgia), a pair will generally only breed twice in three years. However, there is increasing evidence that the rearing period among the Falklands population may be shorter and the cycle can be completed in 10 months. Subsequently birds may breed annually, only occasionally losing a breeding season. A survey of breeding birds carried out in 1987–88 (Strange) found a total of 194 pairs at 7 sites. Allowing for unrecorded sites and the occasional lost breeding season, the total number of breeding pairs is probably between 225 and 240.

Gentoo Penguin *Pygoscelis papua* Pl. 1

Resident: breeding. ⊕ **50 m**

Circumpolar in Subantarctic regions. Length 30 in (76 cm). Stands 22–23 in (56–58 cm). Distinctive species, with deep red bill except for black culminicorn and tip. Juvenile bill dull orange. Feet yellow-orange. Characteristic white patch extends over head from eye to eye and narrow line of white forms an eye ring. In older birds, patch may extend down back of head in a scattering of white feathers. Back and head areas dark, often showing grey-brown tints. Underparts silver-white.

Fairly widely distributed, forming compact breeding colonies of 300–500 pairs. In some areas colonies may collectively form concentrations of several thousand. Majority of breeding sites situated on low, open coastal heath or grassland, usually hundreds of metres inland. Some populations use same site annually while others progress inland selecting new sites each year, which may result in colonies up to 3 m (5 km) inland from original landing area or at an elevation of some 430 feet (131 m). Sites may also be formed in predominantly rocky areas, e.g. Beauchêne Island, West Cays and Fourth Passage Island.

Breeding begins with establishment of colony groups and nest building in late September. Clutch of two eggs laid in mid to late October. Incubation period 33–34 days. Young fully moulted by late January and beginning to enter sea in late February/early March. Feeds extensively on Lobster Krill, evident by dull red excreta at breeding sites. Squid and schooling fish are also an important food.

Fig. 5   Top: typical 'porpoising' action of Gentoo Penguins while travelling at sea. *Below*: the difference in 'porpoising' between Gentoo Penguins and smaller Rockhopper Penguins.

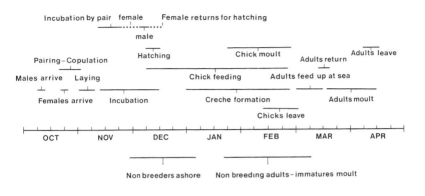

Fig. 6 Chronology of Rockhopper Penguin activities

Adelie Penguin *Pygoscelis adeliae*   Pl. 1

Rare vagrant

Antarctic species. Two confirmed records of species being found on Falkland Islands. Length 28 in (71 cm). Stands about 21 in (53 cm). Small penguin, with distinctive white eyelids and short, dark reddy-brown bill. Black head, throat and back and silver-white underparts. Feet off-white or flesh-coloured.

Chinstrap Penguin *Pygoscelis antarctica*   Pl. 1

Vagrant

Breeds at South Georgia, South Orkney, South Shetland, South Sandwich Islands and Antarctic Peninsula. Colonies often very large, comprising millions of birds. There are several records of this species being found ashore in the Falkland Islands. Length 30 in (76 cm). Very distinctive species, with a black 'chinstrap' line extending from ear to ear across white cheeks and throat. Black crown and back. Bill black and narrow compared with other species. Feet off-white to flesh colour.

Erect-crested Penguin *Eudyptes sclateri*   Pl. 1

Vagrant

Breeds at Bounty, Antipodes, Campbell and Auckland Islands. A single bird was recorded annually on a colony of Rockhopper Penguins at West Point Island between 1961 and 1967 (R B Napier, 1968) and interbreeding was recorded on at least one occasion. A single bird also recorded in 1980–81 on a Rockhopper colony at New Island.Length 28 in (71 cm). Stands approximately 21 in (53 cm). Dorsal plumage dark blueish-black, underparts white. Crest golden yellow with fairly stiff, brush-like feathers which displaying or agitated bird erects at steep angle from position near gape, over eye to back of crown. Bill reddish-brown with pink facial skin around edge to gape. Feet flesh coloured.

Rockhopper Penguin   *Eudyptes chrysocome*   Pl. 1

Breeding: migrant

Subantarctic islands. Three sub-species are recognised, *E. c. chrysocome*, breeding on islands off Cape Horn, Ildefonso Island, Isla Morton, Isla Hornos and Southern Chile, the Falkland Islands and a few pairs at South Georgia. *E. c. moseleyi* at Tristan da Cunha, Gough, St Paul and Amsterdam Islands. E. c. filholi at Prince Edward, Marion, Crozet, Kerguelen, Heard, Macquarie, Campbell, Antipodes and Auckland Islands.

Falklands rockhoppers differ from *E. c. moseleyi* from Tristan da Cunha in having black rather than pink gape and skin at base of bill, and a shorter occipital crest. *E. c. filholi* from Heard, Campbell and Macquarie are also pink faced, while *E. c. moseleyi* of Gough, St Paul, and Amsterdam Islands are black faced but have a longer crest and superciliary plumes.

Length 22 in (56 cm), height 13–14 in (33–35 cm) – smallest of the islands' penguins. Dark blue-black upperparts in new plumage, dull grey-brown in worn or old plumage. Underparts white. Head and chin blue-black. Superciliary stripe or crest sulphur yellow and forms an eyebrow which extends from just above gape to above ear, where short feathers then terminate and long feathers form semi-erect and trailing, plume-like crest. Bill red-brown. Feet flesh-colour. Immature; margin of black and white indistinct at throat, forming an area of grey to below lower mandible. In first year birds, eyebrow much paler sulphur-yellow, indistinct and lacks trailing feathers.

A highly pelagic species which migrates during the non-breeding season. Males return to breeding sites in early October, females ten days later. Egg laying begins first week of November – variations of some 12 days exist between colonies on south east of archipelago, e.g. Beauchêne Island, and those on west of islands, such as New Island, West Point Island and Steeple Jason Island. The most common Falkland penguin, forming dense colonies at some 35 sites, generally on elevated rocky coastlines with deep water approaches on west of archipelago. Feeds largely on squid, Lobster Krill and fish.

Macaroni Penguin   *Eudyptes chrysolophus*   Pl. 1

Breeding: migrant

Subantarctic islands. Extensive colonies at South Georgia, South Sandwich, South Orkney and South Shetland Islands. Also on Antarctic Peninsula, Bouvet, Prince Edward, Marion, Crozet, Kerguelen, Heard and Macquarie Islands. Probably less than 300 pairs in Falklands, usually single pairs found breeding amongst larger numbers of Rockhoppers.

Length 28 in (71 cm). Stands 17·5–18 in (44–46 cm). Larger and heavier than Rockhopper but similar plumage, except for distinctive golden-orange crest which begins in centre of forehead with elongated lateral feathers sweeping back on sides of head and then droops slightly behind the eye. Bill much heavier and deeper in proportion to head than that of the Rockhopper, with distinct light pink skin around base extending to large gape of the same colour.

Breeds in close association with rockhoppers, but about twelve days later. Interbreeding has been recorded on several occasions, resulting progeny exhibit part features of both species. Feeds largely on squid, Lobster Krill and small fish.

Royal Penguin *Eudyptes chrysolophus schlegeli* Pl. 1

Breeding: migrant

Subspecies normally confined to Macquarie Island but a small group of three pairs breeds in the Falkland Islands (Strange, 1987). Taxonomic position unclear; some regard Royal as a colour phase of Macaroni Penguin, but discovery of small, clearly distinct Falklands group suggests that the two forms could be given specific rank.

Length 28–29 in (71–73 cm). Stands about 18 in (46 cm). Significantly larger in build than Macaroni and its bill is about a third larger in depth and length. Colour of gape and facial skin a deep rose-red with blueish tints. Bill a very deep reddy-brown colour. Grey-white bib extends from throat line to lower face and eye. Crest similar in form and colour to Macaroni but thicker and larger with some white feathers at centre of forehead. Breeding period a little later than Macaroni and only one egg apparently laid by Falkland type.

Yellow-eyed Penguin *Megadyptes antipodes* Pl. 1

Rare vagrant

Confined to South Island, New Zealand, Campbell and Auckland Islands. Length 30 in (76 cm). General dorsal colour slate-grey. White underparts. Forehead and crown pale golden, with black shaft marks and a band of yellow feathers beginning at eye and encircling crown. Chin and throat brownish-white. Cheeks pale golden. Bill flesh-coloured with dull reddish-brown on culmen. Feet pale flesh colour.

Magellanic Penguin *Spheniscus magellanicus* Pl. 1

Breeding: migrant

Juan Fernandez Islands in Pacific, islands along coast of Southern Chile to islands off Cape Horn, South Atlantic coast of Argentina as far north as Valdez Peninsula and Falkland Islands. Length 28 in (71 cm). Stands 14–15 in (35–38 cm). All black and white species. Head and upperparts blackish, except for prominent white band of varying width which begins at gape, crosses above eye, with narrow line of white below eye, and continues to lower side of head, joining across throat. Second irregular band of white crosses black upper breast region, and runs under flipper joint and down flanks to meet white of leg feathers and underparts. Bill black, with horn-coloured mark on lower mandible. Facial skin between gape and eye often pink with grey markings. Feet flesh-coloured, heavily marked with grey-black. Immature yearlings, which return to their original breeding sites in December/January to moult, are a dull image of adult, but should not be confused with fledglings which are still attended by adults and bear remains of down.

Migratory population, although occasionally single birds remain in inshore waters until mid-winter (June/July). Breeding season September, when first birds return to their nesting burrows. Amongst the largest populations, on the north coast of East Falkland, birds regularly return about 12–14 September, while in the west the return is generally a few days later. Egg-laying commences mid-October and incubation lasts for 38–41 days. Fledglings leave burrows in late January and adults vacate sites after their moult in March.Widely distributed, found on most offshore tussock islands where species forms 'nest burrows' beneath tussock pedestals. Large populations exist on north east and north coast of East Falkland, but since the introduction of stock and the loss of tussock, burrows are formed on coastal heathland and greens. In some areas birds will nest above ground in cover of Brown Swamp Rush. Feeds predominantly on small schooling fish and squid.

Order **PODICIPEDIFORMES** Grebes

Family **PODICIPEDIDAE** Grebes

Three species of grebe are recorded in the Falkland Islands, two are resident breeders while the Greater Grebe is a fairly regular vagrant from South America.

White-tufted Grebe *Podiceps rolland rolland*   **Pl. 5**

Resident: breeding

Species confined to South America, *P. r. rolland* restricted to Falkland Islands. Length 12 in (32 cm). Height in swimming position about 6 in (15 cm). Adult breeding birds have black head and neck with distinctive, white, fan-shaped patch, marked with a few black feathers, fanning out from bright vermilion eye. When not at rest, usually displays crest. Upperparts blackish-brown, rump red-brown and undertail white. Underparts chestnut-brown. Bill fairly short, narrow and black. Feet large in proportion to bird's body, olive green with lobed toes. Winter plumage: white throat, off-white underparts, brown upperparts and dull reddy-brown foreneck and crown.

Fairly widely distributed. Found in freshwater ponds supporting aquatic vegetation and on slow-moving rivers and streams. Nests under cover of banks and amongst Brown Swamp Rush in shallows of ponds. Nest often a floating mass of vegetation. Begins breeding season in late September with courtship and nest-building. Generally lays in October but sometimes in late December. Adults often carry young on their backs beneath wing fold. Feeds on small fish (*Galaxias* sp.), crustaceans, insects and aquatic plants. In winter, often seen feeding in coastal waters amongst kelp beds and in tidal creeks where it may be confused with Rock Shag.

Fig. 7 Silhouette forms of Great Grebe, Rolland's Grebe and Rock Shag at sea

Great Grebe *Podiceps major* Pl. 5

Regular vagrant

Southern South America, Paraguay, Uruguay, Argentina, Chile and Tierra del Fuego. Length 24 in (61 cm). Height in swimming position 12 in (30 cm). Large and long necked with a long, slightly up-turned bill and crest feathers which protrude from back of crown. Head and back of neck grey, crown blackish. Upperparts greyish-brown, underparts silvery-white and foreneck rusty-red. There are several records of birds in non-breeding plumage (as described here) feeding in coastal kelp bed fringes. Probably an annual visitor and more common than previously believed.

Silvery Grebe *Podiceps occipitalis* Pl. 5

Resident: breeding

Confined to South America, specifically Tierra del Fuego, Chile, Argentina and Falkland Islands. Length 11 in (28 cm). Height in swimming position about 4·5 in (11 cm). Distinct from White-tufted Grebe, generally smaller and holds head and neck lower. Back greyish-brown, with lighter head and chin and distinct black nape patch. Summer breeding plumage has golden, fan-shaped plumes on ear coverts. Throat whiteish and underparts silver-white. Flanks streaked with grey. Bill black. Iris crimson.

Similar distribution to White-tufted Grebe but less common. Appears to prefer ponds with a dense growth of aquatic plants in areas close to coast. Nesting and breeding season generally mid-November but may vary. Frequently dives for food, taking a variety of aquatic life including fish (*Galaxias* sp.) and vegetation. In winter will move to salt water, feeding in shelter of kelp beds.

Order **PROCELLARIIFORMES**
Albatrosses, Petrels, Shearwaters, Storm Petrels and Diving Petrels

---

Family **DIOMEDEIDAE** Albatrosses

There are nine species of albatross found in the southern oceans, seven of these have been recorded at the Falkland Islands, although only one species breeds. Four species breed at South Georgia.

Wandering Albatross *Diomedea exulans*   **Pl. 2**

Regular visitor offshore

Breeds at Inaccessible, Gough, Amsterdam, Auckland, Campbell and Antipodes Islands. *D. e. chionoptera* breeds at South Georgia, Marion, Prince Edward, Crozet, Kerguelen and Macquarie Islands. Can be seen offshore at Falkland Islands but not recorded as landing. Length 42–53 in (107–135 cm), wingspan 100–138 in (254–351 cm) – very large albatross. In all age groups, has mostly white underwings, with blackish primaries and a blackish narrow trailing edge. Adult upperparts mainly white except for black primaries and narrow margin along secondaries. Head white, bill pinkish. Juvenile birds largely brown except for distinctive white face mask. Belly and throat sometimes white. As birds mature upperparts gradually whiten.

Royal Albatross *Diomedea epomophora*   **Pl. 2**

Regular visitor offshore

Circumpolar in southern oceans but only breeds in New Zealand regions. Length 42–48 in (107–122 cm) – very large. Similar to adult Wandering Albatross but lacks the darker immature stages. Bill also pinkish, but cutting edges of both mandibles black.

Black-browed Albatross *Diomedea melanophris*   **Pl. 2**

Breeding: migrant

Circumpolar in southern oceans. Breeds Staten, Falkland, South Georgia, Kerguelen, Heard, Antipodes and Macquarie Islands. Probably the most common and widespread of all albatrosses and the Falklands hold the largest populations. It is the only breeding albatross in the islands.

Length 31–33 in (80–83 cm), wingspan 95 in (245 cm). Stands approximately 25 in (63 cm). Head, upper shoulders and underparts are all white. Dark eyebrow and dark grey-black patch around upper area of eye gives a distinctive look. In breeding birds this eyebrow extends as a light greyish cast around back of head. Bill dull buff-yellow, with salmon-pink tip and upper mandible. Tail light grey. Upperwings grey-black. Underwings have black leading edge, with grey primaries and a grey to blackish-grey trailing edge enclosing an area of white. Feet and legs light grey with blueish-purple tones. Juvenile a dull image of adult

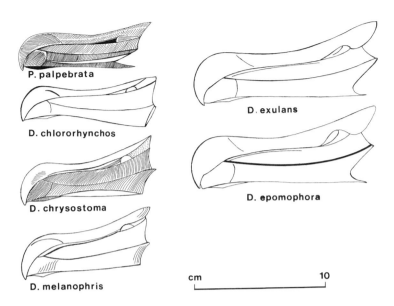

Fig. 8   Bill forms with relative sizes of some southern species of albatross

except underwing largely dark, bill dull black and white of head, nape and collar marked with grey.

Returns to breeding grounds mid-September and egg-laying begins 8–10 October (earlier on Beauchêne Island). Incubation of single egg lasts for 68–72 days and fledglings are reared for 16–17 weeks until they leaving the nest in April. Breeds at 12 sites, with major colonies at Steeple Jason, Grand Jason, West Point, Saunders, New, North, Bird and Beauchêne Islands. Often forms colonies in association with Rockhopper Penguins and generally on elevated sites where birds can use updrafts for flying in and out. Generally scavenge, taking variety of food from sea surface, notably Lobster Krill and squid.

Yellow-nosed Albatross   *Diomedea chlororhynchos*   **Pl. 2**

Vagrant offshore
South Atlantic (with *D. c. bassi* Southern Indian Ocean). Breeds Tristan da Cunha and Gough Islands. Length 28–32 in (71–81 cm), wingspan 70–81 in (178–205 cm) – smallest and most slender of southern albatrosses. Bill black and yellow. Head and neck pale grey with white cap. Otherwise colouration similar to Black-browed Albatross, except for whiter underwing.

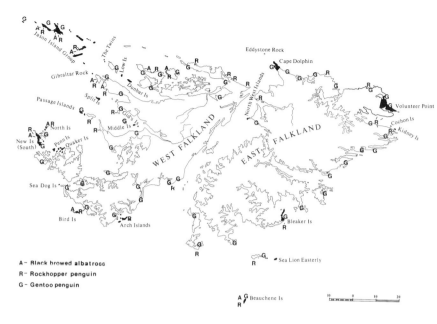

A – Black browed albatross
R – Rockhopper penguin
G – Gentoo penguin

Fig. 9 Known breeding sites of Black-browed Albatross, Rockhopper Penguins and Gentoo Penguins

Grey-headed Albatross *Diomedea chrysostoma*   **Pl. 2**

Annual visitor

Circumpolar in southern oceans. Breeds on South Georgia, Diego Ramirez off Cape Horn, Prince Edward, Marion, Crozet, Kerguelen, Macquarie and Campbell Islands. Recorded a number of times on Black-browed Albatross colonies in the Falklands but does not breed. Length 33 in (84 cm), wingspan 87 in (220 cm). Wing pattern and form similar to Black-browed Albatross, but adults have light blue-grey head with a jet-black bill, with lemon-yellow upper and lower edges; a salmon pink tip to upper mandible; and a distinct white crescent on lower eyelid.

Sooty Albatross *Phoebetria fusca*   **Pl. 2**

Vagrant offshore

Breeds on Prince Edward, Marion, Crozet, Tristan da Cunha, Gough, Amsterdam and St Paul Islands. Length 34 in (86 cm), wingspan 80 in (203 cm). Dark plumage, long slender wings and wedge-shaped tail. Bill black, with yellow groove (sulcus) on lower mandible. Eye partially surrounded by ring of white feathers. Very graceful, soaring flight which distinguishes it at sea from the similar-sized, but heavier built, Giant Petrel.

Light-mantled Sooty Albatross *Phoebetria palpebrata* **Pl. 2**

Vagrant offshore

Circumpolar, breeds South Georgia and in Southern Indian Ocean islands, also off New Zealand. Length 34 in (86 cm), wingspan 84 in (213 cm). Similar in form and flight to Sooty Albatross but very dark head contrasts with pale buff back. Bill has blue sulcus instead of yellow in former species.

Family **PROCELLARIIDAE** Fulmars, Prions, Petrels, Shearwaters

Northern Giant Petrel *Macronectes halli* **Pl. 2**

Regular visitor Sept-Oct. + ⊕ **200 m.**

Southern oceans. Breeds at Prince Edward, Marion, Crozet, Kerguelen, Macquarie, Chatham, Stewart, Auckland, Antipodes, Campbell Islands and South Georgia. Seen off the Falkland Islands and there are two records of single pairs breeding on Beauchêne Island (Strange), may also breed elsewhere. A large and broad-winged bird, length 32–37 in (80–94 cm), wingspan 79 in (200 cm). Body bulky and rather short with a wedge-shaped tail. A conspicuous nasal tube gives the bill a relatively massive appearance. Flight rather labouring compared to albatross. Adults entirely dark grey or greyish-brown, with varying amounts of greyish-white to white on face. Juveniles uniformly sooty-brown. Bill horn-coloured with reddish tip.

Southern Giant Petrel *Macronectes giganteus* **Pl. 2**

Resident: breeding. + ⊕ **200 m.**

Southern oceans. Breeds at Falkland Islands, South Georgia, South Sandwich, South Orkney, South Shetland, Antarctic Peninsula and other Subantarctic islands, except those in New Zealand sector. Also Isla Noir, south of the Magellan Straits (G. Clark).

Length 34–36 in (86–95 cm). Wingspan 81 in (205 cm). Similar to and easily

Fig. 10 Giant Petrels feeding at sea

confused at sea with Northern Giant Petrel, except that adults have largely off-white head and neck, with variable grey-brown flecking which may form darker area on face. Bill light buff-pink to horn colour with light olive-green tip. Some populations show a percentage of light phased birds which range from greyish-white mottling over entire plumage to almost pure white, but uncommon in Falklands, probably originating from populations further south.

Breeding season begins when birds return to breeding sites in September. Courtship takes place in early October. Single egg laid from about 17 October to early November. Unlike the Northern Giant Petrel, which nests alone in sheltered positions, usually nests socially in the open, however, some birds have been found nesting alone in the shelter of open tussock at a number of sites. Incubation period 58–60 days and young fledge in late March.

Commonly seen scavenging inshore by settlement outspills, often giving impression of a large Falkland population although actual breeding population is small, less than 3000 pairs. Presence of this species is an excellent indication of beach strandings (see *Marine Mammals*) and of preying activities by sea lion at penguin landing areas.

Silver-grey Fulmar *Fulmarus glacialoides* **Pl. 3**

Annual visitor

Southern oceans. Breeds at South Sandwich, South Orkney, South Shetland, Bouvet Islands and on Antarctic Peninsula. Common offshore visitor, especially in winter. Length 18–19 in (46–50 cm). Wingspan 45–47 in (114–120 cm). Distinctive pale grey plumage on upperparts, white underparts and underwing, blackish outer primaries. Bill pink with black tip, yellowish subterminal and blue nasal tube. Has very gull-like appearance and flight, interspersed with periods of gliding.

Antarctic Petrel *Thalassoica antarctica* **Pl. 3**

Vagrant

Circumpolar in the higher latitudes of southern oceans. Breeds on Antarctic coasts and islands. Length 16–18 in (40–46 cm). Wingspan 40 in (101 cm). Large fulmar, with beautiful plumage pattern of rich brown and white and white underparts. Underwing white with dark brown margins. Head dark chocolate brown with white markings on neck and throat. Upperparts largely chocolate brown except for white rump and white tail tipped with black. Bill black. Feet blue grey with flesh coloured webs.

Cape Pigeon *Daption capense* **Pl. 3**

Annual visitor

Circumpolar in southern oceans. Breeds at South Georgia, South Sandwich, South Orkney, South Shetland, Bouvet, Crozet, Kerguelen, Heard and Macquarie Islands and on Antarctic Peninsula. With increased fishing activities about the Falkland Islands, this petrel is more evident, particularly in Berkeley Sound an important trans-shipping harbour where it can scavenge from the waste outlets

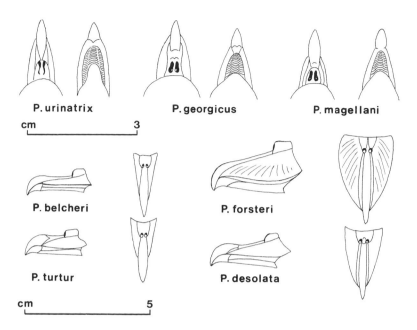

Fig. 11 *Top line*: diagram of dorsal and ventral aspects of bill in three species of diving petrel. *Bottom two lines*: lateral and dorsal aspects of bill in four species of prion.

of fishing vessels. Length 15–16 in (38–40 cm). Wingspan 32–36 in (81–91 cm). Very distinctive species, with boldly chequered black and white upperparts and mostly white underparts except for dark mottled throat and black underwing margins. Bill and feet also black. Has a very characteristic buoyant flight with alternate gliding and wing-flapping. Its common name was probably coined by early whalers because of this pigeon-like flight.

Snow Petrel *Pagodroma nivea*   Pl. 3

Vagrant

Antarctic Continent. Breeds at South Georgia, South Shetland, South Orkney, South Sandwich, Bouvet and Scott Islands and on Antarctic Peninsula. Occasionally seen offshore during Falklands winter. Length 12–14 in (30–35 cm). Wingspan 30 in (76 cm). A distinct species, being the only small, all-white petrel to be seen. Has characteristic erratic, bat-like flight.

Soft-plumaged Petrel *Pterodroma mollis mollis*   Pl. 3

Vagrant

South Atlantic. Breeds at Gough and Tristan da Cunha. Length 12–14 in (32–37 cm). One of the 'gadfly' petrels, named after their swift, dashing, erratic flight made up of rapid wing-beats interspersed with glides. Rather bulky with short, thickset neck and broad tail. Upperparts slate-grey, wings brownish black. Forehead mottled grey and white, crown rather dark, eye area black. Grey collar extends over upper breast. Underbody white with dark grey underwings. Feet flesh coloured with black toes and webs. Bill black.

Blue Petrel   *Halobaena caerulea*   **Pl. 3**
Regular visitor
Circumpolar in southern oceans. Breeds at South Georgia, Marion, Crozet, Prince Edward, Kerguelen and Macquarie Islands and at Isla Freycenet, Isla Deceit and Isla Hornos. Small isolated populations probably breed in the Falkland Islands. Length 11 in (28cm). Wingspan 23 in (58 cm). May be confused with prion species but larger and bulkier, with distinct white tip to square-cut tail. Upperparts blue-grey except for dark grey crown, nape and eye-patch. Forehead white, mottled with grey merging into dark grey of crown. Underparts white. White of chin extends back to form an elongated patch running from eye to below ear. Feet blue-grey, with cream webs. Bill black and bulky with a slight blue tint to lower mandible. Shares twisting, swift flight behaviour of prions.

Broad-billed Prion   *Pachyptila vittata*   **Pl. 3**
Vagrant
Circumpolar in southern oceans. Breeds at Tristan da Cunha, Gough, St Paul, Amsterdam, Snares, Chatham and islets off Stewart Island. Length 10–12 in (25–30 cm). Wingspan 23 in (58 cm). Upperparts blueish-grey with a dark open 'M' mark across upperwings. Tips of central tail feathers black. Feet light mauve-blue. Differs from other prions in respect of its larger, darker head and very broad, glossy black bill (almost as broad as its length) and blue-grey lower mandible.

Dove Prion or Antarctic Prion   *Pachyptila desolata*   **Pl. 3**
Annual visitor
Circumpolar. Breeds at South Georgia, South Shetland, South Orkney, South Sandwich, Kerguelen, Heard and Macquarie Islands. In Falklands, remains found at the plucking sites of Cassins Falcon. Probably more common offshore than originally thought and may even breed in small numbers. Length 10–12 in (25–30 cm). Wingspan 23 in (58 cm). Similar plumage to Broad-billed Prion, except bill is blue and narrower, being twice as long as it is wide at base. Both species have distinct 'hydroplaning' method of feeding, paddling along surface with outstretched wings, sifting the water for small euphausiaceans with their bills.

Slender-billed Prion   *Pachyptila belcheri*   **Pl. 3**
Breeding: migrant
Subantarctic regions of South Atlantic, especially off east coast of South America. Breeds on Isla Nain (Southern Chile), Falkland, Crozet and Kerguelen Islands. Length 10 in (26 cm). Wingspan 22–22·5 in (56–58 cm). Upperparts largely light blue-grey

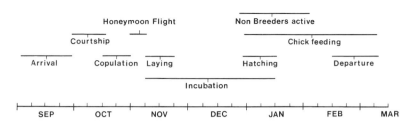

Fig. 12 Chronology of Thin-billed Prion activities

with slaty blue-grey forehead and crown. Lores and broad supercillium, white. Dark grey stripe begins in front of eye and runs below and behind it. Underparts and underwings white. Tip of central tail feathers slaty-blue. Bill bright blue except for black nostril tube, upper surface of culminicorn and sulcus and blue-grey tip. Feet a vivid blue to slate or violet-blue. Webs pink or creamy.

Breeding cycle begins when birds return to breeding grounds in early September. Mating takes place in mid-October and egg laying about 8 November. Incubation of the single egg lasts 46–47 days, with main hatching between 27 December and 12 January. Young fledge 43–54 days later and colonies are clear of young by early March. Nests underground in areas varying from about 5 ft to over 755 ft (1·5–230 m) above sea level. On New Island burrows may be situated on coastal meadows of grass and heathland and on other offshore islands may be found beneath tussock. Colonies have very distinct musty odour. Probably the most common form of petrel in the islands with very large breeding populations on the New Island group and at Bird Island, and smaller groups at other sites, mainly in the west. Feeds largely on amphipods, euphausiaceans and very small squid, picking prey from surface while gliding.

Fairy Prion *Pachyptila turtur*   **Pl. 3**

Breeding

Circumpolar in southern oceans. Breeds on Marion and Prince Edward and is abundant on islands in Bass Strait. Also breeds on islands off New Zealand, Chatham, Snares and Antipodes and on Beauchêne Island, Falkland Islands (Strange, 1968). Length 11 in (28 cm). Wingspan 22 in (58 cm). Plumage very similar to Slender-billed Prion but clearer blue-grey, lacks darker head pattern and has dark-tipped tail across entire width. Bill shorter and deeper. Breeding cycle also similar but probably 10–14 days earlier. The only known Falklands breeding ground is on Beauchêne Island, where birds nest in burrows beneath rock debris and boulders on storm beaches.

White-chinned Petrel *Procellaria aequinoctialis*   Pl. 4

Breeding: migrant

Circumpolar in southern oceans. Breeds on South Georgia, Prince Edward, Marion, Crozet, Kerguelen and Falkland Islands. Length 20–21 in (51–54 cm). Wingspan 58 in (147 cm). A large, glossy-black petrel. Has a conspicuous, light horn-coloured bill with a greenish tinge and edges of bill plates are often outlined with dark grey. Sometimes has white on chin, but on most Falkland birds this is quite small and difficult to see. Might be confused with immature Giant Petrel but smaller, darker and less bulky. Has smooth but powerful flight with deliberate measured wingbeats interspersed with curving glides.

Falkland population quite small, probably only a few hundred pairs widely distributed at four sites. On Kidney Island forms nest burrows beneath tussock stools close to water's edge. On New Island has burrows beneath heathland, 525 ft (160 m) above sea level. Although largely to be seen on their breeding grounds at night, birds also frequently return during day, particularly later in breeding season. Breeding season begins mid-October when adults return to nesting burrows. Egg-laying starts about the third week in November and hatching in mid-January. Incubation lasts approximately 55 days. Young remain in burrows for over 100 days, and depart following the adults in late April/early May.

Greater Shearwater *Puffinus gravis*   Pl. 4

Breeding

Atlantic Ocean. Breeds at Nightingale, Inaccessible, Tristan da Cunha, Gough and Falkland Islands. Small numbers associate and breed alongside Sooty Shearwaters on Kidney Island and probably elsewhere, especially on tussock islands along the east coast of East Falkland. Length 18–20 in (46–51 cm). Wingspan 43 in (109·5 cm). Large and powerfully-built, with distinctive dark-brown cap, white cheeks and an incomplete white nape collar. White uppertail coverts form bar at base of tail. Upperparts mainly dark brown. Underparts mainly white with brownish patch on belly and brown undertail coverts. Underwing white except for dusky wing margins. Bill dark and long with powerful hooked tip. Feet pinkish-flesh. Returns to breeding grounds in September and egg-laying begins last week of October. Young hatch late December and depart in late April.

Sooty Shearwater *Puffinus griseus*   Pl. 4

Breeding: migrant

Pacific and Atlantic Oceans. A transequatorial migrant breeding on islands off Cape Horn, Isla Grafo, off south west coast of Chile, islands off New South Wales and at Snares, Auckland, Campbell, Chatham, Antipodes and Macquarie Islands. Also Falklands, where large population breeds on Kidney Island and smaller populations on north east coast of East Falkland, New, Beauchêne, Dutchman's and Sea Lion Islands.

Length 18 in (46 cm). Wingspan 40 in (101 cm). Plumage generally dark sooty-brown, appearing black at a distance. Underwings and chin lighter grey-brown, often appearing silvery-grey in certain lights. Bill dark horn-colour except for light blue-grey underside of lower mandible. Feet pale purple-grey on top of webs and inside of tarsus, outside and back of tarsus black. Has distinctive rising, twisting and falling flight with very rapid wing beats while gaining height. Generally seen in large numbers. In breeding season birds gather offshore from their breeding grounds before flying in at dusk.

Birds return to breeding grounds in late September/early October. Laying occurs 18–30 November, incubation lasts about 54 days and the eggs hatch in mid-January. By the end of March most adults have left the breeding grounds, young follow in mid to late April, although seasonal variations occur.

Family **HYDROBATIDAE** Storm Petrels

Wilson's Storm Petrel *Oceanites oceanicus*   **Pl. 4**

Breeding: migrant.

Wide ranging, transequatorial migrant. Breeds at South Georgia, Crozet, Kerguelen, Tierra del Fuego, islands off Cape Horn and Falkland Islands. Length 8 in (20 cm). Wingspan 27 in (69 cm). Upperparts largely sooty-black but tail coverts white, forming band on lower back and upper tail region. Underparts and undertail sooty. Flanks show white where uppertail band extends around lower body. Bill, feet and legs black with pale lemon yellow inner web, although this is sometimes indistinct, appearing greeny-black.

Birds return to breeding grounds early November. After pre-laying exodus, egg-laying begins mid-December, continuing into early January. Incubation lasts 38–40 days and young fledge between mid-February and March. Nest burrows are found in a number of different habitats. The large population at Beauchêne Island nests on steep sites amongst rock debris with a covering of peat, clay or vegetation. Elsewhere burrows are formed in the lower parts of tussock pedestals and on Grand Jason Island are placed beneath Diddle-dee heath.

Fig. 13 Tussock stools are used by Sooty Shearwaters to assist their launch into flight

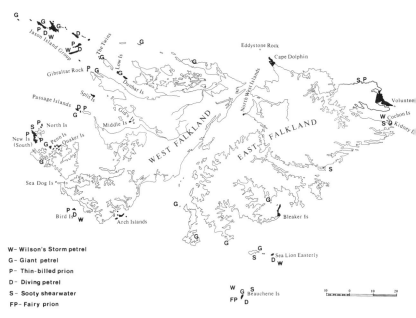

W– Wilson's Storm petrel
G– Giant petrel
P– Thin-billed prion
D– Diving petrel
S– Sooty shearwater
FP– Fairy prion

Fig. 14   Known breeding sites of prion and petrel species

Black-bellied Storm Petrel   *Fregetta tropica*   Pl. 4

Breeding

Southern oceans. Breeds South Georgia, South Orkney, South Shetlands, Crozet, Kerguelen, Auckland, Bounty and Antipodes Islands. Only one known Falkland breeding site, but probably inhabits a number of offshore tussock islands. Length 8 in (20 cm). Wingspan 19 in (48 cm). Sooty-black with white rump. Underparts and upper breast sooty-black and black extends down white belly. Upperwing black. On underwing blackish margins enclose white. Bill, legs and feet black. Forms nest under skirt of Tussock Grass stools at ground level. Little known of breeding behaviour in the Falklands, except that one egg is laid and hatches in the second week of January.

Grey-backed Storm Petrel   *Garrodia nereis*   Pl. 4

Breeding

Southern oceans. Breeds at South Georgia, Gough, Crozet, Kerguelen, Chatham, Auckland, Antipodes and Falkland Islands.Length 6·5 to 7 in (16–18 cm). Wingspan 15·5 in (39 cm). Small and generally ashy-grey with white underwings and belly. Head sooty-grey, lightening on throat and upper breast. Upperparts of back dark grey with slaty-blue tinge. Lower back to rump grey. Tail grey with black tip. Upperwing almost black, except for greater coverts which are grey and form a midwing bar. Underwing white with blackish margins. Bill, legs and feet black. Widely distributed, but loosely colonial on offshore tussock islands where it forms a shallow nesting burrow or cavity in skirt of tussock pedestal. Birds return to breeding grounds in early October, begin laying mid-December and probably leave in late March. Due to its loose colonial habits and comparatively shy nature, little is known of the species' breeding biology.

Family **PELECANOIDIDAE** Diving Petrels

There are four species in this family, all very similar in appearance: small, very stocky, with short neck, small wings, generally black upperparts and white underparts. Share distinctive whirring flight low over sea surface, interspersed with short glides and plunges underwater. Identification of the different species at sea very difficult, mainly vary subtly in size, plumage and bill shape (see diagram of bill shapes.) For this reason only the Falkland species is described in detail.

Magellan Diving Petrel *Pelecanoides magellani*

Confined to extreme southern South America, coasts of southern Chile, Patagonia and Tierra del Fuego.

Peruvian Diving Petrel *Pelecanoides garnoti*

Western coasts of South America, south to Chiloe Island where it overlaps with Magellan Diving Petrel.

Georgian Diving Petrel *Pelecanoides georgicus*

Confined to Subantarctic. Breeds on South Georgia, Crozet, Marion, Kerguelen and Heard Islands.

Common Diving Petrel *Pelecanoides urinatrix*

Southern oceans, the most widespread of the diving petrels, Falklands race is *Pelecanoides urinatrix berard.*

Falkland Diving Petrel *Pelecanoides urinatrix berard*   **Pl. 4**

Breeding

Widely distributed on offshore islands, with extensive populations on Easterly Sea Lion, Bird, Flat Jason, Beauchêne, Elephant Jason and Steeple Jason Islands. Length 8·5 in (21·5 cm). Wingspan 11·5–12 in (28–30 cm). Underparts and throat white, except for faint grey throat band, not always evident. White of cheeks extends up to lower edge of eye and nearly joins at back of head. Upperparts black except for scapulars which are edged light grey to white. Bill black. Feet deep blue-purple with black webs and a black line running up the back of tarsus to knee joint.

Returns to breeding sites in early September and lays third week in October to first week November. Incubation period lasts 48–50 days and young fledge from about mid-February. Nest burrows have been found in varying habitats, low coastal grassland areas, steep clay slopes and in the base of tussock pedestals, but are generally near to the ground. Have been sighted near breeding grounds in mid-winter, suggesting they remain close to the islands all year.

Order **PELECANIFORMES** Cormorants

Family **PHALACROCORACIDAE** Cormorants

Rock Cormorant or **Rock Shag** *Phalacrocorax magellanicus* **Pl. 6**

Resident: breeding

Confined to southern South America. Length 26 in (66 cm). Stands 12–14 in (30–35 cm). Wingspan 36 in (92 cm). Smaller than the King or Imperial Cormorant and distinguishable from the latter by predominantly black head, neck and back and white underparts extending up to lower breast. All but first year birds have reddish facial skin which intensifies to a deep red or brick-red early in breeding season. At beginning of season, adults also develop a white auricular patch and a bottle-green to purple-green gloss to their black plumage. Some have white on the throat, although this varies greatly between individuals and populations. Feet and legs flesh pink and sometimes quite heavily marked with charcoal grey. Bill horn-colour to black. Immature and sub-adult plumages vary considerably, but in general, during first winter, immature is all dark and sub-adult a ghost image of adult, its white underparts heavily covered with brown. Feet and legs black.

Widely distributed but generally confined to near coastal regions, feeding in kelp patches where it is often solitary. Colonial in nesting and roosting but in small numbers. Nests on cliff ledges, often evident by white chalky deposits of guano and nest material. Nest building begins late September/early October and egg laying in November. Young fledge January/February. Characteristic flight with swift but laboured wingbeats and head and neck outstretched, usually close to the sea surface. On the water, body is largely submerged, only the head and neck appear between frequent dives.

Red-legged Cormorant *Phalacrocorax gaimardi* **Pl. 6**

Vagrant

Confined to southern South America. Occasionally recorded in the Falklands – a single bird was regularly observed off the steep west coast of New Island for three years. Length 30 in (76 cm). Wingspan 33 in (84 cm). Distinctive, overall lead-grey except for silvery-grey edges to feathers on back and mantle and white patches on side of head. Bill yellow and facial skin orange. Legs and feet bright red.

King Cormorant or Imperial Cormorant   Pl. 6
Phalacrocorax atriceps albiventer

Resident: breeding

Coasts of southern South America, Subantarctic islands, Antarctic Peninsula. Blue-eyed and King Cormorants, originally treated as separate species, are conspecific in southern South America, treated as polymorphic and called *P. atriceps atriceps*; with *P. atriceps albiventer* restricted to the Falklands and *P. atriceps georgianus* to South Georgia (Devillers and Terschuren, 1978). Here the original common nomenclature is retained.

Length 28 in (72 cm), wingspan 49 in (124 cm). Stands 15–16 in (38–40 cm). Adult plumage, head and upperparts are deep blue-black with a greeny-blue gloss to wing coverts and a white alar bar on the marginal coverts of upper wing. Underparts, foreneck and lower chin white, with demarcation line between dark and white below eye level (see line illustration). At beginning of breeding season, develops a bright purple-blue eye ring, deep orange caruncles and recurved crest on forehead, but as season progresses crest diminishes and colour fades. During courtship and nest building a small patch of filo plumes appears above and behind the eyes, begins to moult prior to egg-laying and disappears by the time the first egg is laid. Facial skin grey, flecked golden yellow. Feet pink to reddy-pink.

Widely distributed, forming extensive colonies, which may number several hundred pairs, on relatively flat but elevated and open coastal situations, often in close association with Rockhopper Penguins and sometimes with Black-browed Albatross. Breeding period varies, but courtship and nest building usually begin mid to late October and egg-laying occurs between third week November and mid-December. The usual clutch size is three with an incubation period of 29–30 days. Young birds fledge in February after a rearing period of 46–50 days. Unlike the Rock Cormorant, generally feeds offshore, often in flocks, pursuing feed, usually small schooling fish, by swimming, diving and short flights.

Fig. 15 King Cormorants feeding at sea

Blue-eyed Cormorant *Phalacrocorax atriceps georgianus*

Resident breeding: South Georgia

Sub-species restricted to South Georgia and Shag Rocks. Plumage similar to King Cormorant, but with a higher line dividing white from black plumage on side of head, giving appearance of white cheeks. Also develops a patch of white feathers on the back in late breeding season and has less developed caruncles.

Order **CICONIIFORMES** Herons, Egrets and Ibises

Family **ARDEIDAE** Herons and Egrets

Fives species of heron and egret have been recorded in the islands, one resident breeder and four vagrants from South America, although the Cattle Egret is establishing as an annual visitor. Three species of the families Threskiornithidae (Ibis and Spoonbills) and Phoenicopteridae (Flamingos) are listed as vagrants.

Cocoi Heron or **White-necked Heron** *Ardea cocoi*   **Pl. 5**

Vagrant/Resident

South America, widely distributed from Panama to Chile and Argentina. Length 48 in (1·20 m). Very large, stands over 3 ft 2 in (1 m) high and has extremely long neck in relation to body size. Back and sides blue-grey, with two black patches on sides of lower breast and white thighs. Two broken black lines run down white neck. Crown and occipital feathers of head black and bill orange-yellow. Feet and legs yellow.

Very shy and solitary, but not uncommonly reported from one or two areas, suggesting a small number of vagrants are resident. Feeds in tidal estuaries, ponds and streams. Has distinctive way of holding neck forward at about 45 degrees while walking and at same angle sideways while fishing. In flight, wingbeats are very slow and deliberate and legs extend beyond tail.

Common Egret *Egretta alba*   **Pl. 5**

Vagrant

South America and North America, widely distributed from Straits of Magellan to northern states of USA. Length 38 in (96 cm). Large, slender heron standing about 30 in (76 cm) high, with all-white plumage, yellow bill and black feet and legs. Develops straight plumes on back in breeding season. In flight, legs extend beyond tail and neck is held in an 'S' shape.

Cattle Egret *Bubulcus ibis*   **Pl. 5**

Annual visitor

Emigrant from Africa now widely distributed in both North and South America; in recent years has spread as far south as Tierra del Fuego. Length 17 in (43 cm). Small, white heron, standing some 14 in (35 cm) high. Bill yellow and very slightly curved.

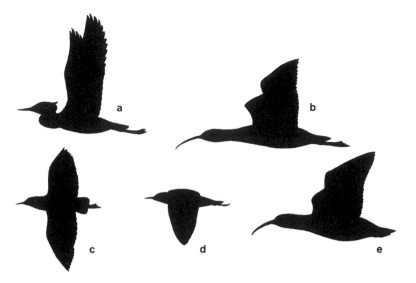

Fig. 16 Flight forms of ibis and heron species: a, Great Egret; b, White-faced Ibis; c, Night Heron; d, Cattle Egret; and e, Straw-necked Ibis

Legs of immatures greenish-yellow to blackish. In breeding birds, plumage on crown, back and breast buff-cinnamon, although very subtle and generally only visible at close quarters in birds that reach Falklands. Prior to 1976 there were no recorded sightings, but in April 1976 (Strange, 1979) a group of three was recorded feeding on a shoreline on East Falkland. Since then, groups of vagrants, often numbering several hundred, have appeared every year in mid-to late April and a small number have been recorded as surviving for some months, feeding on insect and marine life. In time the species will probably adapt to the environment of the Falkland Islands and breed.

Black-crowned Night Heron   Pl. 5
Nycticorax nycticorax cyanocephalus
Resident: breeding
South and North America, Eurasia, Africa, Philippines, Japan, Hawaii. The race *N. n. cyanocephalus* is restricted to the Falklands. Length 21–22 in (53–56 cm). A comparatively stocky heron, standing some 14–15 in (36–38 cm) in height. Adult has predominantly dove-grey to light blue-grey wings, tail and underparts, with creamy-white lower underparts, chin and forehead. Blue-black cap on head trails down nape and from it two white filoplumes extend to the shoulder. Back a lighter blue-black. Bill black with a greenish gape and facial skin. Iris crimson. Feet and legs greenish-buff to pinkish-buff.

First year birds are dark brown to grey-brown with light buff striations on head and foreparts. Back and wings marked with distinctive, light-buff marks 'tear-drops'. Iris golden-yellow. Bill horn-colour with lower mandible largely greenish-yellow. Feet and legs yellowish. Full adult plumage is attained in the fourth year. Widely distributed on most coasts where tidal reaches enable birds to fish in shallows or rock pools. Nests singly or in colonies in variety of habitats; coastal fringes of tussock, low cliffs offering some cover, settlement trees and beds of the tall sedge *Scirpus californicus*. Egg-laying begins mid-October but can extend to late December, probably as a result of birds breeding for the first time, although some possibly have two broods.

Family **THRESKIORNITHIDAE** Ibises

Buff-necked Ibis *Theristicus caudatus melanopis* **Pl. 5**

Annual visitor: resident

Widely distributed in the more open parts of South America, from Tierra del Fuego to Colombia and Venezuela. Annual visitor to Falklands, some possibly resident. Length 29 in (74 cm). Height 16 in (40 cm). Stocky and very distinct. Cinnamon cap, rest of head, neck and upper breast buff. Back silvery-grey. Lower breast, belly, tail and underwings black. Legs a deep red. Iris red and facial skin black. Bill long, black and curved. Very shy, spends much of its time on the ground probing for insect life. When flushed, or on the wing, calls a great deal in a very distinct and loud 'clanging' voice, unlike any other Falkland species.

Order **ANSERIFORMES** Swans, Geese and Ducks

Family **ANATIDAE** Swans, Geese and Ducks

Most numerous family of birds in the islands, with twelve species recorded as breeding and a further four as vagrants, although of these the Cinnamon Teal may breed occasionally. The four geese species all belong to the tribe of Tadornini, Sheldgeese, which are primarily southern South American in distribution.

Coscoroba Swan *Coscoroba coscoroba* **Pl. 7**

Vagrant/resident

South America: Southern Chile, Patagonia, Tierra del Fuego, moves north to northern Argentina in winter. Occasionally recorded in the Falklands as single birds, probably resident, breeding not yet confirmed. In Coscoroba Island, recorded singly. May be confused with all-white domestic geese which in some areas have gone feral, but very shy and wary in comparison. Smallest of the swans, length 44 in (112 cm), and very duck-like, with flattened duck-like, carmine-red bill and legs. All white except for black wing tips. Entire face feathered. Juveniles spotted brownish.

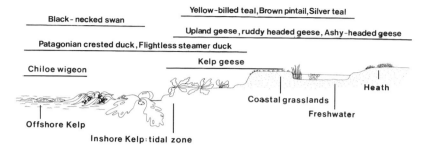

Fig. 17   Feeding zones of different geese and ducks

Black-necked Swan *Cygnus melancoryphus*   **Pl. 7**

Resident: breeding. + ⊕ **400 m.**

South America: Southern Chile, Patagonia, Tierra del Fuego. In winter many move northwards to River Plate area. Falkland Islands. Very large, length 48 in (120 cm), height about 26 in (66 cm). Very distinct, all white except for black head and neck. Has white ocular line behind eye. Bill blue-grey with red caruncle at base of upper mandible, usually larger in breeding males. Legs and feet flesh coloured. Immatures show black tips to primaries.

Not common, total population in 1986 less than 300. Restricted largely to south-east areas of East Falkland, inhabiting larger freshwater ponds supporting aquatic vegetation on which it mainly feeds. In winter gathers in groups on tidal estuaries and sheltered creeks. Begins breeding early August, solitary pairs nesting in remote situations close to water. Very wary and nervous.

Ashy-headed Goose *Chloephaga poliocephala*   **Pl. 7**

Resident/vagrant

Southern South America: Southern Chile, Patagonia, Tierra del Fuego. Rare in Falklands, although individuals and a few pairs occasionally found with groups of the very similar Ruddy-headed Goose and Upland Goose. One pair resident on New Island for some years, but not recorded as breeding.

Length 23–24 in (58–61 cm). Height about 17 in (43 cm). Slightly larger than the Ruddy-headed Goose with more upright stance. Has very distinct ashy-grey head, contrasting with rufous red lower neck and upper breast and barred rufous and black plumage on shoulders and sides of lower breast. Central lower breast and belly white. Lower back predominantly ashy-grey, rump and tail grey-black. Bill black. Eye ring white. Feet and legs chrome-orange with blackish stripe on front of leg and toes. Male slightly larger than female.

Ruddy-headed Goose *Chloephaga rubidiceps*   **Pl. 7**

Resident: breeding

Southern South America: Tierra del Fuego, extreme southern regions of Chile and Patagonia. Falkland Islands. Length 20–23 in (50–59 cm). Stands 15–16 in (38–41 cm). Has reddy-brown to brown-buff head and white eye ring, contrasting with light grey neck. Fine brown and blackish barring on shoulders and breast becomes more distinct on flanks. Lower flanks and trousers often cream. Barring on shoulders merges with grey-brown of back. Tail dark grey. Feet and legs chrome-orange with distinct black marks on knee joints and feet. Bill black. Male larger and utters higher noted whistling call in contrast to lower, short, quacking note of female. Not dissimilar to female Upland Goose, although the latter is larger and heavier with distinct black and white barring on flanks, darker back, wing and tail feathers and yellower legs. Ruddy-headed has a more alert stance, holding head and neck very upright and is noisier and shyer. Common to certain areas but not as widely distributed as Upland Goose. Prefers to graze and breed close to coasts. Lays in early October, two to three weeks later than Upland Goose.

Upland Goose *Chloephaga picta leucoptera*   **Pl. 7**

Resident: breeding

The race *C. p. leucoptera* is generally regarded as restricted to Falkland Islands, while *C. p. picta,* a slightly smaller bird, is found in southern South America. Length 29 in (74 cm). Stands 18–19 in (46–48 cm). Male has white head, neck, breast and underparts, with black barring on flanks and upper back. Lower back and wing feathers dove-grey to dark grey. Tail, bill and legs black. In contrast, female has rusty-red brown head and neck, and black barring on rusty breast and underparts. Barring blends on flanks, changing gradually from brown and white to black and white. Back varies dark grey to grey-brown. Tail and bill black. Legs yellow. Not dissimilar to male and female Ruddy-headed Goose (see above).

Widely distributed, largest populations found on extensive greens in coastal and freshwater pond areas, with smaller numbers inhabiting the margins of streams and other water sources inland. Lays from early September and through October, western populations appearing to lay first. Incubation period lasts 30 days and goslings are usually fully feathered and ready to fly 9–10 weeks after hatching.

In December immatures and non-breeders, often in large numbers, gather to moult and replace their flight feathers by ponds or beaches, where, if disturbed, they can take to the water. In some areas, such as New Island, adult birds also gather to moult in February. Does not migrate, although frequently moves in late summer and autumn to feed on the ripe berries of Diddle-dee, Teaberry, Mountain berry and Pig Vine. Also grazes on small seaweed and kelp, in particular Sea Lettuce *Ulva* sp. and the small brown seaweed *Iridaea.*

Kelp Goose *Chloephaga hybrida malvinarum* **Pl. 7**

Resident: breeding

Southern South America and Falkland Islands. *C. h. malvinarum* restricted to the Falklands and the smaller *C. h. hybrida* is found along coasts of the Beagle Channel, Tierra del Fuego and coasts and islands off Southern Chile.

Length 25–27 in (64–69 cm). Height 14–15 in (35–38 cm). Rather stockier than other Falkland geese. Adult male very distinctive, totally white with clear yellow legs. Bill black, although older birds show pink patch on the culmen. Adult female heavily barred black and white on flanks and breast, with finer barring on neck becoming almost invisible on throat, cheeks and forehead. Nape and back glossy black (breeding birds have white dorsal patch). Lower belly and tail white. Light brown cap, distinct white eye ring and deep pink bill. Legs and feet clear yellow.

Juvenile: female similar to adult but lacks cap and has dark upper tail coverts and a yellowish bill. Juvenile male has a dark head and neck with a white forehead and eyestripe. Primaries dark, scapulars and back darkish with some black bars on neck and flanks. Bill, black. Male loses dark feathers before its first summer, a one year old being recognisable by its remaining dark primaries and secondary feathers.

Breeding begins with egg-laying in third week October/early November. Generally nests near the shore, often immediately above the high tide line. Prefers tussock fringes as nest cover and some mainland populations locally migrate to offshore tussock islands to breed. Incubation period 30 days. Young capable of flight in about ten weeks. Fairly common and widely distributed. Found on most types of coastline where it can graze at low tide on Sea Lettuce *Ulva* sp. and the small brown seaweed *Iridea* sp., although some island populations graze predominantly on grass.

Patagonian Crested Duck or Grey Duck *Lophonetta s. specularioides* **Pl. 8**

Resident: breeding

Southern South America. Coastal regions of Tierra del Fuego, southern Chile and Patagonia. Falkland Islands. Length 20–21 in (51–2 cm). Stands about 9·5 in (24 cm). Brown and buff plumage, with distinct light brown and buff mottling on

Fig. 18 Profiles of crested duck

underparts. Cheeks light buff contrasting with darker brown cap which extends to form crest at back of head. Bill black. Feet and legs dark grey-black. Distinct vermilion eye. On water appears rather slender, with medium length tail held at about 30°. Fairly common marine species, widely distributed on coasts and particularly prolific in more sheltered bays with extensive shallows and tidal reaches, where it forages and dabbles, feeding on a wide range of marine life.

Breeding season very extended, eggs being laid from early August through to April and pairs frequently having two broods. Generally nests close to shoreline with nest well hidden in vegetation and may form a trio, two males attending one female. During display, birds swim rapidly backwards and during breeding season are noisy and aggressive.

Falkland Flightless Steamer Duck *Tachyeres brachypterus* Pl. 8

Resident: breeding

Species restricted to Falkland Islands, although a similar duck, *T. pteneres,* is found on coasts of southern Chile, Tierra del Fuego, Straits of Magellan and Beagle Channel. Length 24–28 in (61–71 cm). Stands approximately 10 in (25 cm). Largest of the ducks found in the Falklands, males weigh 9·5 lb (4·3 kg) and females 7 lb (3 kg), and heavily built with very large bill. Upperparts dark blue-grey and feathers on shoulders and back have a light metallic sheen to their centres. Upper breast blue-grey. Underparts white. Adult males have light grey head, marked grey-brown on forehead, cheeks and chin, but almost wholly white in old birds, and a deep yellow-orange bill. Adult female has a purple-brown head and olive-green bill with black tip. Both sexes have orange-yellow feet and a white eye-ring. Immature plumage similar to adult female.

Common and widely distributed, although noticeably absent from many islands in the Jason group and from Beauchêne Island. Feeds in shelter of kelp beds and close inshore on a variety of marine life, but largely on shellfish such as chitons and limpets *Patella* sp. and *Fissurella* sp. Commonly dives for food, up-ending in shallows, and occasionally forages. Not capable of sustained flight, but by rapid paddle-like wingbeats 'steams' over the surface of the water when escaping from

Fig. 19 Flightless Steamer Duck feeding and 'steaming'

Fig. 20 Profiles of Flightless Steamer Duck *(left)* and Flying Steamer Duck *(right)*

danger or chasing intruders from territory. Very defensive in breeding season, sometimes resulting in male birds killing each other. Begins breeding with egg-laying in mid-September to mid-October. Young are independent within 15–16 weeks. Nests in cover of Diddle- dee heath, patches of brown rush *Rostkovia, Blechnum* fern, grassland and tussock, typically near shoreline but sometimes half a mile inland.

Flying Steamer Duck   *Tachyeres patachonicus*   Pl. 8
Resident: breeding
Southern South America. Beagle Channel, Tierra del Fuego, Patagonia, southern Chile, Falkland Islands. Length 24–28 in (61–71 cm), males proportionately larger. Very similar to flightless species in plumage but slimmer and holds head and tail higher while resting on the water. However, unless viewed together, difficult to differentiate. Flight rather laboured and often only over short distances. Fairly widely distributed but not common. Inhabits both coastal and inland waters, with populations more generally found on freshwater ponds in the breeding season. Breeding begins in September/October with egg-laying. Chooses similar nest sites to flightless species.

Yellow-billed Teal   *Anas flavirostris*   Pl. 8
Resident: breeding
Very common in southern South America, Tierra del Fuego, Chile and Argentina. Small number breed in South Georgia. Smallest of Falkland breeding ducks: length 15 in (38 cm), stands approximately 7–8 in (18–20 cm). Has distinct yellow bill marked black on tip and underside. Plumage buff-grey, with minute dark brown speckles on head and larger, dark markings on breast and sides. Back feathers dark brown, each distinctly marked with buff around edges.

Widespread and common. Probably one of the most adaptable of ducks, inhabiting a variety of environmental niches. In the Falklands, found on both salt and fresh water. Pairs commonly breed on very small streams and ponds in the interior regions of the main islands, on coastal ponds and on small stands of water situated

Fig. 21   Profile of Yellow-billed Teal *(left)* and South Georgia Pintail *(right)*

in dense tussock cover. Begins nesting and egg-laying in August, often rearing two broods. Feeds on aquatic animal and plant life, although in tussock areas appears to feed largely on Tussock Grass seed. Flight very swift with rapid wing beats, usually in groups. Generally quite tame and often curious of human observers.

South Georgia Pintail   *Anas georgica georgica*   Pl. 8

Resident: breeding South Georgia
Larger form, Brown or Yellow-billed Pintail inhabits southern South America and Falkland Islands. South Georgia form sometimes considered a full species. Much smaller, with shorter bill and tail than South American relative. More similar to Yellow-billed Teal both in size and plumage (especially the female), but with longer, sleeker neck displaying light buff on forepart. Also has a more prominent and curved bill and a longer tail. Inhabits tussock ponds and tidal pools, feeding on both plant and animal life including Sea Lettuce *Ulva* sp. and even on the carcasses of dead seals. Begins breeding with egg-laying in November.

Brown Pintail or Yellow-billed Pintail   Pl. 8
Anas georgica spinicauda

Resident: breeding
Southern South America: Chile, Argentina, Tierra del Fuego. Ranges north as far as Colombia. Falkland Islands. Length 20 in (51 cm). Stands about 10·5 in (26·5 cm). Similar to Yellow-billed Teal but much larger and slimmer, with long neck, distinctly longer pointed tail and less yellow bill. Although fairly well distributed, uncommon in the islands, generally recorded as single pairs. Unlike the inquisitive Yellow-billed Teal, it is shy and very wary. Predominantly a freshwater species. Feeds on both aquatic plant and animal life and in Argentina also feeds on stubble fields. May migrate in winter, but little known of its movements in the islands.

Chiloë Wigeon *Anas sibilatrix*   **Pl. 8**

Resident: breeding

Southern South America from Chile and southern Brazil to Tierra del Fuego and Falkland Islands. Length 20 in (51 cm). Stands about 10 in (25·5 cm). Very distinct and unlikely to be confused with other Falkland ducks. Head blackish, with a purple or bottle-green sheen, and contrasts with white face and forehead. Breast marked with fine black and white uneven barring. Flanks rusty-red and back feathers black with white margins. Underparts and rump white. Bill light blue-grey. Legs and feet black. In flight has general black and white appearance. Rather shy species with typical wigeon-like whistling call often made during flight. Flies in rather erratic manner.

Fairly widely distributed, but not common. Frequents both coastal waters, feeding amongst kelp patches and tidal estuaries containing *Ruppia* sp., and fresh-water ponds and rivers where there is aquatic vegetation. On Speedwell Island a small resident population grazes areas of clover. Begins breeding in September and may be double-brooded.

Silver Teal or **Versicolor Teal** *Anas versicolor fretensis*   **Pl. 8**

Resident: breeding

Three races, with *A. v. fretensis* found in southern South America, southern Chile, Patagonia, Tierra del Fuego, and Falkland Islands. Length 18 in (46 cm), height approximately 9 in (23–24 cm) – slightly larger than Yellow-billed Teal and one of the most attractive Falkland ducks. Bill light blue with a canary-yellow basal patch. Head mask-like, with pale cream cheeks and blackish-brown cap to below eye level. Breast buff, dappled with brown. Flanks barred black and white. Hind part silvery-grey and lightly barred. Feet and legs greeny-grey. Back parts mainly dark brown with buff feather margins.

Not widely distributed but fairly common in some specific areas of East and West Falkland where it inhabits weedy ponds. Feeds by dabbling in shallows or by foraging on aquatic vegetation and animal life as it swims. Probably also feeds on seed accumulating in pond margins. Little is known about its breeding but in South America it is capable of rearing more than two broods in favourable conditions. A rather shy, nervous species.

Fig. 22   Profile of Chiloë Widgeon

Order **FALCONIFORMES** Raptors

Three families of the order Falconiformes occur in the Falklands (none in South Georgia): Cathartidae – Vultures; Accipitridae – Hawks; and Falconidae – Caracaras and Falcons. Five species breed and four are recorded as vagrants, one of these, the American Kestrel, is a fairly regular visitor.

Family **CATHARTIDAE** New World Vultures

Turkey Vulture *Cathartes aura falklandica*   **Pl. 9**

Resident: breeding

Has a wide distribution in the Americas from Tierra del Fuego to Canada. The race *C. a. falklandica* is restricted to the Falklands. Length 27 in (69 cm). Stands approximately 16 in (40 cm). Largest and most common bird of prey, clearly identified by its slow, leisurely flight and frequent gliding with its broad wings held at about 30°. In flight, primaries have distinct finger-like appearance. Plumage blackish. Adults have bright red, unfeathered head and face, light blue-grey bill and dull reddish legs and feet. Juveniles have a dusky head, dark bill and dull grey-brown legs.

Begins breeding in September. Commonly nests on tussock islands and in coastal caves. An important carrion eater, feeding on seal excreta, placenta and carcasses and on dead sheep. Much controversy surrounds its effect on sheep farming. Certainly has a much wider distribution due to this industry, sheep being an important food source, but no evidence that it causes economic harm, more likely to assist by clearing the pastures of carcasses.

Fig. 23   Flight silhouette of Turkey Vulture

Family **ACCIPITRIDAE** Hawks

Red-backed Buzzard *Buteo polyosoma* PI. 9

Resident: breeding. + ⊕ **100 m.**

Widely distributed in South America from high Andes in Colombia to Patagonia, Tierra del Fuego and Falkland Islands. Length 20–22 in (51–56 cm). Stands about 13 in (33 cm). Large, broad-winged with 'fingered' but rather rounded tips to wings. Plumage variable but all adults have distinct, light coloured tail with black band near tip. Male head and back usually blue-grey, female back reddy-brown or chestnut. Underparts white with faint barring to sides, but can be buff with brown markings or barred more heavily with leaden-grey in dark-phased birds. Feet and legs yellow. Bill steel-blue with yellow cere. Juvenile plumage generally dark brown with buff markings and a greyish, barred tail. Occasionally immatures have a 'black' phase, all blackish-chestnut apart from 'washed' grey tail.

Widely distributed over East and West Falkland and most larger offshore islands. Breeding sites, used year after year, may be situated on high rocky outcrops, coastal cliffs and even on rolls of unused sheep fencing on plain regions. Begins breeding in early October and both male and female incubate. Young leave nest late December/early January after period of 45–50 days. Takes a variety of prey, including rabbits, rats, mice, small birds and occasionally larger birds such as Dominican Gulls.

Family **FALCONIDAE** Falcons and Caracaras

Striated Caracara or **Johnny Rook** *Phalcoboenus australis* PI. 9

Resident: breeding. + ⊕ **50 m.**

Restricted to the Falkland Islands, islets off Cape Horn and some islands off the south west coast of Chile as far north as Isla Tarlton, (50 22°S 75 19°W). Fairly numerous at Isla Noir (54 28°S 73 04°W) (G. S. Clark).

Length 22–24 in (56–61 cm). Height 14 in (36 cm). Female larger than male. Adult mainly black with very distinct off-white striations on neck, shoulders, breast and nape, where they blend in with dark feathers of head on back of crown. Trousers and underparts light rusty red-brown. White band on tip of tail. Feet and legs pale to deep yellow. Facial skin varies, orange-yellow to pinky-orange. Bill light steel blue. Juvenile birds very drab, largely dark 'bitter' chocolate to brown-black. Tail light brown with light tip, undertail dull chestnut. Lacks distinct striations, having instead small chestnut coloured feathers on nape and shoulders. Bill dull black. Feet light grey. In flight juveniles display a light chestnut bar across primaries and coverts of underwing, while adults show white marks at base of main primaries.

Unusually tame, juveniles especially are very curious towards man. Rarely takes prey on the wing, using instead its ability to run and grasp penguin chicks, eggs and small petrels with its powerful feet and claws. Feeds on a variety of other foods such as insect life, molluscs and carrion, but is nevertheless a specialist

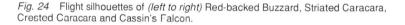

Fig. 24 Flight silhouettes of *(left to right)* Red-backed Buzzard, Striated Caracara, Crested Caracara and Cassin's Falcon.

feeder, its survival during critical winter periods being very dependent on excreta of Gentoo Penguins and Fur Seal.

Largely restricted to offshore tussock islands in specific regions such as Jason Island group, Beauchêne Island and some islands off New Island. Egg-laying begins third week of October to second or third week November. Incubation period 35–37 days. Young fledge in five weeks. Juveniles and immatures tend to move out of breeding areas in March, often concentrating in groups around settlements in search of food, giving the false impression that this rare species is common.

Crested Caracara   *Polyborus p. plancus*   **Pl. 9**

Resident: breeding
Widely distributed in Southern South America from Peru to Tierra del Fuego and Falkland Islands. Length 23–25 in (58–63 cm). Height 14–15 in (36–38 cm). Very distinctly marked. Feathers extending from black cap form small crest at back of head, giving it a rather flat, elongated appearance. Cheeks, nape, neck and breast a contrasting light creamy buff, finely barred with black. Facial skin yellow-orange and bill light steel-blue. Tail white and finely barred, with broad black tip. Back, sides and underparts brown. Legs yellow. In flight the long, broad wings, with 'fingered' feathers, display distinct white patch at base of primaries. Flight slightly laboured, often interspersed with glides. Shy and wary, often giving its position away by harsh, grating alarm call.

Fairly well distributed over main islands, but not very common. Nests on rocky outcrops, usually on high peaks. Begins breeding late September/October. Is both a scavenger and predator, feeding on a variety of animal life: insects, marine creatures, dead birds and sheep. Pellets from one nest were almost exclusively composed of mice remains.

Cassin's Falcon or **Peregrine Falcon**   *Falco peregrinus cassini*   **Pl. 9**

Resident: breeding. + ⊕ **50 m.**

Distributed from Atacama in Chile south to Tierra del Fuego and Falkland Islands. Length 15–18 in (38–46 cm). Stands approx 10–11 in (25–28 cm). The female is the larger. Much darker than northern races, with dark, slaty blue-grey back and dark head. Underparts buff with dark brown horizontal markings forming a broken barring effect. Feet and legs yellow. Bill light blue-grey with light yellow cere. Juveniles much darker and heavily marked with light or chocolate brown 'V' shapes over buff on neck, breast, underparts and flanks – markings gradually widening to form adult barring. Easily recognised in normal flight by short, quick wingbeats interspersed with short glides. During courtship pairs perform nuptial flights with dives and upward swoops or aerial 'tumbles' often accompanied by a great deal of calling.

Egg-laying begins early to mid-October. Incubation lasts 30–31 days. Young eyasses usually make first flight in early January after 40–45 days in the nest. Fairly well distributed, but more frequently found in coastal areas where it nests on cliff ledges. Where prey, such as prion, is abundant, distribution of breeding birds is high. On New Island, with its very large population of Thin-billed Prions, six breeding pairs have been recorded – a density of one pair to 1·2 miles (2 km) of coast. Also takes other small petrels, including Diving Petrel, and small birds and rabbits.

American Kestrel   *Falco sparverius cinnamominus*   **Pl. 9**

Resident/vagrant

Ranges from south-east Peru through Chile, Bolivia, Paraguay, Uruguay, Argentina to Tierra del Fuego. Small, length 10–11 in (25–28 cm), wingspan 17 in (45 cm) and height about 6 in (15 cm). Male back and uppertail rufous to light chestnut with grey-black to dark brown bars. Breast light cream with light rust-brown flecks. Trousers and undertail light buff-grey. Throat and cheeks white with two vertical black bars. Head capped with steel blue. Wing coverts and secondaries blue grey with black spots. Underwings light grey with darker bars. Feet and cere yellow. Bill steel-blue. Female has similar head pattern but is slightly larger and entire upperparts and wings are rufous with black barring.

Rapid, graceful flight interspersed with hovering when hunting prey. When perched it characteristically moves its tail up and down. Feeds on insect life, mice and small birds such as sparrows. Not recorded as breeding, however, sightings of individuals are not uncommon and one pair survived in Stanley for some months, probably preying on resident populations of sparrows. This is an indication that this small falcon could possibly survive and eventually breed in the islands.

Order **CHARADRIIFORMES** Waders, Sheathbills, Skuas, Gulls and Terns

---

A very diverse order of cosmopolitan distribution. Includes several families with many species. Six families, represented by ten breeding species and four regular visitors, can be found in the Falklands and nineteen vagrants have been recorded.

Family **Haematopodidae** Oystercatchers

Pied Oystercatcher or **Magellanic Oystercatcher**   **Pl. 10**
Haematopus leucopodus

Resident: breeding

Southern South America, Straits of Magellan, Tierra del Fuego and islands off the Pacific coast of Chile. Only Pied Oystercatcher found in Falklands. Length 16–17 in (40–43 cm). Stands 8·5 in (22 cm). Upperparts black and white. Underparts, from lower breast to undertail, white. Distinctive deep yellow eye-ring and golden-yellow eye. Bill orange-red lightening slightly at tip. Feet and legs pinkish-white. Female slightly larger with longer bill. Flight swift with rapid wingbeats and high-pitched flight call.

Widely distributed in coastal areas, particularly common where greens or coastal heath border sand beaches and on low coasts with extreme tidal reaches. May also inhabit heathland at fairly high elevations and some distance inland. Feeds on a variety of small marine life including sandworms, small crabs, isopods, chitons, limpets and mussels. Some feed almost exclusively on ground beetles *Lissopterus* sp., turning over stones in search of them.

Breeding begins with egg-laying in mid-September, but can extend to late December. Incubation period 23–24 days. Nest a simple scrape, generally on open ground. Pairs will defend territories, even attacking birds of prey (a Cassins Falcon has been recorded as being speared and killed by an oystercatcher's bill) also known to strike at human intruders. Two-banded Plovers often nest in association with oystercatchers, apparently taking advantage of their defensive nature.

Fig. 25 Pied Oystercatcher displaying

Black Oystercatcher *Haematopus ater*   **Pl. 10**
Resident: breeding
South America; extensive distribution on west coast, from Peru down Chilean
coast to Cape Horn and up east coast to south of River Plate in Argentina. Length
16–18 in (40–46 cm). Stands approx 8·5 in (22 cm). Similar length to Pied
Oystercatcher but heavier build. Unmistakable all-black plumage, although
wings show brown tinge. Bill a deep orange-red with lighter orange-yellow tip.
Eye golden with red eye-ring. Feet and legs creamy white.

Widely distributed to most coasts. Unlike Pied Oystercatcher, inhabits severe
and often elevated coasts. Usually nests close to shore, often in shelter of rock
debris, also found nesting on cliff ledges. Begins egg-laying from third week in
November through to December. Nest sites may be marked by huge accumulations of shells from adults feeding young. Feeds almost exclusively on hard
shelled molluscs – mussels, snails and limpets, and in particular *Fissurella* sp.,
Patinigera deaurata and *Acanthina monodon* (*see Marine Invertebrates*). Much
quieter species than Pied Oystercatcher and less defensive. Flight call a single
note repeated at intervals, often finishing with a series of rapid 'bubbling' notes.

Family **CHARADRIIDAE** Plovers and Dotterels

Southern Lapwing *Vanellus chilensis*   **Pl. 10**
Fairly common vagrant
Widely distributed in South America from Panama to Tierra del Fuego. Length
13–14 in (33 cm). Stands about 10 in (25 cm). Has a long, thin, black occipital
crest, black forehead, breast and centre of throat. Belly white. Nape, neck and
upperparts a light bronzy-grey and medium wing coverts shiny, metallic purplish-
green. Scapulars rosy-bronze. Bill, legs and long, sharp wing spurs reddish.

Typical slow, deliberate flight of a lapwing. Easily alarmed, frequently uttering
loud penetrating call, especially in flight. In Argentina is kept on properties as a
'watchdog' and in gardens as a deterrent to smaller birds. Inhabits open lands,
both wet and dry. In Falklands is more generally recorded on settlement and coastal greens, but appears to be a short period resident only.

Two-banded Plover *Charadrius falklandicus*   **Pl. 10**
Resident: breeding-migrant
Southern South America, breeding from Tierra del Fuego, southern Chile and
Patagonia. South American mainland population migrates north in winter to
northern Argentina, south-eastern Brazil, Uruguay and northern Chile. Falkland
population is not migratory.

Length 7 in (17 cm). Stands 4–5 in (11–13 cm). Small and rather plump. Mainly
light grey-brown back with rich chestnut nape and crown in breeding male,
brownish in the female. Underparts, lores and forehead white, with contrasting
black frontal bar and lower breast band. A second, often incomplete and narrow
band of black is formed round the upper breast. In the adult female, bands are

less prominent and suffused with brown. Bill black, legs and feet greyish-black. Plumage in non-breeding adults duller and lacks the rich chestnut head colouration in the male. Juvenile a ghost image of non-breeding adults.

Tame, but often overlooked due to its habit of running between ground cover rather than flying when disturbed. Locally common, generally inhabits low coastal regions, preferring sand beaches with marginal cover from Sea Cabbage, kelp or driftwood debris. Commonly nests on coastal heath and grassland, in some cases inland on sites where the ground cover is short. Nest a shallow, unlined scrape. Will often nest in close association with Pied Oystercatcher, apparently using this larger species' aggressive nature as a form of defence against predators. Egg-laying begins mid-October. Incubation lasts 25–26 days. Probably broods twice.

Rufous-chested Dotterel *Charadrius modestus* Pl. 10

Resident: migrant: breeding
Southern South America, Tierra del Fuego, Magellan Straits and southern Chile. Most birds migrate in winter to northern Argentina, Uruguay and southern Brazil. Falkland Islands population remains resident.

Length 8–9 in (20–23 cm). Slender, long-legged, standing about 5 in (12·5 cm) high with distinctive upright stance and characteristic head-bobbing motion. In breeding plumage upperparts, nape and crown brown, with contrasting white head band. Face and throat blue-grey. Deep chestnut breast separated from white belly by a black band. Bill black. Feet and legs grey-green. Out of breeding season (March-August) plumage dull, with buff head stripe and brown neck and breast and traces only of black band. Juveniles as non-breeding, but dark brown upperparts speckled with buff.

Fairly widely distributed. During breeding season commonly found inland on heath and grassland, prefers more cover than Two-banded Plover. Egg-laying begins October, but may lay in December/January. It is not known if it is double-brooded.

During February/March flocks of up to 1500 birds gather and engage in what appear to be pre-migration flights, usually in coastal regions, when widely dispersed populations gather and move to winter feeding areas within the archipelago. It is still not clear if all birds migrate to the South American mainland or not, movements are probably dependent on prevailing winter conditions. During mild winters some populations are resident throughout the non-breeding season.

Family **SCOLOPACIDAE** Sandpipers and Snipe

White-rumped Sandpiper *Calidris fuscicollis* Pl. 10

Annual visitor
A transequatorial migrant breeding on Arctic coasts of North America. In northern winter migrates to southern South America. Occurs in the Falkland Islands in large numbers between September and March. Length 6·5 in (17 cm). Stands 3 in (7·5 cm). Small and slender, less erect and rounded than Two-banded Plover

with which it often associates. Runs swiftly and is often inconspicuous, its greyish brown upperparts streaked dark and blending with the grey-quartzite pebbles and rocks of beaches where it is commonly seen. Underparts mainly white, throat area streaked light grey. Off-white eyestripe extends to forehead. Takes flight more readily than Two-banded Plover. Flight much swifter and usually accompanied by a characteristic high, single-note call. Feeds amongst kelp wrecks, tidal mudflats and on sand beaches, but may be seen on oceanic heath and grasslands.

Sanderling *Calidris alba*   **Pl. 10**

Annual visitor
Breeds in Arctic, migrating in northern winter as far south as Tierra del Fuego. Regularly visits Falkland Islands between September and March but in much smaller numbers than White-rumped Sandpiper. Length 7·5–8 in (19–20 cm). Small, plump, about 4 in (10 cm) high. Slightly larger than Two-banded Plover but less erect. Palest Falkland calidrid: distinctive white-grey above, white below. Bill and legs black. Runs swiftly, often hops on one foot. In flight, darker wings show a notable white band. Usually sighted on sand beaches on east of East Falkland. Records suggest that birds use the same favoured sites as migration stopovers.

Whimbrel *Numenius phaeopus hudsonicus*   **Pl. 10**

Regular visitor
Breeds in high northern latitudes. North American race winters south to Tierra del Fuego with small numbers regularly appearing in the Falkland Islands. Length 17 in (43 cm). Stands about 14 in (36 cm). Medium sized curlew with distinct buffish crown stripe and face pattern of contrasting browns and buff. Upperparts dark brown, variably marked whiteish and buffish. Neck and underparts whiteish-buff suffused and streaked brown. Bill dark, almost straight at base but decurved over distal two-thirds. Keeps to coastal regions, feeding in tidal zones. Rather shy and when disturbed takes flight with typical curlew-like but short alarm call. Sightings suggest main movement to the islands is between December and March, although a single bird was recorded as early as 21 August.

Common Snipe *Gallinago gallinago*   **Pl. 10**
and **Magellan Snipe** or **Paraguayan Snipe** *Gallinago paraguaiae*

Resident: breeding
Breeds in South America, some authorities recognise three races. Here *G. paraguaiae* is treated as a single species, distinct from *G. gallinago*. Although some regard them as conspecific, there is a strong case for recognising two species, based on the appearance of two distinct forms in the Falklands. The first, more typical of the Common Snipe, has a proportionately larger, very straight, dark bill, generally darker plumage and more erect stance. It also flushes more readily with a different alarm call and more erratic flight. Appears to be restricted to coastal regions, feeding amongst beach debris, rotting kelp and fringes of coastal ponds.

The Magellan Snipe is 12 in (31 cm) long and stands approximately 4·5–5 in (11·5–12·5 cm). Wingspan 7·5 in (13·5 cm). Bill-length 2·75 in (7 cm). Tail 2 in

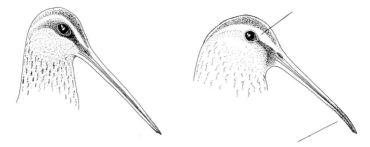

Fig. 26 Two forms of snipe species: Common Snipe *(left)* and Magellan or Paraguayan Snipe *(right)*

(5 cm). Lighter warm buff plumage with generally lighter underparts. Underwings silvery-grey white with small light brown bars on coverts. Bill greenish with black tip, noticeably shorter, with slight decurve over distal quarter. A broad light buff stripe runs through eyes. Legs of both forms a light greenish-grey. Inhabits much drier areas such as heath and grassland bordering tussock fringes. On South Jason Island nests amongst Mountain Blue Grass at an elevation of over 900 ft (275 m) Generally much tamer, preferring to run between ground cover when disturbed. Flight short and more direct. During breeding season territories identified by distinctive, often loud and monotonous 'ticking' call.

Family **THINOCORIDAE** Seedsnipe

Least Seedsnipe *Thinocorus rumicivorus* **Pl. 11**

Vagrant/resident

South America. Nominate (rare) race found in southern Chile, Tierra del Fuego and Argentina. Partly migratory, moving north in winter to northern Argentina and Uruguay. Length 7 in (16–19 cm). Small-headed, dumpy, partridge-like, but standing no higher than pipit. Bill very short, finch-like but curved, yellowish-brown. Legs short and yellow. Male has ash-grey face, front and sides of neck and on breast. White throat is bordered black and lower blackish line borders white belly, the two are joined by a vertical black line in centre of breast. Upperparts brown and buff with scale-like patterning. Female lacks the grey, and has brown rather than black lines. Juveniles ghost image of female. Wings long and pointed with narrow, white, trailing edge and faint whiteish wingbar. Rapid zig-zag flight. Fairly vocal, when flushed, giving snipe-like alarm call, on ground makes a variety of dove-like or mournful calls.

Likes open plain habitats, feeding on seeds, berries and succulent vegetation. A ground-living species, easy to overlook, with a habit of crouching motionless when alarmed and blending well with the predominant buffs and browns of heath and grassland.

Family **CHIONIDIDAE** Sheathbills

Two geographically isolated species: *Chionis alba*, described below, and *Chionis minor*, restricted to Subantarctic islands of Indian Ocean.

Snowy Sheathbill   *Chionis alba*   **Pl. 6**

Resident: Annual visitor
Breeds on Antarctic Peninsula and islands of the Scotia Arc from South Shetlands to South Georgia. Locally common all year, but generally seen in larger numbers during winter. Length 16 in (40·5 cm). Stands approximately 7·5–8 in (19–20 cm). All white and pigeon-like in appearance and movements. Has a short, deep bill, tinted yellow and green with dark tip. Legs and feet bluey-grey, unwebbed and short and heavy in proportion to body. Sluggish flight, with rapid, shallow wing-beats. Tame species, frequenting seabird colonies where it scavenges for spilt regurgitated feed or faeces of Gentoo Penguins containing remains of Lobster Krill. Also feeds on decaying blubber and flesh of stranded cetaceans and is therefore a useful indicator of such.

Family **STERCORARIIDAE** Skuas or Jaegers

Six or seven species in two genera, of which the genus *Catharacta* has a complex and disputed taxonomy and is comprised of a group of closely related species or races widespread in southern oceans and on the Antarctic peninsula. There is one isolated representative in the North Atlantic. Three forms are discussed below, all occur in the South American quadrant: the Chilean Skua, Brown Skua and Falkland Skua.

Falkland Skua   *Catharacta skua antarctica*   **Pl. 6**

Breeding: migrant
Breeds largely in Falkland Islands, but similar form is found at Punta Tombo and south to Camarones on Argentine coast. Length 20–21 in (52–55 cm). Stands approx 12·5–13 in (32–33 cm). Female slightly larger. Very heavily built, with disproportionately small head. Plumage varies from deep chocolate-brown to fairly light brown, although underparts generally lighter than upperparts. May also be heavily streaked or mottled light buff to straw-coloured. When resting, plumage shows no white, but in flight or when displaying shows white flash at base of wing primaries. Bill heavily built, dark horn colour. Feet and legs black but may be marked with white patches on tarsus. Flies fast with fairly rapid powerful wingbeats and can be extremely agile, particularly in pursuit of prey such as Thin-billed Prions.

Widespread and locally common, although a ready supply of prey, such as prions and eggs and young of penguins and cormorants, and a suitable nesting habitat of short, open grass on heathland appear to be prerequisites for a population to establish itself. Individual pairs have been found nesting on islands such as Beauchêne in confined areas of peaty ground, but are not recorded as breeding

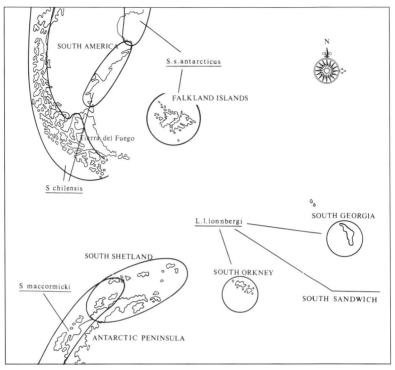

Fig. 27   The range of skuas in the South American quadrant (after Devillers, 1978)

successfully. A migratory species, returns to breeding sites in the last week of October. During third week in November territories are established and egg-laying begins in last days of November to first week of December. Usually two eggs incubated for 29–30 days. Young birds fully feathered by early February and are capable of flight within 35–40 days of hatching. By mid-April birds leave on pelagic migration, latest recorded departure about 28 April.

Antarctic Skua or Brown Skua   *Catharacta skua lonnbergi*

Vagrant

Breeds at South Georgia, other Subantarctic islands and Antarctic Peninsula. Slightly larger than Falkland Skua, but indistinguishable in the field except by its larger bill. Plumage very similar, with considerable variations, from predominant brown to streaked light buff or straw-coloured. Birds return from migration about mid-October and follow similar breeding pattern to Falkland Skua. Return to sea before end of April.

Chilean Skua *Catharacta chilensis*

Vagrant

Breeds almost entirely within islands south and west of Tierra del Fuego and Southern Andes and as far north as Rio Santa Cruz on east coast of Patagonia. Slender and less heavily built than Falkland Skua. Wings proportionately narrower and appear larger. Bill longer, finer and lighter in colour. Underparts bright cinnamon, but not evident in all birds, whereas all have cinnamon underwing coverts. Distinct dark brown or blackish cap is emphasised by lighter, often straw-coloured cheeks, nape and chin. Recorded occasionally but requires careful identification in view of very variable plumage in Falkland type.

Family **LARIDAE** Gulls and Terns

Falkland gulls and terns are generally coastal birds, although some forms may move inland (see Dominican Gull). Nine species recorded, four of them breeding.

Dolphin Gull *Larus scoresbii*   **Pl. 6**

Resident: breeding. ⊕ **50 m.**

Southern South America, Tierra del Fuego, Falkland Islands and Patagonia, north to Puerto Madryn. Length 17 in (43 cm), stands 9·5 in (24 cm) – fairly small gull. Adult plumage very striking, light dove grey on head, neck and underparts, contrasting with deep red bill and legs. Back and upperwings slaty-black, with white tipped tertials, secondaries and inner primaries. In resting bird this white shows as irregular crescent shaped line against black plumage of wings and as series of white crescent marks on the folded primaries. Tail white. Iris golden with red orbital ring and almost complete, white eye-ring. Head, neck and breast of juvenile dark slaty-brown. Back and wings blackish, belly white, tail white, tipped black. Bill dark. Legs grey-brown. After one year underparts similar to adults but darker grey. Head has a brownish-black hood, dark eye and pale pink bill with dark tip. After second year, similar to adults but have a darker dove-grey head tinged brown. Bill and feet reddish but lacking brilliance of adult colour.

Builds nest about third week in November, lays in first days of December, although varies between colonies and seasons. Incubation lasts about 25 days, with first hatching mid-December. By mid-February young are normally fully feathered. Fairly well distributed in coastal regions. Forms dense colonies, often in close association with Dominican and Brown-hooded Gulls and South American Terns. Nest sites may be situated on sand, shingle or boulder beaches, on rocky promontories at quite high elevations and on open coastal heath or grassland. Feeds on a variety of marine life and is an important scavenger of penguin, albatross, cormorant and seal colonies, feeding on spilt regurgitated food and excreta.

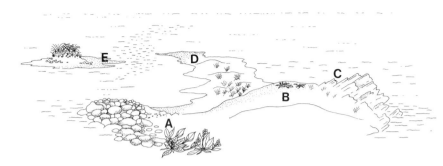

Fig. 28 Nesting habitats of gulls and terns: A, storm beach areas with sand, pebbles and patches of Sea Cabbage – gulls and terns; B, coastal grass and heath – Dominican Gulls; C, rocky coastal promontories – Dolphin and Dominican Gulls; D, sand and shingle points – gulls and terns; and E, offshore reefs and islets of rock and shingle – terns.

Dominican Gull or Kelp Gull *Larus dominicanus*   Pl. 6

Resident: breeding

Southern South America from southern Brazil and Peru to Chile, Uruguay, Argentina south to Tierra del Fuego. Also South Georgia, South Shetlands and Antarctic Peninsula. Race *Larus dominicanus retula* breeds off South Africa, New Zealand. Length 20·5–23 in (52–58 cm), height 12–14 in (30–35 cm). Largest of Falkland gulls. Adults very distinctive, all white plumage apart from black back and most of upperwings. During breeding, bill is a deep yellow with deep red patch on gonys. Feet and legs light yellowish-green. Iris golden with red orbital ring. Juveniles heavily marked grey-brown all over with black band on tip of tail. Bill blackish. Feet and legs fleshy-brown. In third winter, mainly white on head and underparts with few dark feathers on head and neck. Tail white with some dark markings. Bill dull image of adult but retaining some darker markings. Legs similar to adults but colour less clear. Attains adult plumage following summer.

Widely distributed on coastlines. Breeds on West and East Falkland mainlands and other offshore islands, but absent from remote islands such as the Jason Island group and Beauchêne Island. Usually nests in colonies of several hundred pairs on open coastal sites, but will nest on heathland some distance inland. At New Island it has adapted to nesting on cliff ledges. Nest-building begins late November, egg- laying last days of November and early December – dates vary between colonies and between pairs. Incubation 25 days and young are fully fledged and capable of flight by third week February.

Feeding habits have been influenced by sheep farming: in autumn large numbers of culled sheep present readily available food and flocks of largely immature birds concentrate on the killing fields to feed on carcasses. Many young birds rely on this food source and when it is unavailable may die due to an apparent inability to forage for other more natural forms of food.

Brown-hooded Gull or Pink-breasted Gull *Larus maculipennis* Pl. 6

Resident: breeding. ⊕ **50 m.**

Southern South America from Uruguay, Argentina, Tierra del Fuego and Chile. Length 14–15 in (36–38 cm). Stands 9–10 in. Very upright stance and long neck compared to other gulls. Back and wing coverts a light, dove grey. Tail white, underparts white with rosy cast to ventral area. When wings are folded, dark primary markings show as a black tip. Bill and legs dark carmine. In winter plumage the head is white with brown ear spot, and rosy cast on breast intensifies and also appears on the lower back. In breeding season has dark brown hood with white, crescent-shaped eye ring around posterior edge of eye. Juvenile has mottled, light brown back and wings, grey-brown crown, deeper brown ear spot and white tail with a narrow black subterminal band. Bill brownish, suffused reddy-pink with blackish tip. Feet fleshy brown. Flight very distinctive, slow and buoyant, often accompanied by a short, sharp flight call.

Not as common as former two species. Breeds on a number of coastal and inland sites, usually in association with South American Terns and Dolphin Gulls, but appears to prefer some cover such as Sea Cabbage, Tussock Grass perimeters or Swamp Rush. Breeding period similar to other gulls species, although egg-laying may be a few days later. Young fully-fledged and capable of flight by mid-February.

Takes a variety of marine feed, Lobster Krill is an important prey species, scavenging on tideline and feeding amongst kelp beds. Fine shell deposits on colonies suggest they also feed on bivalves, such as *Gaimardia* sp., found on the leaves of kelp.

South American Tern *Sterna hirundinacea* Pl. 6

Resident: breeding. ⊕ **100 m.**

Confined to South America. Tierra del Fuego to Brazil and around 15°S in Peru. Length 16–17·5 in (40–44 cm). Stands 5–5·5 in (12·5–14 cm). Upperparts light blue-grey, underparts white, brushed dove grey. Bill and legs deep vermilion. Tail white, deeply forked. In winter adult plumage is lighter with mottled black and white crown and dull red bill and legs. In breeding plumage has black cap which extends below eye and trails down nape. Juveniles are mottled and barred with buff and blackish feathers. Bill blackish and legs dull orange. Characteristic jerky flight, rather laboured yet swift. When searching for feed often hovers briefly before diving almost vertically to water, although does not appear to dive below surface.

Generally forms dense colonies of several hundred pairs on coastal sites of sand or shingle, often in association with Dolphin, Brown-hooded and occasionally Dominican Gulls. Antagonistic towards intruders but easily disturbed and will often abandon sites where egg-laying is about to commence. Colonies established

Fig. 29   South American Terns in flight

mid-November. Egg-laying begins late November into December. Young are fully fledged by mid-February. During winter birds disperse, probably following feed in adjacent waters just north of the islands. Appears to feed almost exclusively on Lobster Krill and small silver-scaled fish, probably *Clupea* sp. or possibly the fry of Blue Whiting and 'Yellow-belly' (see *Fish*).

Antarctic Tern   *Sterna vittata*   **Pl. 6**
Vagrant
Southern oceans. Four sub-species, completing almost circumpolar breeding range, of which only one, *S. v. georgiae*, which breeds at South Georgia, is discussed here. Length 16 in (41 cm). Resembles Arctic Tern, although in breeding plumage at different times. May also be confused with South American Tern, but darker grey. Widespread at South Georgia, with 40 known breeding sites, varying from scree slopes to coastal flats, but population does not exceed 2500 pairs (Prince & Croxall, 1982). Egg-laying begins in mid/late November, through to early January. Unlike South American Tern, which has a clutch of two, lays only one egg. Believed to be sedentary, remaining close to the island all year.

Order   **COLUMBIFORMES**   Pigeons and Doves

Family   **COLUMBIDAE**   Pigeons and Doves

While pigeons and doves have a worldwide distribution and inhabit all types of country, they have not been successful in establishing in the islands, although the Violet-eared Dove is a fairly common annual vagrant and the Chilean Pigeon, *Columba araucana*, is recorded as a rare vagrant.

Violet-eared Dove   *Zenaida auriculata*   **Pl. 11**

Regular vagrant

Central South America to Tierra del Fuego. The race *Z. a. auriculata* is found in central and southern Chile, Tierra del Fuego and Patagonia. Length 10 in (25 cm). Stands about 6 in (15 cm). A small pigeon with typical pigeon-like movements when feeding on the ground. When rising into flight its tail fans out, displaying lead-grey feathers with a black band and broad white tips. Upperparts generally grey-brown with distinct black spots on wing coverts. Top of head grey and forehead, sides of head and breast pinkish brown. Sides of neck show a metallic purple sheen with two black bars on ear coverts. Legs short and a deep carmine red.

Gregarious, forming large flocks in its normal range, but usually recorded alone in Falklands. However, the sightings of small groups from more westerly islands which lie closest to South America, suggests that the fairly regular appearance of individuals in autumn elsewhere may well have originated as larger movements of birds from this continent.

Order   **STRIGIFORMES**   Owls

Family   **STRIGIDAE** and **TYTONIDAE**   Owls and Barn Owls

Three species are recorded in the Falkland Islands including the Burrowing Owl *Speotyto cunicularia* a rare vagrant not described here.

Barn Owl   *Tyto alba*   **Pl. 9**

Vagrant: resident: breeding

Several races, found on most continents except polar regions. *T. a. tuidana* breeds in South America, from Colombia south to Tierra del Fuego. Length 14–15 in (36–38 cm). Stands some 12 in (30 cm). Upperparts greyish, densely flecked with black, buff and off-white, and with rufous feathers showing through. Face heart-shaped with off-white inner feathers surrounded by a dark ruff. Underparts whiteish buff. Shows long, whiteish, feathered legs. Not uncommonly recorded, although sightings of more than one individual appear to go in phases, numbers being recorded at intervals of four to five years. Small number resident and confirmed as breeding.

Short-eared Owl   *Asio flammeus sanfordi*   **Pl. 9**

Resident: breeding

Breeds over much of the northern hemisphere, Central and South America to Tierra del Fuego, but the race *A. f. sanfordi* is restricted to the Falkland Islands. Length 13·5–15 in (34–38 cm). Stands 11 in (28 cm). Intricately and beautifully marked. The back and wings are a medium to dark grey-brown, blotched with buff. Head, nape and breast generally darker, streaked chocolate brown or a deeper ochre-buff. Face similar, but with off-white bib below bill. Legs heavily feathered,

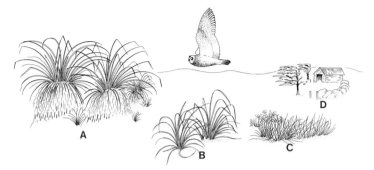

Fig. 30 Nesting habitats of Short-eared Owl: A, Tussock Grass; B, Cinnamon Grass; C, Brown Rush; and D, General habitats of Barn Owl – settlement sheds, gorse, tree cover and cliff crevice.

ochre-buff. Very distinctive flight with slow, deep wingbeats and intermittent glides. May also hover when searching for prey.

Fairly well distributed, but population probably only amounts to a few hundred pairs. Largely confined to offshore tussock islands holding populations of Wilson's and Grey-backed Storm Petrels and Diving Petrels on which it preys. Also feeds on Camel Crickets, other insects and small rodents. Nests under cover of tussock grass and, on main islands, in cover of Cinnamon Grass and Brown Rush. Breeding begins with egg-laying in late September/October. Incubation lasts about 28 days. The young fledge and are capable of flight within about four weeks of hatching, although there are probably variations depending on availability of food.

Order **PASSERIFORMES** Passerines

Ten passerine species, representatives of eight families, breed in the islands, one species only breeds in South Georgia. A further eighteen species have been recorded in the Falkland Islands as vagrants from North or South America (see list of vagrants, p.45).

Family **FURNARIIDAE** Ovenbirds

Tussock Bird *Cinclodes antarcticus antarcticus*　　　　　　　**Pl. 11**

Resident: breeding

Restricted to the Falkland Islands, while a second race, *C. a. maculirostris* is confined to islands south of Tierra del Fuego. Length 7 in (18 cm). Small, height 3·5 in (9 cm), with low stance. Very tame, inquisitive species. Distinctive by its overall dark brown to grey-brown plumage, except for chin and throat which can vary from light brown to birds with a small buff to yellowish-buff throat bar. Bill black,

PLATE 1

Emperor Penguin (p.49)

incubating

King Penguin (p.49)

Gentoo Penguin (p.50)

Erect-crested Penguin (p.51)

Macaroni Penguin (p.52)

Royal Penguin (Falkland type) (p.53)

immature

Rockhopper Penguin (p.52)

immature

Magellanic Penguin (p.53)

Adelie Penguin (p.51)

Chinstrap Penguin (p.51)

Yellow-eyed Penguin (p.53)

PLATE 2

Black-browed Albatross (p.56)

Wandering Albatross (p.56)

Royal Albatross (p.56)

Grey-headed Albatross (p.58)

Yellow-nosed Albatross (p.57)

Sooty Albatross (p.58)

Light-mantled Sooty Albatross (p.59)

Giant Petrel

Northern Giant Petrel (p.59)

Southern Giant Petrel (p.59)

Antarctic Petrel (p.60)

Cape Pigeon (p.60)

Snow Petrel (p.61)

PLATE 3

Blue Petrel (p.62)

Silver-grey Fulmar (p.60)

oft-plumaged Petrel (p.61)

Dove Prion (p.62)

Slender-billed Prion (p.62)

Broad-billed Prion (p.62)

Fairy Prion (Falkland Islands) (p.63)

PLATE 4

Wilson's Storm Petrel (p.65)

Grey-backed Storm Petrel (p.66)

Falkland Diving Petrel (p.67)

Black-bellied Storm Petrel (p.66)

White-chinned Petrel (p.64)

Greater Shearwater (p.64)

Sooty Shearwater (p.64)

PLATE 5

White-tufted Grebe (p.54)

Silvery Grebe (p.55)

Great Grebe (p.55)

Cocoi Heron (p.70)

Common Egret (p.70)

Buff-necked Ibis (p.72)

Cattle Egret (p.70)

immature

adult

Black-crowned Night Heron
(p.71)

PLATE 6

Red-legged Cormorant (p.68)

P.a.georgian

King or Imperial Cormorant (p.69)
P.a.albiventer

Rock Cormorant (p.68)

third winter

Falkland Skua (p.89)

Dominican or Kelp Gull (p.92)

immature

winter

summer
(breeding)

Dolphin Gull (p.91)

Brown-hooded Gull (p.93)

Snowy
Sheathbill
(p.89)

South American Tern

Antarctic T
S.v. georg
(p.94)

South American T
(p.93)

PLATE 7

female
male
Ruddy-headed Goose (p.74)

Ashy-headed Goose (p.73)

female
male
Kelp Goose (p.75)

female
male
Upland Goose (p.74)

Coscoroba Swan (p.72)

Black-necked Swan (p.73)

PLATE 8

Yellow-billed Teal (p.77)

South Georgia Pintail (p.78)

Brown Pintail or
Yellow-billed Pintail (p.78)

Cinnamon Teal (p.72)

Silver or Versicolor Teal (p.79)

Chiloë Widgeon (p.79)

Patagonian Crested Duck (p.75)

Falkland Flightless Steamer
Duck (p.76)

Flying Steamer Duck (p.77)

female

male

Falkland Flightless Steamer Duck
(p.76)

Turkey Vulture (p.80)

female

male

Cassin's Falcon (p.83)

Red-backed Buzzard
(p.81)

Crested Caracara (p.82)

immature

adult

Striated Caracara (p.81)

Barn Owl (p.95)

Short-eared Owl
(p.95)

American Kestrel
(p.83)

PLATE 10

Rufous-chested Dotterel
(p.86)

Sanderling (p.87)

Two-banded Plover (p.85)

White-rumped Sandpiper
(p.86)

Magellan or Paraguayan Snipe
(p.87)

Common Snipe (p.87)

Black Oystercatcher (p.85)

Pied Oystercatcher (p.84)

Southern Lapwing (p.85)

Whimbrel (p.87)

PLATE 11

Least Seedsnipe (p.88)

Tussock Bird (p.96)

Fire-eyed Diucon (p.97)

Rufous-backed Negrito (p.98)

Dark-faced Ground Tyrant (p.97)

Violet-eared Dove (p.95)

Barn Swallow (p.99)

Chilean Swallow (p.98)

PLATE 12

Cobb's or Southern House Wren (p.100)

Grass or Short-billed Marsh Wren (p.9

Rufous-collared Sparrow
or Chingolo (p.103)

Black-throated Finch (male)
(p.103)

House Sparrow (male) (p.105)

Black-chinned Siskin (male) (p.104)

Falkland Thru
(male) (p.10(

Falkland Pipit
(p.101)

Long-tailed Meadowla
(male) (p.102)

PLATE 13

female

adult male

Falkland Islands Fur Seal (p.130)

female

adult male

Southern Sea Lion (p.129)

adult male

female

Southern Elephant Seal (p. 135)

Weddell Seal (p.137)

Leopard Seal (p.137)

Fuegian Marine Otter or Sea Otter
(p.127)

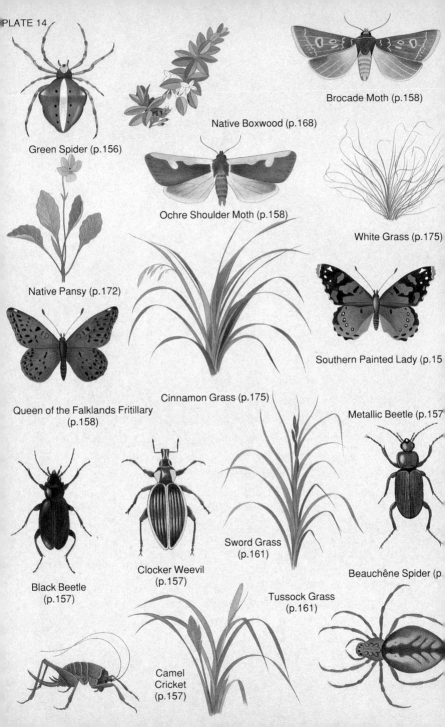

PLATE 14

Green Spider (p.156)

Native Boxwood (p.168)

Brocade Moth (p.158)

Ochre Shoulder Moth (p.158)

White Grass (p.175)

Native Pansy (p.172)

Southern Painted Lady (p.15

Cinnamon Grass (p.175)

Queen of the Falklands Fritillary
(p.158)

Metallic Beetle (p.157

Black Beetle
(p.157)

Clocker Weevil
(p.157)

Sword Grass
(p.161)

Beauchêne Spider (p.

Tussock Grass
(p.161)

Camel
Cricket
(p.157)

Mountain Blue Grass (p.162)

PLATE 15

Native Woodrush (p.162)

Blue Couch Grass (p.162)

Brown Swamp Rush (p.164)

Spiky Grass (p.166)

Scurvy Grass (p.172)

Sea Cabbage (p.166)

Sundew (p.165)

Diddle-dee (p.170)

Marsh Marigold (p.165)

Wild Celery (p.161)

Mountain Berry (p.170)

Teaberry (p.170)

Fachine (p.168)

Gaultheria (p.170)

Yellow Daisy (p.162)

PLATE 16 TREE KELP *Lessonia* sp.
(p.178)

Storm-beached
stem of *L. flavicans*

L. frutescens

L. nigrescens

L. flavicans

Sea lettuce
Ulva sp. (p.179)

Iridaea sp(p.179)

Durvillea antarctica (p.179)

root system

Giant Kelp or Basket Kelp (p.178)

Durvillea caepest
(p.179)

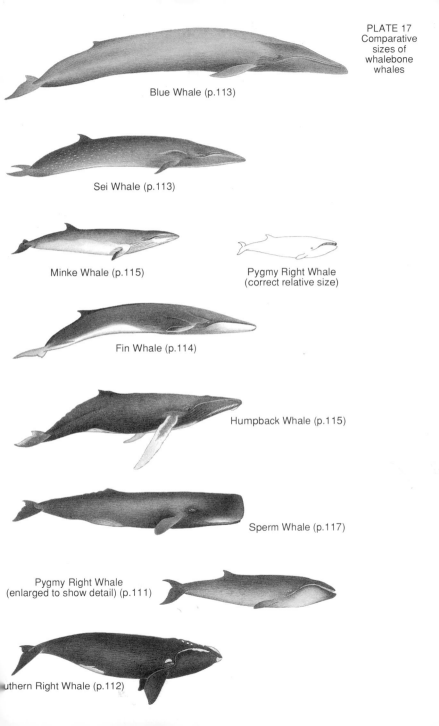

PLATE 17
Comparative
sizes of
whalebone
whales

Blue Whale (p.113)

Sei Whale (p.113)

Minke Whale (p.115)

Pygmy Right Whale
(correct relative size)

Fin Whale (p.114)

Humpback Whale (p.115)

Sperm Whale (p.117)

Pygmy Right Whale
(enlarged to show detail) (p.111)

uthern Right Whale (p.112)

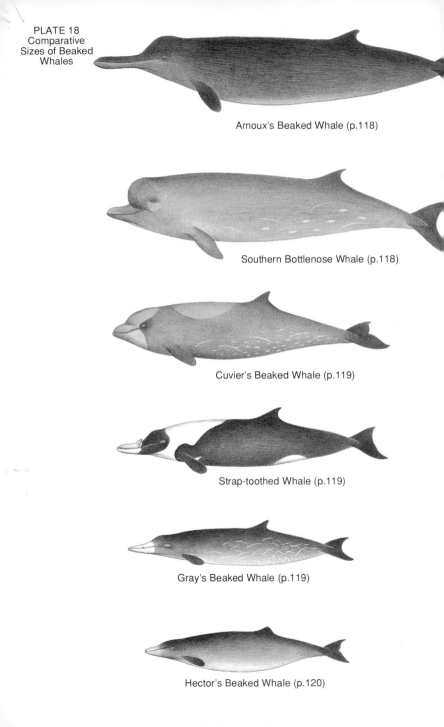

PLATE 18
Comparative
Sizes of Beaked
Whales

Arnoux's Beaked Whale (p.118)

Southern Bottlenose Whale (p.118)

Cuvier's Beaked Whale (p.119)

Strap-toothed Whale (p.119)

Gray's Beaked Whale (p.119)

Hector's Beaked Whale (p.120)

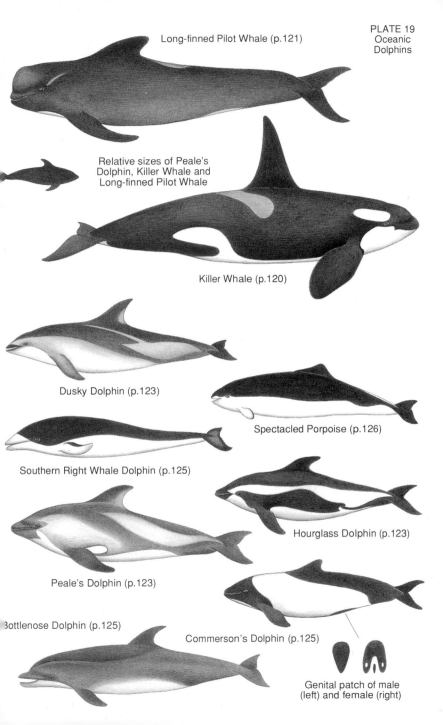

Long-finned Pilot Whale (p.121)

PLATE 19
Oceanic
Dolphins

Relative sizes of Peale's
Dolphin, Killer Whale and
Long-finned Pilot Whale

Killer Whale (p.120)

Dusky Dolphin (p.123)

Spectacled Porpoise (p.126)

Southern Right Whale Dolphin (p.125)

Hourglass Dolphin (p.123)

Peale's Dolphin (p.123)

Bottlenose Dolphin (p.125)

Commerson's Dolphin (p.125)

Genital patch of male
(left) and female (right)

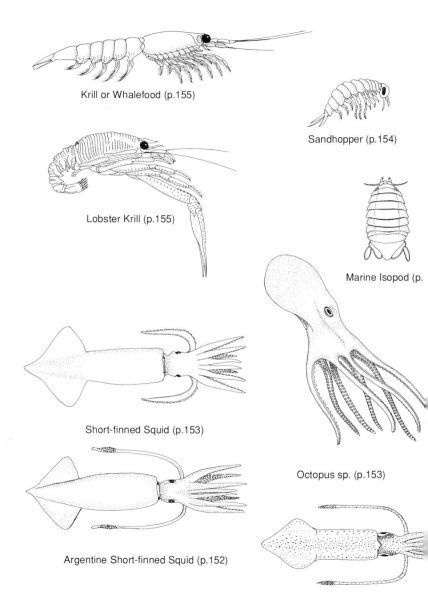

PLATE 20
Marine
Invertebrates

Krill or Whalefood (p.155)

Sandhopper (p.154)

Lobster Krill (p.155)

Marine Isopod (p.

Short-finned Squid (p.153)

Octopus sp. (p.153)

Argentine Short-finned Squid (p.152)

Patagonian Squid Loligo (p.152

slightly down-curved and long, 0·6–0·75 in (1·6–2 cm), in proportion to head. Feet and legs black. Juvenile birds show a more pronounced yellow to yellow-orange gape. Often on the ground. Flies rapidly, often closely following the contours of the ground. Adults mark territories with raised wing display accompanied by a rapid trilling call.

Common on outer islands which remain free of rodents or cats. Not restricted to tussock islands but appears to favour tussock environment. Scavenges beaches and shorelines, taking a wide range of food, including seal and seabird excreta, marine amphipods and scraps of regurgitated feed from seabird colonies. Camel crickets and other insect life found in the tussock habitat represent another important food source. Nests below ground under loose pieces of stone in old petrel burrows and fissures, often within or on the perimeter of a tussock stand. Breeding normally begins in October and two or three eggs are laid. Incubation period is about 12 days, young fledge in 12–15 days. Species is normally double brooded with second laying between December and January.

Family **TYRANNIDAE** Tyrant Flycatchers

Dark-faced Ground Tyrant   Pl. 11
Muscisaxicola macloviana macloviana
Resident: breeding
Restricted to the Falkland Islands, although similar race *M. m. mentalis* breeds in southern Chile, Patagonia and Tierra del Fuego but migrates north to Peru and Uruguay in winter. Length 6·5 in (16·5 cm). Small, very slender bird about 4·5 in (11·5 cm) high. Stands very erect on slender black legs. Upperparts grey-brown with darker grey-brown on top of head. Underparts light grey and off-white on undertail coverts. Tail dark grey with off-white to buff stripe down outer edges. Bill black.

Very agile flight, sometimes hovering to catch prey on the wing and tending to make short flights between elevated perches, dropping to the ground to pick up ground moths and other insects. Has distinctive habit of flicking its wings when alighting. Call note almost inaudible. At beginning of breeding season male adopts a wing-raising display. Fairly common and widely distributed both inland and on coastal areas, where rocky outcrops, stone runs or coastal cliffs offer nesting sites in the form of deep and well-sheltered crevices. Breeds in October through December but little is known about the cycle, although it is probably double brooded.

Fire-eyed Diucon *Pyrope pyrope*   Pl. 11
Vagrant
Very similar to Dark-faced Ground Tyrant, but slightly larger, less slender species, with a distinctive ruby-red eye. Observed on a number of occasions but should be considered a rare vagrant.

Fig. 31 (Top): flight patterns of Chilean Swallow. Generally frequents settlement areas. Rapid wingbeats interspersed with gliding. *Bottom*: Barn Swallow prefers open camp. Flight generally low zig-zag with rapid wingbeats.

Rufous-backed Negrito *Lessonia rufa*   **Pl. 11**

Vagrant

Southern South America, from Arica in northern Chile to Tierra del Fuego and Staten Island, north through Patagonia to southern Brazil. Southern race breeding in Tierra del Fuego, migrates north in winter. Not recorded in Falklands annually, but may be considered to be one of the more common vagrants. Length 5 in (13 cm). Small terrestrial species, rather restless. Male plumage distinctive, black with a chestnut-red back. Female back brown and cinnamon. Underparts grey spotted brown. Short black tail.

Family **HIRUNDINIDAE** Swallows

Several vagrant species have been recorded (as well as those visiting species described below): Southern Martin *Progne modesta elegans*; Purple Martin *Progne subis*; Rough-winged swallow *Stelgidopteryx ruficollis*.

Chilean Swallow *Tachycineta leucopyga*   **Pl. 11**

Regular visitor

Breeds in southern South America, Tierra del Fuego. Southern populations migrate north to Brazil in winter. Regular visitor to Falklands, small numbers usually seen in September/October and again in March. Length 5·5–6 in (13–15 cm), a small swallow. Blue-black above with distinct white rump and half-collar and white underparts. Tail short, slightly forked. Tends to glide, with occasional rapid wingbeats. Might be confused with White-rumped Swallow *Tachycineta leucorrhoa* which has white forehead and half superciliary, but is not as shy as Chilean Swallow.

Barn Swallow *Hirundo rustica erythrogaster* **Pl. 11**

Regular visitor

A North American race of the European Swallow. Migrates to South America, wintering in the austral summer as far south as Tierra del Fuego. Its occurrence in the Falkland Islands and as a rare vagrant in South Georgia coincides with its movements south in October/November and northwards in March. Length 6 in (15 cm). Flies low with rapid zigzagging flight. Shining dark blue above. Forehead, throat and upper breast rufous chestnut with blue-black breast-band and buff underparts. Wings and tail blue-black, tail deeply forked with white subterminal patch on inner web. Juveniles are generally duller and more often recorded.

Family **TROGLODYTIDAE** Wrens

Grass Wren or **Short-billed Marsh Wren** **Pl. 12**
Cistothorus platensis falklandicus

Resident: breeding

Confined to the Falkland Islands, other races occur in South America as far south as Cape Horn. Length 4–4·5 in (10–12 cm). Smallest of resident birds, stands approximately 2–2·5 in (5–6 cm). Has distinctive whirring flight, usually of very short duration. Upperparts dark brown with light fawn stripes which commence on the head as flecks, increasing in length as they progress down the back. Tail reddish-brown with dark brown bars. Underparts a light buff, undertail light brown. Has a buff eye-stripe. Bill horn colour. Legs and feet buff.

Fairly widespread but confined to moister regions with dense cover in Cinnamon Grass, Brown Swamp Rush, Sword Grass or Tussock Grass. Although there are no records of this species' status before the introduction of sheep and cattle, it was probably far more common before much of its preferred habitat was grazed out. Breeding season commences with nest-building and egg-laying in October.

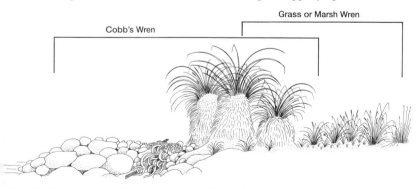

Fig. 32 Habitat zones of Grass and Cobb's Wren, showing boulder beach with Tussock Grass fringe and inland stands of rush, Cinnamon Grass and Sword Grass

Nest usually a ball of grass, fine roots and other vegetable fibres, built in cover of grasses just above ground level. Feeds on a variety of insect fauna and on grass seeds.

Cobb's Wren or Southern House Wren PI. 12
Troglodytes aëdon cobbi

Resident: breeding
Confined to the Falkland Islands, other races inhabit North and South America. Length 5 in (13 cm), height 2·5 in (6 cm) – small. Fairly tame, often skulking between beach boulders rather than flying. Upperparts generally light rusty-brown. Wings cinnamon brown with small darker grey-brown bars and uppertail similar but with darker brown bars. Underparts slightly lighter and underwings light grey. Undertail light grey with darker bars. Bill slightly curved and fairly long 0·75 in (1·6 cm). Feet and legs brown. May show colour variations between different island populations.

Restricted to outer tussock islands and some others which remain rodent and cat free. Appears to favour loose boulder beaches with deposits of kelp adjacent to stands of Tussock Grass. Nests in the dry skirt of tussock or in cavities formed in coastal banks of peat, clay or rock. Breeds October through December. Fledglings found both early and late in the season suggest it is double-brooded. Feeds on small amphipods and insect life found amongst kelp wrecks, Camel Crickets and larvae.

Family **TURDIDAE** Thrushes

Falkland Thrush *Turdus falcklandii falcklandii* PI. 12

Resident: breeding
Confined to the Falkland Islands, with the race *Turdus falcklandii* inhabiting Tierra del Fuego, Staten Island, Cape Horn, Patagonia and Southern Chile. Length 10 in (25 cm). Very upright stance, about 5·5 in (14 cm) in height. Spends much of its time on the ground. Has distinctive movements, hopping, bounding and running for short distances with wingtips held below level of tail. Adult upperparts ochre-brown and head blackish, male usually shows a darker cap. Tail blackish. Throat a lighter buffy-ochre streaked blackish and underparts buff. Has distinctive orange-yellow legs, deep yellow bill and yellow eye-ring. Fledglings have spotted blackish underparts and upperparts streaked with buff, changing in late summer to adult plumage but with brownish bill and dull yellow-brown legs.

Widespread and common, inhabits the more rocky inland regions and coasts. Is locally abundant on offshore tussock islands and in settlements, where it has adapted to nesting in peat sheds and other buildings. Inhabits trees (*Cupressus*) and bushes, in particular Gorse *Ulex europaeus*. Nests often quite large, usually of dried grass and other vegetation. One female under observation built a complete nest in 48 hours, the main structure, less the lining, being built in less than eight hours. Gathered during a period of heavy rain, it was composed of green and dead material and remained wet and green some days after the bird had commenced incubation. Nesting commences in mid August and breeding continues through to late January. Usually has three or even four broods. Incubation period varies, but usually 12–13 days and young fledge in 14–18 days. Breeding cycles may be as little as 8–9 days apart. Food largely larvae and earthworms, although in dry summer conditions feeds largely on ground beetles and moths. Readily takes berried fruits, both cultivated and the berries of Diddle-dee and Teaberry. In settlement areas birds feed on scraps, in particular fat and meat.

Family **MOTACILLIDAE** Pipits

Falkland Pipit *Anthus correndera grayi* **Pl. 12**

Resident: breeding

Breeds only in the Falkland Islands. Other races inhabit South America, from Peru, Bolivia and Brazil south to Tierra del Fuego. Length 5·5 in (14·5 cm), height 3·5 in (9 cm) – small. Slight species with very finely built legs and feet and an exceptionally long hind claw 0·5 in (1·2 cm). Plumage generally buff-brown to light buff, heavily streaked dark brown on the back and breast. Tail narrow, with small terminal fork. Eye feathers shaded lemon-yellow. Back feathers shaded a golden yellow and primaries and secondaries edged yellow. Feet and legs buff. Bill horn-coloured with rosy hue. Has a typical 'meadow pipit' song flight and can climb to such a height that it is difficult to see with the naked eye. Descends on a churring note. Flight jerky and undulating.

Fairly widespread, appearing to prefer open grasslands, in particular dense swards of White Grass. Also inhabits coastal heath and open tussock. Spends a lot of time on the ground, moving quickly through the cover of grass and other vegetation. Breeding commences in September. On New Island in the extreme west, birds are in full song from mid-August to December. Probably has three broods. Nest is a finely built cup, well concealed on the ground amongst grasses and other vegetation. Feeds on small grubs, ghost moths and other insects. Dense population on New Island feeds on small ground spiders.

South Georgia Pipit *Anthus antarcticus*

Resident: breeding, South Georgia

Restricted to South Georgia. Was probably derived from the South American and Falkland Islands species but is now considered to be distinct. Length 6·5 in (17 cm). Similar in appearance and habits to Falkland Pipit but slightly larger and has reddish tan upperparts marked with dark brown and light buff and lacks yellow feather shading. Largely confined to offshore islands and areas of the main island protected from rats. Prefers coastal habitats, feeding along the shoreline or in tussock cover. Feeds on flies and their larvae, beetles and marine copepods. Breeding season extends between November and January. Species is double-brooded. Nests close to the ground, usually in cover of tussock.

Fig. 33   Long-tailed Meadowlark in typical feeding habitat

Family **ICTERIDAE**   Orioles

Long-tailed Meadowlark or **Military Starling**   **Pl. 12**
Sturnella loyca falklandica

Resident: breeding

Restricted to the Falkland Islands, although another race is found in southern South America to Tierra del Fuego. Length 9·5–10 in (24–27 cm). Stands 4–5 in (10 to 12·5 cm). Adult male has deep vermilion breast and throat and red lores extending into an off-white eye stripe. Bill is heavily built and pointed, appearing oversized in relation to head. Top of head, back and rump dark brown with golden-buff edged feathers, giving a streaked effect. Cheeks, flanks and undertail black brushed off white. Bill and feet horn coloured with steel-blue areas. Female has much paler red breast, generally lighter plumage and is slightly smaller than the male. Juvenile a ghost image of the female. Spends much of its time on the ground, probing for larvae and other insect life. Walks quickly, very similar to the European Starling, hence the local term 'starling'. Usually has a low, almost crouching stance, but when alarmed holds head erect. Male has a loud, rather harsh song, female call much weaker and shorter.

Fairly widespread, but more generally inhabiting settlement areas and coastal regions. Commences breeding in mid-August and continues through to January. Nest usually built of grass, often situated beneath clumps of grass with entrance tunnel, occasionally nests low down in Gorse bushes. Incubation lasts 12–13 days. Young fledge in periods varying from 11–15 days. Raises two, possibly three broods.

Takes a variety of food, including earthworms, caterpillars, larvae, pupae and marine invertebrates such as amphipods. Female appears to be solely responsible for collecting and feeding the young, often collecting and stockpiling food before taking it to the nest. The male visits the nest to remove droppings. Although very territorial and isolated during the breeding season, flocks of both adults and immatures gather in late summer, remaining together throughout the winter. Falkland population does not migrate but may move locally.

Family **FRINGILLIDAE** Finches

Alongside residents, five vagrant species have been recorded in the islands: Yellow-bridled Finch *Melanodera xanthogramma*, Patagonian Sierra Finch *Phrygilus patagonicus*, Gray-hooded Sierra Finch *Phrygilus gayi* and Mourning Sierra Finch *Phrygilus fruticeti*.

Black-throated Finch   *Melanodera melanodera melanodera*   **Pl. 12**
Resident: breeding
Confined to the Falkland Islands, while *M. m. princetoniana* is restricted to southern South America, Tierra del Fuego, Straits of Magellan and Patagonia. Length 6 in (15 cm), height approximately 3 in (7·5 cm) – small. A ground-loving species, often overlooked due to its quiet nature and colouration which blends in with ground cover, particularly in the case of immatures and females. Male bird has distinctive blue-grey head, contrasting with a black bib and face mask, edged with white. Back and flanks brushed blue-grey and light yellowish-green. Breast and underparts similar, but predominantly yellowish-green. Tail slightly forked, greyish with two yellow outer feathers. Primaries and inner edge of tertials black-ish-brown. Leading edge of folded wing shows bright yellow. Feet black. Male bill blue grey and female horn-coloured. Female plumage largely streaked brown and grey-buff with faint tinges of yellow on the underparts. Tail brownish-grey with feathers finely edged with white. As in male, outer tail feathers yellow, but lighter. Wings dark brown with feathers edged with white. Has faint buff eye stripe.

Fairly common and widespread, found inland but prefers coastal regions. Also inhabits some dense Tussock Grass islands, but more common on those with inner areas of grass and heath. Feeds on seeds of tussock, Mountain Blue Grass and other grasses. In autumn and winter takes seed from the berries of Diddle-dee, Teaberry and Mountain Berry. On Elephant Jason Island finches were observed gathering Diddle-dee berries which were then pushed into a large Balsam Bog while the birds extracted the seeds – a practice probably accounting for the occurrence of Diddle-dee growing from some larger Balsam plants. Breeds between September and late December producing two, possibly three, broods. Nest usually well concealed on the ground, in dense White Grass or under cover of other vegetation. Also nests in shallow crevices beneath rocks.

Rufous-collared Sparrow or **Chingolo**   *Zonotrichia capensis*   **Pl. 12**
Regular vagrant
Several races have been described, inhabiting both tropical and temperate regions of South America. *Z. c. australis* inhabits southern regions of South America and is one of the other races identified as reaching the Falkland Islands. Length 5·5 in (14 cm). Small, sparrow-like, height about 3 in (7·5 cm), but with finer proportions. Has distinctive grey head and crown feathers which form a small crest flanked by heavy black lines. Throat white with a semi-collar of cinnamon on the nape. Breast and flanks light grey. Upperparts brown streaked with black, bill brown-grey and legs brown. Fairly

common vagrant, usually observed near settlements where it spends much of its time on the ground, feeding both on seeds and insects.

Black-chinned Siskin *Carduelis barbata* Pl. 12

Resident: breeding

Species widespread in wooded areas, particularly edges of Beech *Nothofagus* sp. forests of Tierra del Fuego, Straits of Megellan, Patagonia and Chile. Length 5 in (13 cm). Very small finch about 2·5 in (6·5 cm) high. Male has generally olive-green plumage on back, suffused yellow-green on rump, flanks and cheeks. Underparts brighter yellow-green. Has distinct black cap with small black chin. Tail brown, with small amount of yellow on basal sides. Wings, blackish to brown, with two bright lemon-yellow bars. Female plumage similar but duller and lacks black cap and chin. Bill dark blue-grey above, light horn below. Feet blackish-brown.

Largely confined to some offshore tussock islands and settlement areas with mature growths of introduced trees, shrubs and Native Boxwood. Although seemingly common in some areas, the Falkland population is probably small. Usually seen in small groups or flocks. Easily identified and detected by rather noisy and fairly constant twittering song. Begins breeding in September and continues through to December. Nests about 6 ft (1·8 m) above the ground in tussock, Boxwood, *Cupressus* and other shrubs which provide dense cover for the delicate cup-shaped nest. Normally has three broods. Feeds largely on small seeds, but probably also takes small larvae, recorded as an important food in its South American habitat.

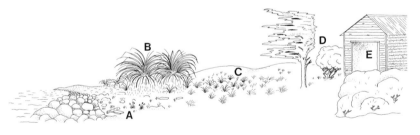

Fig. 34 Habitats of some passerine species: A, vegetated storm or boulder beaches – Black-throated Finch, Ground Tyrant; B, coastal Tussock Grass – Siskin and Falkland Thrush; C, open grassland and heath – Pipit, Black-throated Finch; D, introduced trees, gorse and Native Boxwood – Siskin and Falkland Thrush; and E, settlement out-buildings – Thrush, House Sparrow

Family **PLOCEIDAE** Sparrows

House Sparrow *Passer domesticus* **Pl. 12**

Resident: breeding

At one time confined to Europe, North Africa and Asia, it is now a fairly cosmopolitan species having been introduced to North and South America, Australia and New Zealand. Apparently introduced to South Georgia during the whaling era but its present status there is unknown. Small, length 5·5 in (14 cm), height 3 in (7·5 cm). Fairly plump species with generally brown plumage, streaked darker brown on back, greyish underparts and a light wing bar. Male has a black bib on throat and upper breast, a grey crown and light cheeks. Female is dull brown and grey-white below, lacking any distinctive markings.

Species restricted to Stanley and a small number of settlements where it nests in cavities formed by double roofs or walls and occasionally in trees. Believed to have been introduced to Stanley in 1919 (Woods, 1975) and subsequently spread. Its colonisation of the Falklands has not been over-successful and populations remain small and isolated, however, with the recent establishment of very large building complexes such as Mount Pleasant Airport this may change.

MAMMALS

CHECKLIST

The following list covers all known breeding species of land and marine mammals, both indigenous and introduced species, found in the Falkland Islands and South Georgia. Those recorded only from South Georgia are marked (SG).

Brazilian free-tailed Bat   *Tadarida brasiliensis* (single vagrant recorded from Golding and Pebble Islands)

European Rabbit   *Oryctolagus cuniculus*
Cottontail   *Sylvilagus* sp.
European Hare   *Lepus europaeus*

House Mouse   *Mus musculus*
Norway Rat   *Rattus norvegicus*
Black Rat   *Rattus rattus*

Pygmy Right Whale   *Caperea marginata*
Southern Right Whale   *Eubalaena australis*
Blue Whale   *Balaenoptera musculus*
Sei Whale   *Balaenoptera borealis*
Minke Whale   *Balaenoptera acutorostrata*
Fin Whale   *Balaenoptera physalus*
Humpback Whale   *Megaptera novae-angliae*
Sperm Whale   *Physeter macrocephalus*
Arnoux's Beaked Whale   *Berardius arnuxii*
Southern Bottlenose Whale   *Hyperodon planifrons*
Cuvier's Beaked Whale   *Ziphius cavirostris*
Layard's Strap-toothed Whale   *Mesoplodon layardii*
Gray's Beaked Whale   *Mesoplodon grayi*

Hector's Beaked Whale   *Mesoplodon hectori*

Killer Whale or Orca   *Orcinus orca*
Long-finned Pilot Whale   *Globicephala melaena*
Dusky Dolphin   *Lagenorhynchus obscurus*
Hourglass Dolphin   *Lagenorhynchus cruciger*
Peale's Dolphin   *Lagenorhynchus australis*
Bottlenose Dolphin   *Tursiops truncatus*
Southern Right Whale Dolphin   *Lissodelphis peronii*
Commerson's Dolphin   *Cephalorhynchus commersonii*
Spectacled Porpoise   *Phocoena dioptrica*

Fuegian Marine or Sea Otter   *Lutra felina*

Patagonian Fox   *Dusicyon griseus griseus*

Southern Sea Lion   *Otaria flavescens*
Falkland Islands Fur Seal   *Arctocephalus australis australis*
South Georgia Fur Seal   *Arctocephalus tropicalis gazella* (SG)
Southern Elephant Seal   *Mirounga leonina*
Leopard Seal   *Hydrurga leptonyx*
Weddell Seal   *Leptonychotes weddelli* (SG)

Guanaco   *Lama guanicoe*
Eurasian Reindeer   *Rangifer tarandus* (SG)

Order **LAGOMORPHA** Hares, Rabbits and Pikas

Family **LEPORIDAE** Hares and Rabbits

This is the principal family of Lagomorpha comprising about 70 species spread worldwide. Two species have been introduced to the Falkland Islands, the rabbit being represented by two sub-species.

Brown Hare *Lepus europaeus*
Introduced: breeding
Length, head and body, 25–27 in (63·5–68·5 cm). Ears 4·5–5 in (11·5–12·5 cm). Fur a greyish brown, underparts whitish. Ears have black patch on tips. Top of tail dark, underside white. Much larger than any of the introduced rabbits and has a more upright stance, sometimes lifting up onto hindquarters to look around. Distribution restricted to East Falkland mainland, where it is locally fairly common on open coastal heath and grassland. Unlike the rabbit, it is not a social animal, individual animals remaining apart except in the breeding or 'rutting' season. Feeds mainly at night and rests during the day in a depression or 'form' made in long grass. Population status not known and there are no known records indicating when the hare was first introduced.

European Rabbit *Oryctolagus cuniculus*
Introduced: breeding
Small rabbit about 18 in (45·5 cm) in length. Ears shorter than head and, unlike Brown Hare, lacks black patches. Fur a greyish- brown with buff-coloured flanks and a tail which is dark on top and white underneath. Occasionally all-black animals are recorded. Breeds in a few localities on East Falkland, especially on the northern parts of the east coast, where it was originally introduced. Also found on Saunders Island, West Tyssen Island and until some years ago on Keppel

Fig. 35 Brown Hare

Fig. 36   (Left): Wild Rabbit. *(Right)*: North American Rabbit or Cottontail

Island. The complete history of introduction is not fully known. Rabbits were introduced to Saunders Island by Byron in 1765 and were recorded by both Moody and Whittington in the early 1840s as being common in valleys around Port Louis on East Falkland. Being of a European type, it is possible that this particular population was first introduced by the French in 1764.

Cottontail   *Sylvilagus* sp.

Introduced: breeding

About 17 in (43 cm) in length (head and body). Ears about 3 in (7·5 cm), distinctly longer than head. General colouration greyish with silver flecks. Has distinct rusty-red nape patch and white on tops of legs. Tail small, whitish. Ears have black line on tips. Does not make a warren but lies in a partially hidden 'form' in dense patches of *Poa erecta* grass, Tussock Grass or in thickets of Gorse *Ulex* sp. Also uses abandoned Magellan Penguin burrows and crevices beneath rocks. Appears to have a preference for higher, drier areas. In summer feeds on various grasses and on the bark of Gorse. Appears to be restricted to New Island, probably having been introduced by American whalers and sealers who used the island as a base in the late 1700s – early 1800s. Resembles the Eastern Cottontail *Sylvilagus floridanus* of the eastern side of North America.

Order **RODENTIA**   Gnawing Mammals

Family **MURIDAE**   Old World Rats and Mice

The family of rats, mice and Eurasian voles is divided into eight sub-families. The family Muridae comprises 250 species, distributed throughout the world, including three in the Falklands: the House Mouse, Black Rat and Brown Rat. The existence of a fourth species or even possibly a species from the sub-family Cricetinae of the New World should not be discounted.

Fig. 37 The two forms of House Mouse found in the islands: long-tailed large-eared form *(top)* and House Mouse *(bottom)*

House Mouse *Mus musculus*

Introduced: breeding

A small, greyish-brown mouse with grey or light brown belly and scaly tail. Length of head and body 3–3·5 in (7·5–8·5 cm), tail 2·75–3·75 in (7–9·5 cm). Fur short. Ears medium size. Locally common both in settlements and in the field, where it feeds on seeds and berries. During winter tends to appear more frequently in settlements. Probably introduced during the period of early settlement in the late 1700s. Recorded on Saunders Island, site of the first British settlement, in 1774 and in Port Louis in 1842. On Steeple Jason Island there exists a long tailed, large eared form of mouse, not dissimilar to the Long-tailed Mouse or Woodmouse *Apodemus sylvaticus* of the Old World (or Deer mouse *Peromyscus maniculatus* of the New World). The origin of such a form on a remote outlier is not known, but presents the interesting possibility that it might have emigrated from the New World by way of American whalers and sealers who worked this island in the late 1700s and early 1800s.

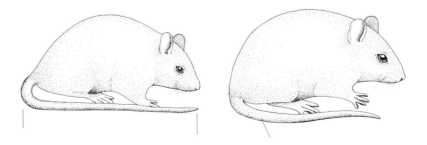

Fig. 38 Black Rat and Norway Rat

Norway Rat or **Brown Rat** *Rattus norvegicus*

Introduced: breeding

Head and body 7–10 in (17·5–25 cm), tail 5 in (12·5–20 cm). Distinguished by its greyish-brown colour and rather long scaly tail. Belly greyish with 12 mammae or milk teats. Inhabits both settlements and other areas. At South Georgia lives mainly in dense Tussock Grass which provides a major part of its diet throughout the year. Also found on a number of Falkland offshore tussock islands. Being omnivorous not only eats roots and growing points of the tussock but also insect life, carrion, marine invertebrates and ground nesting birds, such as petrels, and their eggs. Islands with populations of this species are noticeably clear of smaller, ground-nesting species. A ground-loving species, usually nesting in burrows either beneath buildings or in Tussock Grass. Forms well-marked trails, often under cover of vegetation, with separate faecal areas. Falkland breeding habits have not been studied, although it probably breeds all year round.

Black Rat or **Ship Rat** *Rattus rattus*

Introduced: breeding

Slightly smaller in body length than the Brown Rat, 7–8 in (18–20 cm), but noticeably longer tail measures 8·5–10 in (21·5–25·5 cm) and is longer than head and body length. Tail naked and lacks scales. Fur dark brown, sometimes greyish on belly. Ears more than half as long as head. Ten mammae. Unlike the Brown Rat it does not burrow, preferring to live in tops of buildings and in generally drier conditions. Also probably not as prolific, although known to populate the main islands and some inhabited larger offshore islands. Prefers Tussock Grass and field areas near settlements, probably being more dependent on man for its survival. Although introduced to South Georgia at different times it is not known to have survived. Nothing is known of its breeding habits.

Order **CETACEA** Whales, Dolphins and Porpoises

Sub-order **MYSTICETI** Whalebone Whales

There are three families representing the Mysticeti, members of two of these are found in southern waters. In place of teeth, all the Mysticetes possess baleen plates, or whalebone blades – triangular, hairy plates situated either side of the mouth, used to collect and sieve the small organisms which form their food. Also all have paired blowhole, forming two longitudinal slits on the top of the head.

Fig. 39 Identification of Right Whale at sea

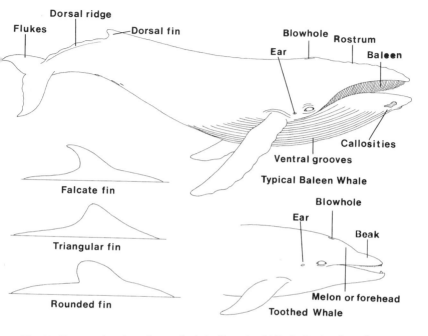

Fig. 40 Topography of two forms of whale, Humpback Whale *(top)* and small toothed whale *(bottom)*, and illustration of different dorsal fin forms

Family **BALAENIDAE** Right Whales

Pygmy Right Whale *Caperea marginata*   **Pl. 17**

Found in the southern hemisphere in waters north of the Antarctic Convergence. Shares features of Southern Right Whale (below) but much smaller, largest known specimen 19 ft 5 in (5·9 m) long. Also more streamlined and has a less disproportionately large head and a small falcate dorsal fin. Lower jaws are bowed and the upper jaw arched. The rostrum is tapered. Flippers are small, narrow and slightly rounded at the tip. The tail flukes are broad. Dorsal areas grey to dark grey, with white ventral regions extending to lower half of lower jaw. Dark flippers stand out against lighter body. Has 230–250 pairs of small, yellowish-white baleen plates, the largest about 70 cm in length. Sightings are rare and usually of lone individuals or pairs, sometimes observed in company of dolphins or Pilot Whales.

Southern Right Whale   *Eubalaena australis*   **Pl. 17**

Believed to be isolated from the Northern Right Whale by the tropical belt, roughly 20°N and 20°S, although it is not clear if they are distinct. Robust whales whose large heads make up 25% of their body length. Grow up to 55 ft 9 in (17 m) with a weight of more than 60 tons. Rostrum long, narrow and arched and from it hang about 250 pairs of black baleen plates; bowed lower lips close over it on either side (see line drawing). On the top of the head are a series of growths or callosities, the largest, the 'bonnet', appears on the rostrum in front of the two blowholes. Also form on sides of head, chin, lower lips and around the eyes. Black or very dark grey all over, except for callosities and occasional irregular white patches on throat and belly. Patches and callosities vary greatly, facilitating identification of individuals. Lacks dorsal fin or ridge. Flippers large and broad. Tail flukes have a broad, smooth and concave rear margin, with a deep notch. Slow swimmers, rarely exceeding 4 miles (6 km) per hour, and identified at sea by their slow movements and characteristic 'V' shaped spout (see line drawing). When diving, tail flukes are lifted clear of the surface.

Historically found seasonally off the coasts of South America and were probably the main quarry of early whalers working out of Falkland harbours. However, like the northern populations, they were hunted to near extinction, the last Right Whale taken in Falkland waters was in the early 1900s by the Salvesen Whaling Station at New Island. In the last twenty years the species has shown a slow recovery and has been seen in small numbers in their old recorded habitats. At Golfo San Jose, on the Peninsula Valdez in Patagonia, they appear in numbers each year between July and November, giving hope that they may again be seen in numbers in Falkland waters.

Family **BALAENOPTERIDAE**   Rorquals

Six species make up this family, of which five are recorded in southern waters. 'Rorqual' is derived from an old Norse term meaning 'grooved whale' – a reference to the grooves or pleats on the underside of the throat and chest. All these

Fig. 41   Identification of Blue Whale *(top)* and Sei Whale *(bottom)* at sea

whales have pointed flippers, a dorsal fin and a flat upper jaw, the lower jaw is bowed outwards.

Blue Whale *Balaenoptera musculus* Pl. 17

Long and slender, may exceed 98 ft (30 m) in length in the southern hemisphere, with an estimated weight of 160 tons. Dark slaty-blue with lighter mottling on flanks and belly. Some show a yellowish colouration caused by diatom accumulations forming a film on the skin after long periods in colder waters. When viewed from above, rostrum appears broad, flat and nearly 'U' shaped. A single ridge extends from raised area in front of blowhole to near tip of snout. Flippers are long and slim and the flukes broad and triangular, with a slightly notched but otherwise smooth rear edge. Extremely small dorsal fin is set very far back on body and is rarely visible until whale is about to dive, when the tail stock lifts slightly out of the water. Has 55–88 throat grooves extending back to the navel. Slender, vertical blow (see line illustration) may be up to 29 ft 6 in (9 m) high.

Usually occur singly or in pairs and may follow well-known routes at specific periods during their long migrations. Relatively shallow feeders, taking krill from the shallower depths of the sea. In the southern hemisphere, generally stay south of 40°S during summer, moving north in winter. Now very rarely sighted off the islands, although in past years it was regularly seen during migration.

Sei Whale *Balaenoptera borealis* Pl. 17

Distributed worldwide but favour temperate and oceanic waters, although do not extend as far polewards as the Blue or Fin Whale. In the southern hemisphere, found primarily south of latitude 30°S in winter and south of 40°S in summer, although remain common around South Georgia in late summer and autumn.

In the Antarctic males reach a length of 58 ft (17·7 m) and females 69 ft (21 m). In dorsal view, appears slim and streamlined with a less rounded snout than Blue Whale. Viewed from the side, the head is slightly arched. A single prominent rostral ridge extends from blowhole to tip of snout. Belly is marked by 38 to 56 ventral grooves which end well before naval. Flippers relatively small and pointed at tips, flukes also relatively small. Dorsal is far more prominent than that of Blue Whale, strongly falcate and situated much further forward, more than one third of body length forward of the fluke notch. Dark grey on back and sides and often marked with grey or white scars. Ventral groove area marked by an area of greyish white. Baleen plates, 300–400 on each side, are black with greyish fringe.

Travel in groups of 2–5, but may gather in larger numbers on feeding grounds. Largely surface feeders and do not dive deeply. The head rarely emerges at a steep angle, instead the blowholes, much of the back and dorsal fin are visible almost simultaneously and may remain visible for long periods. Blow is an inverted cone (see illustration) but spray lower and less dense than that of Fin Whale. Submerge by slipping below surface and remain only a few metres down, their progress marked by a series of ripples as they move their flukes.

Fin Whale or Razorback *Balaenoptera physalus*   Pl. 17

Distributed world wide, but more common in temperate, arctic and antarctic waters than in tropical regions. In the southern hemisphere, migrate between the warmer breeding grounds to summer feeding grounds in the Antarctic. There are several populations, those sighted off the Falklands probably winter off the Brazilian coast.

Not quite as large as Blue Whale, but grows to some 85 ft (26 m) in the southern hemisphere. Head flat, with a single ridge running from raised area in front of blowhole. Rostrum is narrower and more 'V' shaped than 'Gothic arch' shape of the Blue Whale. On the dorsal surface a distinct ridge runs from the fin to the flukes, hence its name 'razorback'. Dorsal fin may be more than 24 in (60 cm) tall (nearly twice the height of that of the Blue Whale and similar to Sei Whale but less falcate) and is positioned about one third along body length, forward from the tail flukes.

Dark grey to brownish-black, but lacks Blue Whale mottling and rarely as scarred as Sei Whale. Behind the head and along the back is a greyish-white chevron, its apex running along the midline and its arms pointing down the sides. Undersides, including undersides of flippers and flukes, are white. Dark, asymmetric colour on head reaches further down on left than on right. Lower right lip, mouth cavity and about 20–30% of the right front baleen are yellowish-white, on some animals the right upper lip may also show lighter colouration. The remaining plates are striped with alternate bands of yellowish-white and blueish-grey. There are between 260 and 480 baleen plates on each side. The ventral grooves number 56–100 and extend to the navel or beyond.

Occasionally seen singly or in pairs but usually in pods of three to seven – pods making up herds of larger numbers. However, individuals of one herd may be miles apart. Tall, 13 ft (4 m) blow, shaped like an elongated, inverted cone. When moving slowly, dorsal is exposed shortly after the appearance of the blowholes. When surfacing from a deeper dive they may blow, submerge the blowholes, then arch the back and dorsal high above the surface. Flukes not shown when diving. Was probably one of the more common Falkland species and one of the main quarries of the New Island Whaling Station which operated between 1908 and 1916. Sightings now rare.

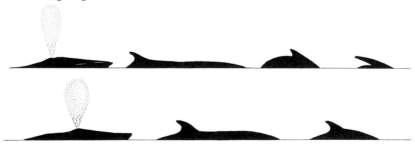

Fig. 42 Identification of Fin Whales *(top)* and Minke Whales *(bottom)* at sea

Fig. 43 Identification of Humpback Whale *(top)* and Sperm Whale *(bottom)* at sea

Minke Whale or Lesser Rorqual   *Balaenoptera acutorostrata*   Pl. 17

Smallest of the Balaenoptera. Northern and southern populations differ, some authorities recognise two or even three sub-species. Widely distributed in tropical, temperate and polar waters. Maximum length for a female in the southern hemisphere is about 32 ft 9 in (10 m), with a weight of about 10 tons (10·16 tonnes). The male is slightly smaller. Slender and very streamlined, with distinctive, extremely narrow, pointed snout. Viewed from above, the rostrum is triangular, with a single prominent head ridge. Flippers slim with pointed tips. Flukes broad and smoothly concave along the rear margin. There are 50–70 ventral grooves which end before navel, often just behind flippers.

Tall, falcate, dorsal fin lies about two thirds of the body length back from snout. Generally black above and white below from chin to tail flukes, including flippers. On northern hemisphere populations there is a diagonal band of white across the middle of the top surface of the flippers. Often also have two light grey areas on their sides, one just above and behind flippers, another just in front and below dorsal fin. The 300–325 baleen plates are white or yellowish white, although southern hemisphere animals often show dark grey on the baleen.

More commonly seen as single animals, pairs or trios. Often swim close to shores, entering bays and inlets. Blow is low and inconspicuous. Like Fin Whales, they often arch the back high above the surface when diving, but do not show tail flukes. May also breach, leaping completely clear of the water. In the South Atlantic migrates to and from around 42°S, mature whales ranging south to the ice edge, while immatures remain between 50° and 20°S.

Humpback Whale   *Megaptera novae-angliae*   Pl. 17

Very distinct from other rorquals and thus placed in a separate genus, *Megaptera,* meaning 'big wing', a reference to this whale's enormously long flippers. Widely distributed in all oceans, ranging from tropical wintering grounds around islands and continental coasts to the edges of polar ice zones.

Very thick-set and robust. Female humpbacks grow to around 52 ft 6 in (16 m), males are slightly smaller. Viewed from above, head is broad and rounded and the head ridge indistinct and marked by a line of fleshy knobs, which also appear elsewhere on head and lower jaw. Also has a very characteristic rounded projection near tip of lower jaw. Dorsal fin lies about one third of the body length from the flukes. Size and shape varies, from a small triangular projection to a more sharply falcate fin. Dorsal frequently includes a hump or step, from which the species derives its common name. Enormous elongated flippers, with knobs or lumps along the leading edge, may equal one third of body length. The flukes are broad and marked on the rear margin by serrations and irregularities. About 14–35 broad ventral grooves extend to the navel. Usually black or grey, with a white region varying in area on the throat and belly. Flippers are white underneath and may be all white. Underside of flukes are partially or completely white. The 270–400 baleen plates are black to olive-brown.

Often found alone or in groups of 2–3, except in their breeding and feeding areas where they form larger groups. Blow is about 9 ft 7 in (3 m) high and bushy (wide relative to height). As they dive, flukes are raised high in the air. Slow swimmers,

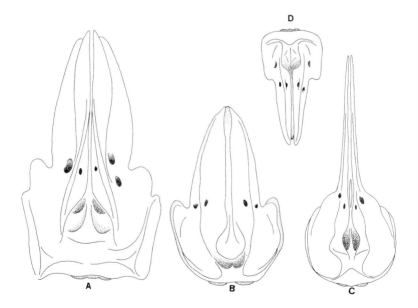

Fig. 44 Forms of some whale skulls: A, Killer Whale; B, Pilot Whale;
C, beaked whale; D, dolphin

generally travelling between 4 and 7·5 miles (6 and 12 km) per hour. Known for their breaching, when they can leap clear of the water. Humpbacks make extensive seasonal migrations to their wintering areas, following coasts or keeping to island groups. Probably common in the Falklands before the earlier whaling era but sightings now rare, although single animals sighted in Port Philomel in the austral summers of 1984 and 1985 suggest they are reappearing.

Sub-order **ODONTOCETI**
Toothed Whales, Dolphins and Porpoises

Comprises seven families. All Odontocetes have teeth, although not always visible, and asymmetrical skulls, the right side of the frontal section being larger than the left. They have a single external nasal opening or blowhole. There are also differences in the skeletal makeup between the Odontoceti and Mysticeti.

Family **PHYSETERIDAE** Sperm Whales

Sperm Whale *Physeter macrocephalus*   **Pl. 17**

Widely distributed throughout the world, although only the larger males penetrate the colder waters of high latitudes. By far the largest of the toothed whales, males may reach a length of 60 ft 8 in (18·5 m), females grow only to 36 ft 8 in (11·2 m). Distinctive, enormous head makes up about one third of the total bulk. The blunted, almost square, snout, which projects beyond the tip of the lower jaw, houses the spermateceti organ, a specialised tissue producing a wax important for maintaining hydrostatic balance. The blowhole is situated well to the left of the midline and far forward on the head. The back has a rounded or triangular dorsal hump followed by four or five smaller low humps. Ventral keel on tail stock may be visible when diving. Flippers are small and rounded. Body surface is often irregularly corrugated. Generally dark brownish-grey with a greyish to off-white belly and front of head. The skin around the mouth is white. Narrow lower jaw contains 18–25 conical, slightly curved teeth. Very small, rudimentary teeth are sometimes found in upper jaw.

Blow is generally bushy, rising about 6 ft 6 in (2 m) high (see line illustrations, p.115) at a sharp angle towards the left of head. The flukes are broad and triangular, straight on the rear margin, and have a deep notch. When diving, the flukes are thrown high in the air. Four separate strandings (all male) have been recorded in the islands over the last 20 years, in one case a group of 18 animals stranded.

Family **ZIPHIIDAE** Beaked Whales

Medium-sized toothed whales, characterised by an extended, beak-forming snout, small flippers and a small dorsal fin, set well back on the body. There are

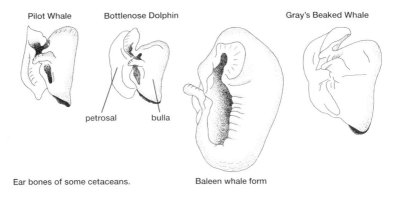

Pilot Whale   Bottlenose Dolphin   Gray's Beaked Whale

petrosal   bulla

Ear bones of some cetaceans.   Baleen whale form

Fig. 45 Earbones of some cetaceans

no documented sightings of live beaked whales in Falkland waters, excepting an unidentified species returned to sea after being stranded at Hill Cove in 1985. However, six identified species of beaked whale have been recorded from the islands as stranded specimens. This number representing a large proportion of the total recorded strandings of whales. This could mean that there are much larger populations of beaked whales than was originally believed.

Arnoux's Beaked Whale *Berardius arnuxii*   **Pl. 18**

May be two forms, the northern form is known as Baird's Beaked Whale. Length 36–39 ft (11–12 m), females being the larger. Elongated and rotund with a prominent, bulbous forehead sloping smoothly but steeply to a rather long, tube-like beak. At the front of this forehead, or 'melon', there is a visible hollow. In the centre of the head is a crescent-shaped blowhole, its rounded edge facing forward, a characteristic unique to the genus Berardius. The lower jaw extends slightly beyond upper jaw. The flippers are small and rounded at the tips. The dorsal is small and triangular-shaped, positioned less than one third of the body length from the flukes. A pair of triangular teeth are positioned near the tip of the lower jaw, in older animals a smaller pair appears behind these. Larger forward teeth are exposed outside the mouth. Generally slate-grey with light grey to white underparts and often marked with light-coloured scars.

Southern Bottlenose Whale *Hyperodon planifrons*   **Pl. 18**

This southern species has a circumpolar distribution with a northern limit at about 20°S. Known to be deep divers, remaining submerged for long periods (an hour or more), which may account for the rarity of sightings. Dolphin-like, but much larger, over 23 ft (7 m) in length. Has a very bulbous forehead or 'melon', due mainly to the presence of an oil reservoir, particularly pronounced in larger species and distinctive of adult males. The crescent-shaped blowhole is located in a hollow behind the forehead. The snout is short, the lower jaw protruding slightly beyond the upper and bearing on its tip a pair of large conical teeth. In older animals the tip protrudes beyond the gum. Has short, pointed flippers and a small, hooked dorsal fin, about 30 cm high and one third of the body length from the flukes. Generally dark grey to blueish-black, slightly lighter below. Very old males may have a white head. Nothing is known about the seasonal movements of the southern species.

Cuvier's Beaked Whale *Ziphius cavirostris* **Pl. 18**

Widely distributed in all oceans of the world. Stranded specimens occur in the islands and as far south as Tierra del Fuego, but species does not extend into higher latitudes. Maximum known length is 24 ft 6 in (7·5 m). Long and robust with a relatively small head without bulbous forehead. Forehead slopes gradually so that the short beak is less well-defined. The lower jaw extends beyond the upper and has a pair of conical teeth at its tip which are exposed in male animals, but do not pierce the gum in females. The flippers are small and the dorsal fin smoothly falcate or low and triangular and located behind the midpoint of the back. Colouration varies from a dark brown, slate grey or fawn, underparts and head are generally lighter. The back and sides are usually covered with linear scars and the belly with white or cream-coloured blotches. Often observed in close schools of three to ten. A stranded specimen, an old 24 ft 6 in (7·5 m) male, was collected at Whaler Bay on West Falkland in October 1964.

Layard's Strap-toothed Whale *Mesoplodon layardii* **Pl. 18**

Circumpolar in the southern hemisphere, with a northern limit of about 30°S, there are no records of this whale being found in Antarctic waters. Spindle-shaped, tapering at both ends and taller than wide, and usually about 19 ft 6 in (6 m) in length. Has a small head with well-defined beak. The lower jaw extends slightly beyond upper jaw. In males a strap-shaped pair of teeth emerges well behind the tip of the lower beak and extends upwards and backwards beside the upper jaw, curling over to prevent the mouth opening fully. The dorsal fin is triangular or falcate, situated behind the centre of the back. A female collected at the Falkland Islands had an almost non-existent dorsal fin. Flippers are small and narrow, usually pressed close to the body where they rest in depressions in the sides. Dark grey to black, with a lighter belly and a number of white areas around the face, behind the flippers and around the genital slit. A stranded specimen was collected at Bleaker Island on East Falkland in May 1964. This was an old female measuring 20 ft 8 in (6·3 m). Curiously, a specimen of the same species was collected in the same locality in 1880.

Gray's Beaked Whale *Mesoplodon grayi* **Pl. 18**

Circumpolar in the southern hemisphere. Most strandings recorded in New Zealand, although it has been recorded from the South West Atlantic, both in Tierra del Fuego and in the Falkland Islands. Length 16 ft – 19 ft 8 in (5–6 m). Head

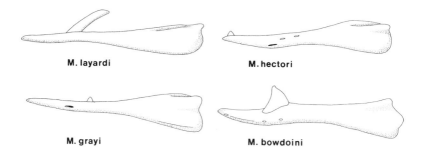

Fig. 46 Lower jaws of some beaked whales *Mesoplodon* sp.

small with a long and narrow beak. Two mandibular teeth, triangular in shape, are located about 8 in (20 cm) from the tip of the snout, but only visible in adult males. There are also 17–22 small, slightly recurved teeth on each side of the upper jaw. A stranded specimen of a young Gray's Beaked Whale was found on Saunders Island in 1981.

Hector's Beaked Whale *Mesoplodon hectori*   Pl. 18
Probably confined to temperate latitudes of the southern hemisphere where it might be circumpolar. Has been recorded from Tierra del Fuego, Falkland Islands, South Africa and New Zealand. Length about 13 ft – 14 ft 8 in (4–4·5 m). Has the typical spindle-shaped body of the genus Mesoplodon and a small head with medium-length beak. Flippers small. Dorsal fin relatively small and almost triangular-shaped. There are two mandibular teeth, small, triangular and flat, situated near the tip of the lower jaw. Upperparts dark, underparts lighter, the flanks can have linear and oval scars.

Family **DELPHINIDAE** Oceanic Dolphins

Killer Whale or **Orca** *Orcinus orca*   Pl. 19
Cosmopolitan, occurring both in polar regions and in equatorial regions. Males grow to 31 ft (9·5 m), although females rarely exceed 23 ft (7 m). The body tapers anteriorly, while the head is rounded except for a very indistinct beak. The most conspicuous external feature is the dorsal fin; in females and immature males this is falcate, in males it is much larger, almost triangular and reaches heights of 6 ft (1·8 m). In larger, older animals the top of the fin may visibly bend to one side. Flippers are also impressive, being large and rounded. Overall colour deep black, with well defined creamy-white oval eye patches, white chin, throat and white on the undersides of the flukes. White throat patch continues along the ventral

midline and branches into three segments posterior to the navel – two of these are visible on the flank, one on each side, the other continues beyond the anus. Behind the dorsal fin is a light-coloured saddle, in Falkland populations this is a faint grey colour. In a calf accompanying a cow the creamy-white areas were noted as having a deep pink hue.

Not common but regularly sighted in certain areas. Groups or 'pods' vary in size from two to seven, the largest recorded in the islands being composed of eleven animals. In the Falklands, movements of Killer Whales may be seasonal, being controlled largely by the movements of their main prey, which, observations suggest, is seal. At Sea Lion Island a known group was observed to follow certain routes at regular times, their appearances just off the breeding beaches of Elephant Seal apparently regulated by the seasonal movements and breeding stages of the seal. Elsewhere, they have been observed patrolling close inshore to coastlines inhabited by Fur Seal.

Long-finned Pilot Whale or 'Blackfish' *Globicephala melaena*   Pl. 19

Abundant and widely distributed in the colder temperate waters of the North Atlantic and the southern hemisphere. There are believed to be two separate populations, sometimes recognised as sub-species *melaena* in the north and *edwardi* in the south. Males grow to about 19 ft 8 in (6 m) – the largest of a group of around

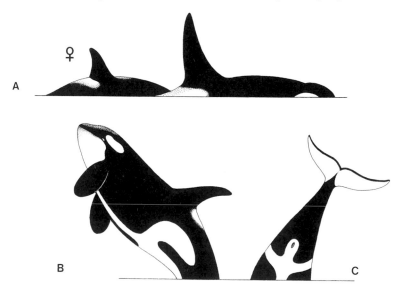

Fig. 47 Surface characteristics of Killer Whale: A, dorsal fins of female and male; B, breaching, showing side markings; and C, diving, showing ventral markings

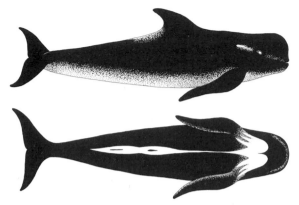

Fig. 48 Identification of Pilot Whale: side aspect *(top)* and ventral aspect *(bottom)*

200, recorded on West Falkland in 1984, measured 5·79 m, approximately 19 ft. Females are about 16 ft (5 m). Viewed from above, body is wedge-shaped, the head a blunt end to the thick end of the wedge. In profile, head is very bulbous and beak very indistinct, effectively replaced by a thickened upper lip. Mouthline curves upwards slightly. Crescentic blowhole lies slightly to the left of centre on top of head. Flippers are open, sickle-shaped and distinctive by their length, being one fifth or more of the body length. Distinctive dorsal with long base and rounded tip is generally falcate, but low in profile. Overall very dark greyish-black (locally known as 'Blackfish'), with characteristic white to light grey mark on underparts, extending from lower chin to surround anal parts (see line illustration). Some larger animals also have a whitish 'saddle' immediately behind dorsal. In a stranding of some 200 animals at Dunnose Head on West Falkland (May 1984), many animals had a small, light grey 'sunbeam-like' streak above and behind the eye, rising at an angle of 30° to the eye.

Gregarious, often forming very large groups of several hundred animals. In Falkland waters they have been recorded in most months, except mid-winter to early spring June/September. Strandings are not uncommon, an analysis of available records indicating that at least one occurs in most years. Numbers involved vary from single animals, or small groups of less than ten, to a maximum record of some 500 whales. The reason for strandings remains a mystery. In one case, where 340 animals became stranded on a sand beach at low tide, a large bull swam ashore first, followed by mixed groups at different points along a 984 ft (300 m) stretch of beach. As the tide rose, they left and re-beached closer to the leading bull. For three days all except the leading bull and some calves voluntarily left on high tides to swim around offshore, but eventually beached again, apparently quite deliberately attempting to keep up with the bull.

In a second incident a dead Pilot Whale was observed offshore and then a small calf and an adult were found dead ashore. At the same time a large group remained offshore, apparently in a resting state, while a second group was noticeably more active and excited. Within a day or two, about 130 became stranded on a flat rocky shoreline 1·9 miles (3 km) away, with a second group of 40 stranding in a third locality 1·2 miles (2 km) away; the two larger groups were 3 miles (5 km) apart. On examining the records, certain beaches show evidence of more than one such stranding over a period of years.

Dusky Dolphin *Lagenorhynchus obscurus*   Pl. 19
Inshore species with a circumpolar range in warm and cold temperate waters of the southern hemisphere. Fairly common around Peninsula Valdez in Argentina and recorded in the Magellan Straits and at the Falklands, although there is no known resident population in the islands. Length about 5 ft (1·5 m) – 6 ft 6 in (2 m). Beak indistinct. Dorsal fin tall and very erect with slight recurve and a blunt tip. Flippers moderately long and distinctly curved, tapering to a blunt point. Colouration complex, not dissimilar to Peale's Dolphin, but more distinct. Entire dorsal region is blueish-black, with black tail and snout. Dorsal fin black with light grey rear portion. Flippers light grey. A light grey area runs from the snout, through the eye and sweeps down over the flanks to the underside about two thirds along the body length. The belly and throat sections of this area are white. On the dark dorsal region a fine grey streak extends along the flank, meeting another grey blaze or streak starting below the dorsal fin line and sweeping back over the tail stock. May be confused with Peale's Dolphin, although the latter has a dark face and throat, a dark blaze across the midback and less defined pigmentation.

Hourglass Dolphin *Lagenorhynchus cruciger*   Pl. 19
Circumpolar in the Antarctic and Subantarctic regions, it is the only dolphin likely to be seen in the southern polar waters with a dorsal fin. Appears south of Cape Horn especially in the cold currents associated with the West Wind drift. Small, probably reaching no more than 6ft (1·8 m). Has a fairly well defined beak and a prominent dorsal fin, wide at the base and strongly recurved. The flippers are tapered and swept back and there is a heavy keel on the top and bottom of the tail stock or peduncle. Most distinctive feature is its striking, clearly defined, black and white marking (see plate illustration). The beak, dorsal surface, fin, tail and flippers are black. The sides and flanks are bi-coloured, the white areas forming a crude 'hourglass' shape. The patterning is most striking about the head, giving a white masked appearance. On the lower sides, level with the anus, there is also a dark crochet-hook shaped line. A pelagic species not commonly seen in the coastal waters of the islands. In December 1981 a freshly dead specimen was found beached on New Island, but a skull-hunting visitor dismembered this rare find before all-important field drawings could be made.

Peale's Dolphin or Peale's Porpoise   Pl. 19
Lagenorhynchus australis
Confined to the coastal waters of southern South America in the region of Cape Horn to about 57°S, Straits of Magellan, Tierra del Fuego and the Falkland

Islands, where it is fairly common. Comparatively large, up to an estimated 8 ft 2 in (2·5 m) in length. Dorsal fin erect and slightly swept back with a blunt point, flippers also swept back and medium length. Dorsal surface, head and snout dark grey. Dorsal fin dark with a lighter rear portion. Flukes dark. Flippers of Falklands population are light grey. From anus to throat, the white belly is fairly well demarcated from the light grey flanks and the broad, diagonal, dark grey area which sweeps down the sides from the forward dorsal area. Might be confused with Dusky Dolphin, although in the latter demarcation between dark and light is more distinct.

A coastal species usually seen moving in small groups of three to eight animals along the outer edges of kelp beds. Observations of known groups indicate a strong attachment to specific areas and routes within limited home ranges. Swims slowly, surfacing at regular intervals and occasionally diving after prey. Can be very acrobatic, leaping and tail slapping and will also ride bow waves, but wary of boats especially in areas with a history of hunting or disturbance.

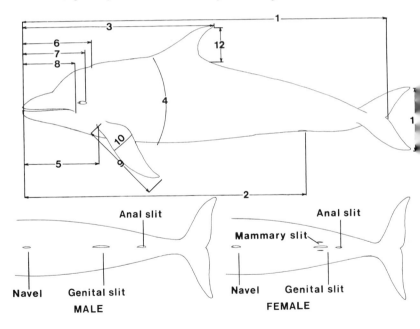

Fig. 49 Required measurements and sex identification of stranded whales: 1, upper jaw to notch between flukes; 2, upper jaw to anus; 3, upper jaw to dorsal fin; 4, maximum girth; 5, upper jaw to forward insertion of flipper; 6, upper jaw to blowhole; 7, upper jaw to eye; 8, length of gape – upper jaw to corner of mouth; 9, length of flipper; 10, maximum width of flipper; 11, width of tail flukes, tip to tip; 12, height of dorsal fin

Bottlenose Dolphin *Tursiops truncatus* **Pl. 19**

Cosmopolitan except in very high latitudes.Maximum size is 12 ft 9 in (3·9 m); a stranded male measured 10 ft 5 in (13·2 m). Beak and head may be rather short, or rather slim in form with a fairly long beak. Beak is always well demarcated from forehead by a sharp crease. Flippers are fairly slim, of moderate length 16 in (40 cm) with pointed tips. Dorsal fin falcate and fairly tall – 12 in (30 cm) in stranded male above. Grey to dark grey with lighter pigmentation on lower underparts. A poorly defined 'cape' mark commences at apex of forehead, broadens from the blowhole to dorsal fin and then narrows to a thin line. In two stranded male specimens there were 22 and 19 teeth on each side in upper jaws and 21 and 22 in lower jaws. Both stranded with a group of about 200 long-finned Pilot Whales on West Falkland in May 1984. There are no other records of the species being found in the islands.

Southern Right Whale Dolphin *Lissodelphis peronii* **Pl. 19**

Circumpolar but prefers temperate waters. May extend south of the Antarctic Convergence but most sightings are to the north of this line, in the West Wind Drift and Falkland Currents. A pelagic species, remaining in deeper waters. Very distinct and slim. Maximum length about 8 ft 2 in (2·5 m). Has no dorsal fin. Striking black and white colouration is clearly demarcated. White area covers beak and forehead, sweeping below eye level to the nearly all-white flippers and, from the rear of the flipper joint, continuing over the flanks to the tail in a gentle curve. Flukes are pale grey shading to white on the leading edge. Beak is short but clearly demarcated from forehead. Swims very fast, its movements at sea a series of bouncing leaps not unlike those of Gentoo Penguins. Groups of two to more than a thousand have been recorded. Little is known about the natural history of this species.

Commerson's Dolphin *Cephalorhynchus commersonii* **Pl. 19**

Known only from east coast of southern South America, from Peninsula Valdez, Argentina, to Tierra del Fuego; common in the Magellan Straits and south of 50°S on the Chilean coast. Also recorded off South Georgia and is fairly common in Falklands. Small, maximum length about 5 ft 5 in (1·7 m), with a rather short and stocky body, hence its local name of 'puffing pig'. Lacks a distinguishable beak, sloping forehead runs down to a small indentation marking the snout. Dorsal fin is distinctly rounded and set past the middle of the back. Flippers are elliptical with rounded points. Very distinctive colouration, cannot be confused with any other species of the region. Black of head extends to include flippers and form a sharply pointed area on the underside which projects back towards navel. A clearly demarcated area of white starts at the back of the head and covers the forepart like a saddle, extending back along the flanks and underparts. A second saddle of black covers the remaining back parts, including the dorsal fin area, tail stock and flukes. Has a distinctive white pear-shaped mark on chin and throat and a black 'teardrop' surrounding the reproductive aperture of males. The female has a horseshoe mark.

A

B

Fig. 50 Surface characteristics of A, Peale's and B, Commerson's Dolphins

Locally common, preferring comparatively sheltered waters. Some frequent almost land-locked stretches of water which Peale's Dolphin is less likely to enter, although the two may usually be found in relatively close company outside such areas. Usually observed in small groups of 2–8, although at least one recorded population numbered between 30 and 40 animals. Observations indicate that populations keep to quite well defined territories. Frequently ride bow waves and do not appear to be as shy as Peale's Dolphin. Small calves seen in mid-summer (December) suggest that young are born in early summer.

Family **PHOCOENIDAE** True Porpoises

Spectacled Porpoise *Phocoena dioptrica*   **Pl. 19**
Usually found in western South Atlantic. Off the South American mainland it has been recorded from the mouth of the River Plate south to Tierra del Fuego. In the Bahia San Sebastian, north east Tierra del Fuego, over 200 stranded specimens have been collected, indicating that it is probably the most common species in that region, yet apparently rarely seen at sea (Natalie Goodall, 1978). Also recorded from South Georgia and the Falkland Islands. Reaches a length of some 6 ft 6 in (2 m). Has no forehead or beak. Mouthline curves slightly upwards. Dorsal fin smoothly rounded, triangular shape. Flippers small with rounded tip. Distinct colouring, black above and white below, with a demarcation line running from snout, just above eye and longitudinally to near flukes where it then rises to dorsal surface. Edges of mouth are black.

Order **CARNIVORA** Otters and Dogs

Family **MUSTELIDAE** Otters

Fuegian Marine Otter or **Sea Otter** *Lutra felina*   **Pl. 13**

Introduced: rare: resident

Widely distributed from Tierra del Fuego and up west coast of Chile, living in the maze of channels of this region.Similar in general appearance to the Common Otter of Europe, but smaller, about 3 ft 4 in – 4 ft (1–1·2 m) from tip of nose to tip of tail. The body is long with short legs and a broad rather flat tail. The rather pointed head is flattened, with small ears and stout vibrissae or whiskers. Coat is dark brown when wet and lightish brown when dry. Swims swiftly with only the head showing. When diving, body bends in a marked curve, the middle of the back breaking the surface briefly. Dives may be frequent and long. While feeding may bring prey ashore to eat or may feed while floating on its back. In its native habitat it is largely a marine creature, living amongst dense belts of coastal kelp. Its holts or burrows are formed beneath rocks or in the dense coastal undergrowth of dwarf beech.

Introduced to the islands in the early 1930s, but present status unknown. However, brief sightings in the south west and south east and evidence of spraints (faeces) in suitable coastal habitats suggest that a small population probably still exists in certain more remote coastal regions. The abundance of kelp, offshore islands with dense Tussock Grass cover and rich inshore feeding grounds offer an ideal breeding ground.

Family **CANIDAE** Dogs

Patagonian Fox *Dusicyon griseus griseus*

Introduced: breeding

Inhabits southern South America, Patagonia, southern Chile and Tierra del Fuego. Introduced to the Falklands in the early 1930s. Restricted to five islands, namely

5 cm   LH

Fig. 51 Field marks of Fuegian Marine Otter

Fig. 52 Patagonian Fox

Staats Island, Weddell Island, Beaver Island, Split Island and River Island, all in West Falklands. Small, 32–36 in (81–91 cm) in length, from tip of tail to nose. Weight 6·5–10 lb (3–4·5 kg). Overall colour light grey, with light reddy-buff on lower parts of legs, tops of ears and head and muzzle. Tip of tail black with broken line of black on top edge (see illustration). Very short legs, appears to 'trickle' over contours of the ground.

In its native range it is an animal of the open plains. In the Falklands, where populations are restricted to comparatively small islands, it has adapted largely to a coastal habitat. Much of its feeding is by scavenging tidal zones for marine life, often feeding on small Dogfish which hide beneath loose rocks at low tide. Has thus developed the interesting habit of lifting quite large pieces of rock by inserting forepaws beneath stones and turning them over by springing body up and backwards. Also feeds on Diddle-dee berries and large numbers of insect life. On Split Island, where foxes have a restricted area of coast on which they can feed, population feeds almost exclusively on insect life, mainly Camel Crickets, ground beetles and weevils. Not known to dig an earth, relying on available cover such as Tussock Grass, Boxwood thickets or loose rock debris for establishing a den. Nothing is known about the breeding habits of the Falkland populations.

Order **PINNIPEDIA** Sea Lions, Seals and Walruses

The Pinnipedia are divided into two main groups – the Otarioidea (sea lions, fur seals and walruses) and the Phocoidea, a group known as 'true' seals, which includes species such as elephant seals. The main external differences between the two are connected with their method of locomotion on land. The Otarioidea can walk or lope using both fore and hind flippers, the latter being turned forward and used with the fore flippers in a rudimentary four-footed method of movement. This group of seals also has external ears and scrotal testes. The Phocoidea cannot turn their hind flippers forward to assist movement on land, therefore they depend on body muscles for locomotion in the form of a rippling or loping movement, the fore flippers being used for little more than support. These seals have no external ear appendage and the testes are internal.

Family **OTARIIDAE** Sea Lions and Fur Seals

Southern Sea Lion *Otaria flavescens*   **Pl. 13**
Resident: breeding
Distributed on Atlantic and Pacific coasts of South America from northern limits of Peru, south to Tierra del Fuego, the Falkland Islands and north on the Atlantic coast to Isla de Torres off the coast of south east Brazil. Adult males reach a maximum length of about 8 ft (2·6 m) and, when raised on fore flippers, some 5 ft (1·6 m) in height. Weight estimated at between 500–700 lb (226–320 kg). Have characteristic heavily built head and neck, large in proportion to body. Forepart of head is rather flat and blunted and eyes are relatively small. On land, when dry, neck hair stands out, giving appearance of mane and effectively making animal look larger. Colour may vary from deep brown or chocolate-brown with lighter brown on mane, to brown with a reddish cast. Underparts usually lighter than back. Naked area of flippers black.

Adult females reach a length of 6 ft (1·96 m) and weigh about 300 lb (136 kg) – about two thirds the size of males. When dry, body colour varies from a gold-

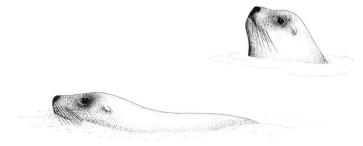

Fig. 53 Sea Lion at sea

129

en-buff to light grey-brown and the head is light silvery-buff. Eye region often appears dark due to secretion or weepage. Head quite small in relation to body, with finer, less blunted shape than male. While upright and resting, will often hold head back over body. When wet, both sexes and all ages have similar, very dark colouration, may also appear lighter when hauled out on dark rocks. Pups are black.

Fairly widely distributed, with about 60 breeding sites. Breeds at a number of sites on East Falkland mainland, but is largely absent from West Falkland mainland coast. Majority of sites are situated on offshore tussock islands. Breeding grounds are typically on rocky beaches of slab or broken rock, boulder and sometimes shingle – few on sand. All are protected on seaward side by reefs, or more commonly by kelp beds, usually of *Macrocystis pyrifera*, and generally backed by low lying cliffs or, more typically, by stands of Tussock Grass. Breeding groups rarely enter the shelter of Tussock Grass but, usually in the non-breeding season, use it for hauling out.

Breeding commences in December when adult bulls establish territories, while females tend to stay at sea to feed up prior to pupping. The first return to pup in about the third week in December, the last pups being born about mid-January. During this period breeding bulls become very defensive of their harems, five or six cows held in a tightly formed territory. Two or three days after giving birth the female is mated and then allowed by the bulls to go to sea to feed up, returning at intervals of a few days to suckle the pups. Towards the end of January, pups gather into groups or 'pods', but may remain dependent on the cows for 12 months or more. In February there is a break-up of territories, bulls leaving to feed up after their long, self-enforced period of fasting ashore. During breeding non-breeding animals may form fringe colonies a little distance from breeding territories. But between March and October there is no apparent segregation, although old breeding bulls, no longer capable of holding a harem, move away to a partly solitary existence.

Main foods are octopus and squid, with some Lobster Krill and fish. Usually feed in kelp beds and often at night. Also not uncommonly recorded preying on penguins, particularly Gentoos, observation suggests that this is carried out very largely by lone rogue bulls. Similar incidents have been recorded when newly born Elephant Seal pups have been taken, although the reason for this is not entirely clear, it is probably connected with territorial behaviour.

A population survey carried out in 1965 (Strange) gave a total of 30,000 animals of all ages. In 1990 a further survey by the author realised a figure of 3385 of all ages. This dramatic decrease has yet to be explained, but does mean that this species is now becoming quite rare in the Falkland Islands.

Falkland Islands Fur Seal   Pl. 13
Arctocephalus australis australis

Resident: breeding

Southern hemisphere Fur Seals all belong to the single genus Arctocephalus but are classed into seven species. The Falkland Fur Seal is a sub-species of the South

IX Typical breeding habitat of Southern Sea Lion in the Falkland Islands – a boulder beach on a small offshore tussock island.

X Gently shelving sand and shingle beach on the north-east coast of East Falkland. Typical breeding and hauling out area for Sea Elephant. A harem bull, back right, prepares to defend his territory and his breeding cows against the intruding bull further along the beach to the left.

XI Typical Falkland Island Fur Seal habitat. Formidable coastline, often with deeply under-cut, shelving cliff faces rising out of deep water.

XII Falkland Fur Seal colony. Note gently inclined rock slabs with access to shade and proximity of deep water. Such sites are carefully chosen because they are clean, the seals defecate directly into the water or onto rocks that are frequently washed by the sea.

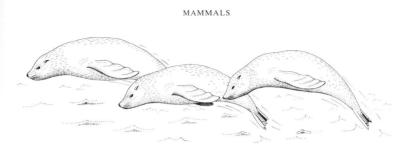

Fig. 54 Typical 'porpoising' action of Fur Seal travelling at sea

American Fur Seal *A. australis.* On the South American continent it is represented by *A. a. gracilis,* from northern Chile to Staten Island and at various localities on the Atlantic coast north to Rio de Janeiro. Another sub-species, *A. a. galapagoensis,* is found in the Galapagos Islands.

Adult males are about 6–6 ft 6 in (1·9–2 m) in length and weigh about 300–350 lb (136–158 kg). Females reach a length of about 4 ft (1·2 m) with a weight of 100–120 lb (45–54 kg). Adult males have a characteristically heavily built neck and a fairly pointed muzzle. Females are much smaller and better proportioned, with a fairly slim, pointed head. When dry, colour is an even grey-brown and in some light conditions reflects a silvery-grey off tips of the guard hair. Males are generally darker. Pups are black.

Has breeding grounds at some 10 sites, mainly in the north west and south west, characteristically on rocky sites with deep water approaches. Elevated sites with shelving rock faces or steep incised strike ridges are favoured. Many sites are shaded or near shade. Not found on open beach sites or within the cover of Tussock Grass. Forms large colonies of 1000–3000 and, although individual groups of less than 100 occur, such groups are sited sufficiently close together for there to be some interaction.

Breeding season commences in early November when adult harem bulls establish territories. The first females arrive late November, a few days before they are due to pup – there are usually 5–9 cows in a harem. The earliest pups have been recorded on 30 November but main pupping is generally in the mid two weeks of December. Mating occurs some days after pupping, then females depart on feeding trips, returning to suckle their pup every few days. After the first departure, pups tend to wander outside their territories. By mid-January they form into groups or 'pods', dispersing to suckle when cows return. Cows tend to feed in groups, animals from given areas of a colony appearing to keep together, and commonly leave rookeries in the evening returning early in the morning. It is not known if feeding is carried out at night.

Lactation lasts over six months, some pups still suckling in October. It is not clear when harem bulls depart, but appearance of younger bulls in late January probably coincides with a period when they leave to feed up after their enforced fast. Reappear in March to moult. When others moult is not clear, but by early

Fig. 55 Profiles of Fur Seal female *(left)* and adult male *(right)*

May pup coat is similar to that of adult and yearlings have completed moult and now bear distinct silvery-grey coats.

Unlike some species of Fur Seal, does not migrate, but during July, August and September breeding colonies are probably 'rested' and many move to what appear to be winter hauling-up grounds. The movement of other classes has yet to be studied, but yearlings and non-breeders may occur on rookeries at any period. Pups and cows may go to sea for periods of time to feed up.

At sea, moves in groups and has a distinctive porpoising action, clearing the surface of the water while travelling at speed. While resting or playing on the surface, has a distinctive way of rolling or partly submerging the body while holding a hind or fore flipper above the surface. Main food is Lobster Krill, squid and some fish are also taken. Population surveys (Strange, 1984) give an estimated total of between 18,000 and 20,000 animals.

South Georgia Fur Seal *Arctocephalus tropicalis gazella*

Breeding: migrant (South Georgia)

A sub-species of *A. tropicalis*, Kerguelen Fur Seal, breeds on South Georgia, South Sandwich, South Orkney and South Shetland Islands. A northern sub-species, *A. t. tropicalis,* is found north of the Antarctic Convergence on Tristan da Cunha, Gough, Marion, Kerguelen and Amsterdam Islands. Adult males are 5–6 ft (1·5–1·8 m). Females are smaller, about 4 ft 6 in (1·3 m). General colouration greyish-brown, although females show a creamy throat and breast. In the male a heavy mane, showing many white hairs, extends over the neck and shoulders and a dark yoke extends upwards from the fore flippers over the shoulders and behind the mane. Differs from Falkland Fur Seal in having a more prominent mane and, in the female, showing more creamy-buffs.

Breeds on generally rocky, boulder-strewn beaches near Tussock Grass or other vegetation. Breeding habits are very similar to those of the Falkland Islands species, except that the season is shorter, lactation lasts about five months only. Between late May and September they desert their breeding grounds and take to the sea. Their main feed is krill *Euphausia superba*, fish and squid are also taken. Estimated South Georgia population exceeds 300,000 breeding cows (Headland, 1984).

Family **PHOCIDAE** True Seals or Earless Seals

Southern Elephant Seal or Sea Elephant *Mirounga leonina*   **Pl. 13**

Resident: breeding

Circumpolar, found on most Subantarctic islands including South Georgia. Breeding colonies are also found on the southern South American coasts of Tierra del Fuego and at certain localities north to Punta Norte on the Argentine coast. Largest of all seal species, an adult male reaches 18 ft (6 m) and weighs about 3·5 tons (3·55 tonnes). Females are smaller, measuring 10–12 ft (3·4–3·9 m) and about a quarter of the weight. When first ashore, older male animals are golden-brown to light brown. The newly moulted coat is dark grey. Females are generally darker brown. On younger animals the coat varies from light silvery-fawn to light grey-buff. At birth the pup is black. A distinctive feature of adult males is the inflatable proboscis. Although female snout and muzzle are heavily built, there is no enlargement (see illustration). In adult males the neck area is usually deeply scarred as a result of fighting between harem bulls. Females may also bear scars resulting from biting during mating. Fore flippers of both are small in relation to body size.

Least common of the three breeding species in the archipelago, but may be found in fairly large numbers (200–300 animals) at a number of sites mainly in the north west, north, east and south east. Prefer beaches of sand or shingle for breeding, with an approach over a gradual shelving sea bottom. However, may haul up on any type of beach it can negotiate with its limited ability to move on land. Breeding season begins when adult bulls arrive on beaches, generally in

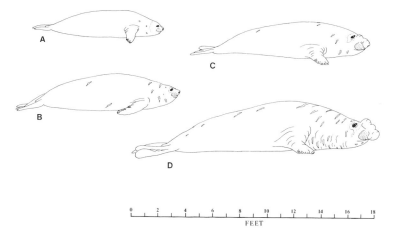

Fig. 56   Age and sex profiles of Elephant Seal: A, female 5 years old; B, female 15 years old; C, sub-adult male 6 years old; and D, harem bull 15 years old

second week of September, although the earliest animals arrive in late August. Cows arrive about a week later, gradually forming harem groups which vary greatly in number, from 6–50 cows attended by one bull. Sampling gave an average of 29 cows. The first pups are born about mid-September, main pupping is in the first and second week of October. Pup is fed for some 23 days, during which time cow remains ashore and is mated, after pup is weaned she leaves for sea. During the formation of harems, dominant bulls become very aggressive to other mature non-breeding bulls which come ashore and attempt to mate cows or to challenge them. By early November harems diminish as most cows depart. By mid-November most breeding bulls have also left for the sea in order to feed up after self-enforced stay ashore.

At birth pups are about 4 ft (1·2 m) in length and weigh between 80–90 lb (36–41 kg) and gain weight rapidly. By the time they are weaned, in just over three weeks, they may weigh 400 lbs (181·5 kg), with a length of 5 ft 3 in (1·6 m). After 10–12 days they moult and the black natal coat is replaced by silvery-fawn. The first of these silver-coated young are seen on breeding beaches in the third week of October, when they are around 34 days old. At this stage they may enter the sea for short forays, or gather in small groups some distance from the original breeding sites before leaving on their first feeding trip.

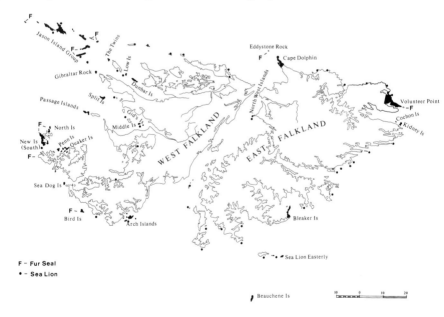

Fig. 57 Sites of main seal colonies and wildlife reserves

In late November/early December there is a gradual increase on the beaches of yearlings and non-breeders which have come ashore to moult. These are followed by adults, usually females, in January/March and then by bulls in March/April. During the winter months of April, May and June most adults stay at sea, although some beaches remain partly inhabited in most months of the year. It is not known how far the Falkland population moves away from the islands, although sightings of marked animals in the Falkland Islands from Punta Tombo in the Argentine coast shows that animals from other populations move considerable distances.

Diet is largely composed of squid and fish, probably taken at considerable depths. Their only known natural enemies are Killer Whales and Leopard Seals and occasionally adult bull sea lion are known to take young pups. At certain breeding sites, notably at Sea Lion Island, Killer Whales can be seen frequently patrolling inshore, close to the breeding beaches and have been observed taking seal, probably accounting for the mortality in pups when they first leave the colonies. In the last 30–40 years the Falklands population has become re-established after its near extinction in the 1800s (see *History of depredation*). A survey (Strange, 1965) estimated that no more than one thousand pups were being born annually. Over the last 15 years colonies have increased noticeably, with the present annual production of pups estimated at about 5000.

Leopard Seal *Hydrurga leptonyx*   Pl. 13

Visitor

Essentially solitary and circumpolar in distribution, usually on outer edges of pack ice, but does range widely to most Subantarctic islands, including South Georgia and the Falklands. Adult females, considerably larger than males, reach a length of some 12 ft (4 m), males about 10 ft (3·5 m). Upperparts darkish grey and underparts light grey, with spotting on throat, shoulders and sides – amount of spotting varies. Overall appearance rather reptilian, with a disproportionately large head for its long, slim body line. At close quarters the wide gape and three-pointed cusp-type teeth are distinctive.

Now fairly uncommon, although at one time was a regular visitor to certain beaches. There is one unconfirmed record of breeding. More commonly seen in winter, but may haul out at any period of the year. Appear to prefer open sandy beaches, or perhaps they are simply more difficult to spot on rocky surfaces. Feeds on a wide range of food, taking squid, fish, krill, other species of seal and penguins. Perhaps due to its carnivorous habits and appearance, has a rather bad reputation for being fierce towards man; however, there are no recorded incidents of unprovoked attacks. Perhaps in time this reputation will change in much the same way as it has done with the Killer Whale.

Weddell Seal *Leptonychotes weddelli*   Pl. 13

Rare vagrant

A peri-antarctic species. Circumpolar and coastal. Common in the South Orkneys, its most northerly limit of range is South Georgia where there is a small breeding

Fig. 58 Guanaco

colony. Occasionally recorded in the Falkland Islands. Adult females generally larger than males, measuring about 9 ft 4 in (2·8 m) in length. Males are about 9 ft (2·7 m). Colour varies, but usually blackish on the back with whitish blotches and streaks increasing in size and number down the sides of the lighter underparts. In summer, coat may fade to a light greyish-brown.

Cows come ashore in late August and pup in September/October. Suckling lasts about six to seven weeks, the pup entering the water before lactation ends to augment its diet with small crustaceans. After weaning, cows are ready to mate again. Fish is the usual feed, although squid and crustaceans are also taken.

Order **ARTIODACTYLA** Camels, Llamas, Reindeer

Family **CAMELIDAE** Camels, Llamas

South American Guanaco *Lama guanicoe*

Introduced: breeding

A South American species and the most widespread of the llamas, found in the Cordillera of the Andes and southwards to Patagonia and Tierra del Fuego. Stands about 4 ft (1·2 m) at the shoulder and about 5 ft 5 in (1·7 m) to the top of the head. Long-legged, long-necked animals with a camel-like head. Known as the camels of the New World. Woolly coat is fairly thick, light-fawn coloured on the back, flanks, neck and outer edges of legs, white on underparts and inner parts of legs. A guard hair grows through the wool, giving a rather ragged appearance and a highlight of reddy-brown to the fawn coloured coat. The short, brush-like tail is dark.

Forms small herds composed of one adult male and several females, plus off-spring of different ages. Introduced to Staats Island in the south-west of West Falkland. In the Falklands, young, 'Guanaco-chico', are born fully developed in early September after 11 months gestation, and within 24 hours are capable of running with the herd. Cared for by mothers for about six months, but then if male driven out of the herd by the dominant male. Non-breeding adult males and young males form herds which run separately from breeding herds. November rutting season is frequently marked by violent battles between males.

Feed is composed mainly of Diddle-dee, although during periods of over-population will eat most forms of vegetation. Introduced to Mare Harbour on East Falkland between 1862 and 1871, but how long these animals survived is not recorded. Again introduced in 1937 and placed on Staats Island where their descendants remain today. In 1982 this population amounted to 136 animals of all ages, divided into some six herds, some all-male, some breeding.

Family **CERVIDAE** Reindeer

Eurasian Reindeer *Rangifer tarandus*

Introduced to South Georgia: breeding

Small deer about 6 ft (1·8 m) in length and standing some 3 ft 5 in (1·06 m) at the shoulder. The only deer where both sexes bear antlers, those of the male being larger. The hooves are widely splayed to assist movement over snow. Colour is generally brown with white or greyish hair on lower parts and rump. South

Fig. 59 Eurasian Reindeer

Georgia population was introduced by the whaling industry for the purpose of providing meat. Three introductions were made between 1911 and 1925, the stock originating from Norway. Introduced to two geographically different areas, there are now two genetically distinct populations on South Georgia (as yet unnamed). Whereas in the northern hemisphere they graze over large areas on lichens, the South Georgia reindeer rely heavily on Tussock Grass, its availability ultimately controlling the population. Population is estimated to total about 2000 animals (Headland, 1984).

FISH

At least 80 species of fish have been recorded in Falkland waters and it is very possible that many more are yet to be recorded. A wide variety of forms and types exist from the small Rock Eel to large and diverse forms such as skates, tunnies, sunfish and sharks. The purpose of this section is to list a small number of fish recorded as prey species of some Falkland birds and mammals. A few of the larger fish occasionally found on the shores of the archipelago are also included.

Family **GALAXIDAE** Galaxids

Falkland Minnow *Galaxias maculatus*

Three species of Galaxidae are recorded from inshore waters. *G. maculatus* is one of two indigenous freshwater species which inhabits rivers, streams and some ponds in the islands. Recorded as an important food for both Rolland's and Silvery Grebes. *G. attenatus*, locally known as 'smelt', is also found in some freshwaters but is probably more common in brackish waters of estuaries and coastal regions at certain times of year. This small, silver-coloured fish attains a length of about 8 in (20 cm).

Family **APLOCHITONIDAE** Aplochiton

Falkland Trout *Aplochiton zebra*

Locally referred to as the native or local 'trout' and the only other indigenous freshwater fish recorded in the islands. Reaches a length of about 12 in (30 cm)

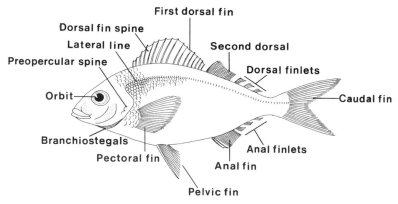

Fig. 60   Topography of a fish

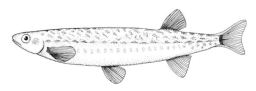

Fig. 61   Falkland Trout

and is not dissimilar to the minnows in shape and colour, but is marked on the back and sides with a series of vertical bars in brown and reddish shades. Inhabits streams and rivers and can also be found in coastal waters. Numbers have diminished greatly from rivers and streams since the introduction of Brown Trout *Salmo trutta*, which apparently preys on the smaller local species. The small fry are probably taken by both species of grebe.

Family **ZOARCIDAE**   Eelpouts

Rock Eel   *Austrolycus depressiceps*

A number of species belong to this family, one of the most common forms being the Rock Eel. This small, dark, smooth-skinned, eel-like fish, with a single back fin formed by the fusion of the dorsal, caudal and anal fins, is generally found hiding beneath rocks and stones in medium to low tide zones. An important prey of the Black-crowned Night Heron. Another species, *Phucocoetes latitans*, inhabits the rhizomes or basket-like roots of kelp and is probably taken by Rock Cormorants commonly seen feeding amongst kelp beds.

Family **NOTOTHENIIDAE**   'Antarctic Cods'

One of the most common fish of the Antarctic and Subantarctic waters, with some 16 species recorded from the region of the Falkland Islands. Many inhabit off-shore waters, several species are common in shallow inshore waters and some inhabit intertidal zones. In the islands the name 'Rock Cod' is given indiscriminately to all species of Notothenia.

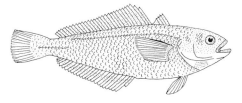

Fig. 62   'Yellow Belly'

Notothenia tessellata

One of the more common species of Notothenids found in the Falkland archipelago but widely distributed in the Straits of Magellan, southern Chile and northwards to Chiloe Island. Attains a length of about 10 in (25 cm). Dull greyish-brown, marbled, spotted and blotched with darker brown. First dorsal fin is largely covered by a black spot, second dorsal variegated with a series of dark spots. Margins of fins are clean white. Appears to prefer shallow waters, often inside kelp zone, although in winter may move to deeper waters. Although not specifically identified as a prey species, it is probably the most common form taken by sea lion and by those species of bird which feed largely in the inshore zones.

Notothenia ramsayi

The most common species of Notothenia offshore. Also the largest of those species found in the waters between the Falkland Islands and Patagonia, attaining a length of some 17 in (43 cm). Has not been specifically identified as a prey species, but young fish are probably an important food during those periods when certain penguins and seals are constantly at sea.

Notothenia macrocephala 'Yellow-belly'

Widely distributed, circumpolar in Subantarctic waters, being recorded from New Zealand, Macquarie Island to Patagonia, Straits of Magellan, Chile and the Falkland Islands. Locally referred to as 'Yellow-belly'. Grows to about 12 in (30 cm). Greyish-olive, blueish-grey or golden-brown above, shading to a rich golden-yellow, with bright orange-yellow branchiostegal membranes situated below the gills. Dorsal fins blue-grey. Fairly common in the littoral zones during summer, moving to deeper waters in winter. The silvery young are mainly pelagic and have been recorded as a species taken by terns.

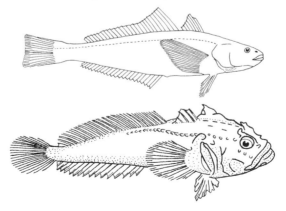

Fig. 63 Mullet *(top)* and Dogfish *(not to scale)*

143

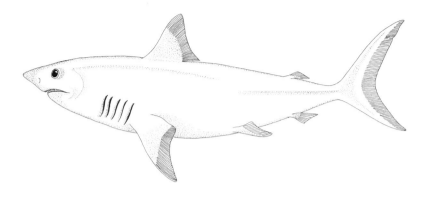

Fig. 64 Porbeagle Shark

Family **ELEGINOPS** Mullets

Mullet *Eleginops maclovinus*

Inhabits coastal waters of Argentina, Patagonia, Chile and the Falkland Islands. Known locally as Mullet, it is one of the more common fish inhabiting shallower waters in creeks and estuaries. Enters brackish waters and on the north coast of East Falkland a population has adapted to fresh water. In this case a one-time salt water tidal inlet has been blocked by a storm beach, trapping the fish in what is now a large inland area of water known as Loch Head Pond. Commonly grow to some 16 in (40 cm) and can attain a length of 23·5 in (60 cm). Brownish-grey with pale belly. Body may be mottled darker. This genus differs from the Antarctic Cods in having a rather small mouth and a differently shaped pectoral fin (see illustration). In some specific areas it is a prey of sea lion.

Family **HARPAGIFER** Dogfish

Dogfish *Harpagifer bispinis*

Sometimes referred to locally as Dogfish. Differs from Antarctic Cods in having a naked body and hooked operculum. Small, usually 2·5–3 in (6–8 cm). Head large in proportion to body with two distinct 'horns' or spines. Colouration very variable, but often creamy white to buff with dark bars or blotches. Inhabits close shore areas, shallow waters beneath kelp and is common in tide pools and under stones and rocks. Probably an important prey species of the Black-crowned Night Heron. Patagonian Foxes have also been observed feeding on this species.

Family **LAMNIDAE** Mackerel Sharks

Porbeagle Shark *Lamna cornubica*

Voracious sharks, feeding mainly on fish, although specimens recorded off the Falkland Islands were found to have been eating squid. Grows to some 13 ft (4 m). Dark blueish-grey with lighter areas beneath. Tips and posterior edges of fins pinkish, although this quickly fades. Snout pointed and overlaps crescentic mouth. Has three or four rows of teeth, slender, awl-shaped with smooth edges. In October 1983 a Porbeagle Shark was found beached at West Point Island in the north west of the archipelago. In 1988, during April, 17 sharks, the majority of them female, were caught in trawls, apparently while they were attempting to snatch squid from the mouth of nets. At least five of these had 4–6 well-formed embryos.

Family **CETORHINIDAE** Basking Sharks

Basking Shark *Cetorhinus maximus*

Largest of temperate water sharks, growing to some 34 ft 5 in (10·5 m). Sluggish, and non-ferocious. Derives its name from habit of lying still on the surface of the sea. Snout is bluntly pointed and overhangs the mouth which has several rows

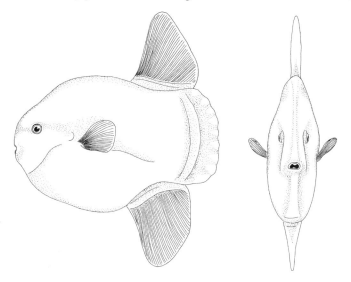

Fig. 65 Side and front view of Sunfish

of small conical teeth. Very large external gill-clefts extend far around the neck. Blueish-grey to black, generally paler on the lower parts. Feeds almost entirely on small shrimp-like crustaceans and plankton. Nothing is known about the movements of these sharks in the waters about the Falkland Islands, possibly an occasional visitor. There are two records of this species for the islands.

Family **MOLIDAE** Ocean Sunfishes

Sunfish *Mola mola*

Distributed in warm and temperate oceans. There is one record for the Falkland Islands, a specimen found beached at New Island, West Falkland, with a body measurement of 7 ft 6 in (2·3 m) by 5 ft (1·5 m). Very distinctive, almost circular in profile but laterally compressed to resemble two dinner plates joined face to face. Caudal fin absent, the tail being replaced by a scalloped fringe of thick skin. Dorsal and anal fins deeply set in body. Pectoral fin very small. Mouth circular and very small in relation to size. Skin very leathery with no scales. Light to medium grey with off-white lower body. Feeds on animal plankton and very small fish.

Family **RAJIDAE** Skates

Rays *Raja* sp.

At least nine species of skates or ray of the genus Raja have been recorded from Falkland waters. Three species, *R. griseacauda, R. multispinis* and *R. scaphiops*, are more commonly recorded as stranded specimens. Many of the species are very

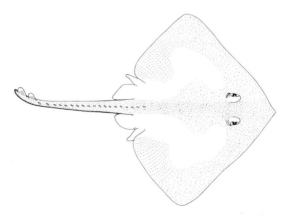

Fig. 66 Ray

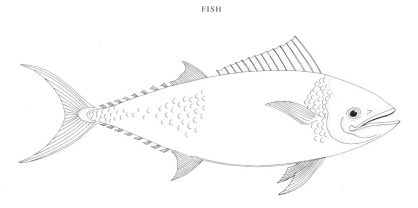

Fig. 67 Tunny

similar, but in general the flattened disc-like body is quadrangular or roughly circular, with a snout which projects forward from the front of the head. The eyes are prominent and set fairly close together. The mouth forms a nearly straight slit on the underside of the head. The teeth are small and set in several rows. There are two dorsal fins positioned almost at the end of the tail, but the caudal fin is virtually non-existent. The upper surface of the disc is mainly smooth but with areas of small spines or spinules, the size and positioning varying according to species.

Family **SCOMBRIDAE** Tuna and Mackerel

Tunny *Thunnus* sp.

Pelagic migratory fish which feed on shoaling fish. By means of gill filters they are able to sieve small fish larvae from the water. Also take larger prey such as squid and surface species of fish. Great wanderers, roaming over large areas in search of prey, and built for speed, the body being oblong and robust but beautifully streamlined. The slender peduncle of the caudal fin has a keel on each side, in addition to a pair of keels at the base of the fin. The body is covered with scales which are larger and heavier on the shoulder. The jaws have a single row of pointed teeth with bands of very small teeth on the roof of the mouth. Behind the soft dorsal and anal fins there are eight to ten finlets. Immediately behind the pelvic fins is a deep groove in which fins lie when the fish is swimming at speed. Similar depressions take the spinous dorsal and pectoral fins. Colouration, dark metallic blue above and silvery-white on belly. Nothing is known about its movements in Falkland waters, however, the occasional strandings of individual specimens suggest that some populations may follow migratory routes close to the islands.

MARINE INVERTEBRATES

Phylum **MOLLUSCA**
Chitons, Marine Snails, Bivalves, Squids and Octopods

Over 200 species recorded in Falkland waters, divided into five classes, of which three are confined to the sea. This work confines itself to marine molluscs and in particular to a small number recorded as important prey species of Falkland mammals and birds.

Class **POLYPLACOPHORA**   Chitons

Chitons have an elongated, flattened body and carry a series of eight articulating shell plates, each with a separate shell muscle. Share habitats of limpets, occurring on rocks and stones. Articulating plates enable them to crawl over irregular surfaces and, in the event of being torn off rocks in heavy seas, to curl up and avoid damage. Live largely on plant material, microscopic algae rasped or scraped from the surface of rocks or holdfasts of kelp.

Most Falkland species appear to be confined to lower shore or offshore regions amongst the stems and holdfasts of *Lessonia* and *Durvillea* sp. of kelp. Often well camouflaged, not uncommonly covered with thin layers of white or pink encrustations of polyzoa. The individual shell plates are butterfly-shaped and usually a turquoise colour inside. Length is about 2·5 in (6 cm), width 1·5 in (3·5 cm) in some larger forms. Apparently an important element in the diet of the Flightless Steamer Duck. Adult birds have been observed taking large specimens which are swallowed whole. Remains of chiton shells on Dominican and Dolphin Gull colonies indicate that chitons are also taken by these birds.

Class **GASTROPODA**   Marine Snails, Limpets, Whelks, etc.

Largest of the molluscan classes. Unlike other molluscs, gastropods are fundamentally asymmetrical due to torsion, i.e. many are typically spirally twisted, although no outward trace of this may remain (as in the case of limpets). Shell is always of one piece.

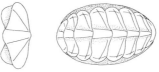

Fig. 68   Chiton: shell plate and complete shell

Fig. 69 Forms of limpets. *Top, left to right:* Rough Thorn Drupe, Smooth-shelled Limpet and Common Limpet. *Bottom:* Painted Keyhole Limpet and Coppery Limpet

Painted Keyhole Limpet   *Fissurella picta*

Cone-shaped shell represents the greatly enlarged body whorls, the apical whorls having disappeared. There is no columella and the animals are usually attached by a horseshoe-shaped muscle. Water currents enter shell, pass over head and gills and exit, together with faecal material, through hole (foramen) in top of shell. Feeds nocturnally on algae. Often attractively coloured with purple-brown to reddish-tan rays, usually twelve in number. Commonly found attached to rocky areas of the shore in mid to lower tidal zones, often in shaded crevices. Grows to around 3·5 in (9 cm) by 2·5 in (6 cm).

Common Limpet   *Patinigera deaurata*

Very common, belonging to the super family Patellacea. Surface rough with a series of pronounced ribs radiating from domed apex to the bottom edge. Light brown to greyish-buff. Size 3 in (8 cm) by 2 in (5·5 cm), height of dome about 1·5 in (4 cm). Largest of the Patellidae found in the Falkland Islands. Grows singly or in small groups but not dense. Generally attaches itself to smooth surfaced rocks, on both vertical and horizontal planes in medium to low tide zones. Appears to be widely distributed on both sheltered and exposed coastlines. From collection of empty shells, some measuring up to 3 in (7·5 cm) by 2 in (5·5 cm), taken at nest sites of Black Oystercatchers, appears to be the most common food of this species. Striated Caracara have also been recorded as feeding on this limpet.

Coppery Limpet   *Patinigera deaurata delicatissima*

Fairly small and low domed, 1·5 in (4 cm) by 1 in (3 cm). Has a thin white shell, often transparent with golden brown, irregular markings which radiate from the apex to the edge. Apex usually well forward of centre and smooth, while rest of shell has numerous small ribs. An attractive species which is found below the low tide zone, occasionally on kelp stems washed ashore. Sometimes found amongst other shells at sites of Black Oystercatcher nests, probably taken from 'wrecks' of kelp washed ashore during storms.

Smooth-shelled Limpet *Nacella mytilina*

Fairly small, 1·5 in (4 cm) by 1 in (2·5 cm). Has smooth, thin shell with a shiny backed apex situated at one end. Edges of shell are very slightly scalloped. Colour varies from a pale grey-buff or light brown in larger specimens to a deep khaki or grey-green in smaller specimens. Inside shell is a pale silver-grey sheen. Appears to inhabit zones below the low tideline, probably on the stems and leaves of kelp. Small specimens found in very large numbers on Dominican and Dolphin Gull colonies, probably taken from the surface layers of kelp beds.

Rough Thorn Drupe *Acanthina monodon*

Typical whelk shell form, about 2·5 in (6 cm) in length by 1·5 in (3·5 cm). Shell aperture has siphonal groove. On the lower shell margin is a labial spine used to wedge or force apart mussels or other bivalves on which it preys. Also acts as a brace while it employs an alternative method of attack, drilling into the shell of prey. On beached specimens this spine is often broken off. Shell is generally thick and has many spiral ridges. Main body whorl reddish-brown with lighter apex whorls. Interior white. Intertidal, inhabiting rocky shores. Commonly found at nest sites of Black Oystercatchers. Has also been identified as prey of some Striated Caracara populations.

Class **BIVALVIA** Bivalves, Mussels, Scallops, Clams

The two-part shell enveloping a bivalve is usually symmetrical and their basic shape oval, triangular or nearly circular. The outer surface of most is sculptured,

Fig. 70 Bivalves. *Top left*: Clam with hole drilled by Rough Thorn Drupe. *Top right*: Blue Mussel. *Bottom left*: Kelp Bivalves. *Bottom right*: Ribbed Mussel

may have broad or narrow ribbing, furrows or ridges. Mussels, clams and scallops are widespread in the Falkland Islands. Only the mussel is commonly taken as food by some species, although small clams in the late veliger larva stage may also be taken.

Blue Mussel *Mytilus edulis chilensis*

May grow to 3·5 in–4 in (9–10 cm), with either an oblong, oval or almost rhombic shape. Fairly smooth with concentric lines. Deep blue-black, blue or light blue in older shells. Surface usually covered with a thin layer, known as the periostracum, a protein substance which gives a black-brown appearance, which in dry specimens quickly erodes away. Inside of shell is white, with a mother of pearl layer on the area adjacent to the hinge, gradually changing to blue on the outer regions. Forms dense beds or mats, attaching itself by its byssus threads, usually to rocky substrates. May also form clusters of shells. More generally forms beds within the low to medium tide zones, where they may be covered by a maximum of some 8–10 ft (2·5–3 m) of water. Common in the islands but largely confined to more sheltered coastal bays and inlets. Important feed for Pied and Black Oystercatchers and for Dominican and Dolphin Gulls. In the late veliger larva stage mussels may also be taken by Steamer Duck and Crested Duck.

Ribbed Mussel *Aulacomya ater*

Large, growing to a maximum size of about 7 in (17 cm), tends to be larger than Blue Mussel. Deeply ribbed, brownish-black with purple highlights. Interior of shell white with purple marks on outer edges. An offshore species, grows below lowest tide zones on rocky sea bed and may also attach to kelp, *Lessonia* sp., holdfasts. On some beaches appears in large numbers, washed ashore with kelp holdfasts and may then be taken by scavenging species, especially in winter. Specimens have been found at nest sites of Black Oystercatcher, but only rarely.

Clam *Humilaria exalbida*

Fairly large, about 3 in (8 cm) in diameter. Shell rough, white or buff-white, very thick with numerous concentric ribs. The umbones are pronounced, pointing forward at a slight angle. Found in sand often up to 1 ft 8 in (0·5 m) below the surface. Appears to be fairly well distributed and common on gradually shelving sand beaches. Edible but not exploited.

Kelp Bivalve *Gaimardia trapesina*

Small, delicate bivalve with a rounded triangular or oblong shape. Rarely larger than 1 in by 0·5 in (2·5 cm by 1·5 cm). Shells have smooth, glassy surface but may also have concentric ribs. Colour varies from a delicate golden-buff to pinky-buff. Attaches itself by its byssus threads to the leaves of kelp, *Macrocystis* sp. – leaves are often covered with these shells, but generally only in the shallower surface layers. Probably the most important form of bivalve taken as food by all species of gull and marine ducks found in the islands.

Class **CEPHALOPODA**   Cuttlefish, Squids and Octopuses

Cephalopods are the most complex of the molluscs, having an elaborate structure and being much more active than other forms. All are predacious carnivores. Can dart very rapidly through the water using a form of jet propulsion, whereby, by muscular means, water is expelled with great force through a funnel formed from the modified molluscan foot. Also able to change colour instantaneously and to discharge sepium, a black ink-like substance, as a form of protection. Four main species of squid are known from Falkland waters. Three are listed here as important prey species.

Patagonian Squid or **Loligo**   *Loligo gahi*   **Pl. 20**

Known from Peru, Chile and Argentine coasts. Common on the continental shelf from Tierra del Fuego to Golfo San Jorge in Argentine waters. In Falkland waters appears to be common in certain areas off the east coast of East Falkland, especially prolific off the south east of Beauchêne Island, where it forms an important food source for the large Black-browed Albatross and Rockhopper Penguin colonies.

One of the smallest squid found in these waters, reaches a maximum size of 12·5 in (32 cm). Purplish-brown. Little is known about natural history except that they collect in very large numbers. During reproduction they produce enormous amounts of gelatinous spawn on the sea bottom, after which the adults die. Life cycle is completed in about a year. Evidence suggests that different populations vary in the timing of their life cycle, with one population spawning about March and another in September/October. One of the most important prey species of the islands' seabird and seal colonies, particularly of Rockhopper Penguins. At certain periods of the penguins' breeding season, especially when large amounts of food are being brought ashore to feed chicks, sites become stained with the light purple-coloured excreta of birds feeding on squid.

Argentine Short-finned Squid or **Illex**   *Illex argentinus*   **Pl. 20**

Distributed on Atlantic coast of South America south of Uruguay to Tierra del Fuego. Common on the continental shelf around Falklands. Larger than Loligo, growing to around 15·5 in (40 cm), with a comparatively larger head and tentacles. Reddish-brown. Little is known about its natural history. Appears to have a seasonal movement in Falkland waters, adult squid appearing to the north in latter half of summer. This movement is made in a southerly direction, against the northerly flow of the Falkland Current. In late summer/early winter, the movement is reversed. As with other Cephalopods, grows very quickly, spawns once and dies soon after, living for about one year. Spawning is believed to take place in May. Occasionally large numbers of adults strand on sand beaches. An important prey of albatross, penguins and Fur Seal. The seasonal movement of some seabird and seal species is probably related to the northerly winter movement of Illex.

Short-finned Squid *Martialia hyadeshi* **Pl. 20**

Distributed in Argentine waters south of 38° south to the Falkland Islands and in waters south of Tierra del Fuego. Similar size to Illex, mantle length about 15·5 in (40 cm). Tentacles short and robust, about half the length of mantle. Reddish brown but dark on the dorsal surface of mantle. Nothing is known about the natural history of the species. Has been recorded as a prey species of penguins but not apparently as common a food during the breeding season.

Octopus *Octopus* sp. **Pl. 20**

Widely distributed in the sub-littoral zones, inhabiting kelp beds and crevices among rocks. Has a sack-like body with four pairs of tentacles all the same length with which it crawls, although it is capable of swift darting movements by employing jet propulsion. Beached specimens are rare, probably because it is capable of leaving and entering the water by use of its tentacles. Sea Lion commonly hunt octopus in beds of the giant kelp *Macrocystis*. Having secured their prey, they bring it to the surface and thrash it to pieces with a series of violent head movements.

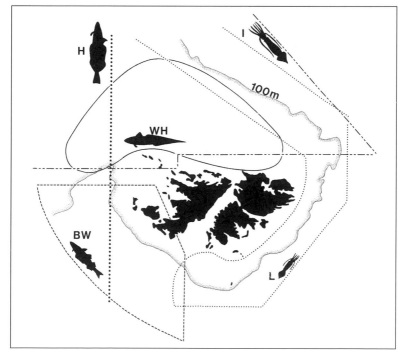

Fig. 71 Zones of main fish and squid species found off the Falkland Islands: I, Argentine Short-finned Squid; H, Hake; WH, Whip-tailed Hake; L, Patagonian Squid; BW, Blue Whiting

Phylum **ARTHROPODA**

Arthropods are the most numerous and widespread group of animals and include such diverse forms as insects, crustaceans, spiders, centipedes and millipedes. All are characterised by having paired jointed limbs and the entire body is encased in a thick cuticle or protective shell which has to be shed or moulted periodically as the animal grows. The Falkland Islands have a large and diverse collection of Arthropods. This work is confined to describing a small number of Crustacea and a selective list of insects.

Class **CRUSTACEA**

Crustaceans are the third largest group of arthropods and include Crabs, Lobsters, Shrimps, Barnacles, Fish Lice and Woodlice. Four forms are described as important or common forms of feed for certain species of bird or mammal.

Order **ISOPODS**   Pl. 20

A large and important group with many marine species. In general form they resemble woodlice. The body is flattened and composed of a number of plates or segments. Eyes are set close to head. The outer antennae are usually large. When disturbed they are very active, tending to roll up into a ball. Inhabit different zones from about the mid-shore, where some species will be found under stones or sheltering beneath the leaves of kelp, to lower shore and beyond where they inhabit kelp beds. An important food of marine ducks, especially Crested Duck and Flightless Steamer Duck, which will feed by dabbling in small tide pools or between kelp and seaweeds at low tide.

Order **AMPHIPODA** 'Sandhoppers'   Pl. 20

Typical amphipods found on most beaches are the *Gammaridae* or *Talitridae*. Whereas isopods tend to be flattened and broadly oval, amphipods are usually compressed from side to side and are hence more shrimp-like. *Gammaridae* are a typically compressed, curved shape and usually found wriggling on their sides. May be found at extraordinary heights above sea level, under stones on cliff tops, or some distance inland, but generally only where such sites are subjected to some sea spray. *Talitridae* are jumping animals which walk and stand upright. Very common form of amphipod, typically found in piles of rotting kelp amongst sand and shingle, usually in those zones above and below the high tide levels. Amphipods are taken by several species of bird, in particular tussock birds, Falkland Thrush, Cobb's Wren and snipe.

Order **EUPHAUSIACEA** Krill

Krill or **'Whalefood'** *Euphausia* sp.   **Pl. 20**

Krill, the principal food of baleen whales, are pelagic crustaceans. Shrimp-like but differ from the true shrimps in not having the first three pairs of thoracic links modified as mouth parts. Most are coloured red or pinky-red from the caroteroid pigment astacene in their chromatophores (pigment-containing cells). Owing to their habit of congregating in large dense swarms, the surface layer of the sea may at times appear reddish. At night euphausiaceans may be equally noticeable due to their bright luminescence, produced by photophores, light-producing organs which the animal can flash on and off or keep brightly lit for some minutes. In the Subantarctic waters of the Falkland Islands two species, *E. vallentini* and *E. lucens*, appear to be common. Euphausiaceans in general are important in the feeding ecology of many seabirds, although little is known about their distribution and seasonal movements in these waters.

Order **DECAPODS** True Shrimps, Lobsters, Crayfish, Crabs

Lobster Krill *Munida gregaria*   **Pl. 20**

A free-swimming decapod, which, like other forms of decapod, has ten thoracic legs including two pincer-tipped appendages like those of a lobster. Has appearance of a very small lobster. May reach a length of some 2·5 in (6 cm). Like euphausiaceans they are generally red and are frequently seen in very dense swarms. In the warmer Subantarctic waters of the Falkland Islands, Lobster Krill takes the place of the Antarctic Ocean's *Euphasia superba*, the one species crucial to the Antarctic food chain and the only species properly called 'krill'.

Forms a very substantial part of the food of many seabirds and is probably the major prey species of the Falklands Fur Seal. Its presence in the waters about the islands throughout most months of the year, is evident by the brick-red remains in the excreta of Fur Seal and of Gentoo Penguins. However, there is a noticeable population increase in the latter half of the summer breeding season and autumn, when enormous swarms may be seen on the surface waters, giving a reddish cast to the sea. In late March/April many beaches may be covered with stranded Lobster Krill and even after their remains have broken down sand will be left stained with a pinky residue from the caroteroid pigment.

TERRESTRIAL INVERTEBRATES

Phylum **ARTHROPODA**

Class **ARACHNIDA**
Order **ARANEAE** Spiders

Nineteen species of spider have been recorded from the Falkland Islands (Usher, 1983) although it is very probable that many more exist. Little is known of their ecological role in, for example, controlling potential pests. However, they are known to be an important element in the diet of several species of birds. For the purpose of this work only two species are described, one a common species and easily identified, the other a large species recorded from one island in the Falklands and found nowhere else in the world.

Green Spider *Araneus cinnabarinus*   **Pl. 14**

One of the largest and best known spiders, often found inhabiting *Veronica* and *Hebe* hedges in settlements and on thick stands of *Blechnum* fern. They are passive predators which wait for flies and moths to fly into their webs rather than hunt for prey. Depending on the habitat, their colour varies from those with a bright green abdomen and white centre stripe to spiders with a green-brown body and buff stripe. Juveniles are reddy-brown, but after moulting they gain some yellow speckling and gradually change to the brilliant green of the adult. During January, the austral summer, females begin to spin cocoons of a golden-brown silk in which their eggs are held and by March many can be found often with females in attendance. The cocoons probably remain intact until the spring when the young spiders emerge.

Beauchêne Spider *Emmonomma beauchenicum*   **Pl. 14**

An endemic species, to date only recorded on the remote outlier, Beauchêne Island. Unlike the Green Spider, does not appear to require a plant habitat and is found beneath rock debris where little plant life exists. Very large with a body measurement of some 0·5 in (1·3 cm). Nothing is known about the natural history of this species.

Class **INSECTS**

Falkland insect fauna has not been thoroughly studied and is generally under-collected. Some 254 species in 10 orders are presently recorded (Robinson, 1988) but undoubtedly many more species have yet to be found. A large number of Falkland species exhibit the classical oceanic-subantarctic adoption of complete wing- loss. A small number of the more common forms are described below, emphasis being placed on those known to be important in the feeding ecology of certain birds.

Order **COLEOPTERA** Ground Beetles and Weevils

Black Beetle *Lissopterus quadrinotatus*   **Pl. 14**

A large, shiny black beetle with reddish highlights, especially noticeable on its legs. Very common. Feeds on other insects and invertebrates. Nocturnal and generally found beneath large clumps of Diddle-dee or under the litter of Tussock Grass. Very active runner and when disturbed moves very quickly in order to hide from the light.

Metallic Beetle *Metius blandus*   **Pl. 14**

Smaller than the former species, with a greeny metallic sheen to their overall black colouration. An extremely common species of ground beetle, generally found beneath clumps of Diddle-dee or ferns or beneath stones, but appears to prefer dry areas. Nocturnal and probably carnivorous. An important prey species of the Pied Oystercatcher, and in some areas it is not uncommon to see groups of these birds moving over a piece of ground turning over small stones in their search for these beetles.

Clocker Weevil *Caneorhinus biangulatus*   **Pl. 14**

One of the largest and most striking weevils found in the Falkland Islands, large specimens attain a length of 1 in (2 cm) or more. The head is prolonged to form a beak or rostrum which carries jaws or mandibles at its tip. Colour varies but generally a dark brown with light fawn markings on the head. The edges of the elytra (horny front wings) are also marked with buff or fawn, giving the back a striped appearance. Unlike the Falkland beetles, weevils are slow-moving and when disturbed often feign death. Like most weevils, probably feeds on vegetation. Commonly found in areas of heathland, appearing to prefer drier areas of vegetation.

Order **ORTHOPTERA** Crickets

Camel Cricket *Parudenus falklandicus*   **Pl. 14**

Resemble typical crickets, but wingless. In comparison with other Falkland insect life they are large creatures, having a body length of 1 in (2·5 cm), with legs and antennae of a similar length. Omnivorous, but prefer animal food, especially beetle larvae. Widely distributed and found in a variety of habitats which offer dense cover. Tussock islands appear to be particularly important habitats, they live amongst tussock litter and in the skirts of tussock plants. Also not uncommonly found in the underground nest burrows of petrels and Magellan Penguins. Whether this is by accident or intent is not known, although there is a possibility that they feed on waste food from these birds.An important food of Tussock Birds, Thrushes, Cobb's Wren and the Short-eared Owl.

Order **LEPIDOPTERA** Moths and Butterflies

Lepidoptera forms quite a large component of the Falkland Islands' insect fauna, Noctuidae moths being one of the more common forms. Sometimes referred to as Owlet Moths these are fairly heavily built and commonly attracted to light. A number of the small moths are flightless, probably as a result of development in a generally exposed environment with a high wind factor. There are two butterflies on the islands, both fairly commonly recorded, one breeding, the other a probable migrant. Before the 1900s a small 'blue' butterfly, probably a species of Parachilades, was commonly seen, although never collected and identified. Similar sightings are still made every two or three years, suggesting a small population still exists in some remote area of the islands.

Ochre Shoulder Moth *Caphornia ochricraspia* **Pl. 14**

One of the largest and more attractive Noctuidae moths found in the islands. Commonly inhabits grass and heathlands. In the late summer numbers are so large in certain areas they constitute swarms. Fairly distinct brown and ochre patterning.

Brocade Moth *Pareuxoina falklandica* **Pl. 14**

Another species of Noctuidae commonly found in the grass and heathlands of the islands. Grey-browns and light buffs are the dominant colours, with distinctive, intricately patterned front wings.

Queen of the Falklands Fritillary *Issoria cytheris cytheris* **Pl. 14**

Belongs to one of the largest of all butterfly families, the Nymphalidae. Occurs widely in Argentina and Chile, but the Falkland Islands population represents a distinct race. Fairly small. Not generally seen in large numbers, but locally common in a few localities during mid-summer. Adults have been noted feeding from a variety of different flowers. The host plant for the caterpillars is not known, but probably one of the Violaceae.

Southern Painted Lady *Cynthia carye* **Pl. 14**

Another member of the Nymphalidae and closely related to the well known Painted Lady, an extraordinary migrant and one of the most cosmopolitan of all butterflies. Restricted in its range, occurring along the high Andes, south from Colombia to Argentina and Chile. Sightings on the Falklands are not uncommon, usually in the latter half of the summer, from January to March. It is not clear where these come from but, like the Painted Lady, known to be migrant. Probably fly from South America assisted by the predominantly westerly winds. Or alternatively, but less plausibly, there could be a small breeding population on the islands which migrates to South America during the winter. Larger than the Falkland Fritillary and has a much swifter zig-zag flight.

PLANTS

There are 164 flowering plants and vascular cryptogams known to be native to the Falkland Islands and a further 92 introduced species. Here 45 species have been selected either as important nesting or feeding habitat species, or because they are in themselves of interest. This section is divided up into the different plant communities, and different species are listed under these. Except for a few variations, these communities follow the accounts of Skottsberg (1913), Davies (1939) and Moore (1967). A section on marine algae describes some of the more common seaweeds and kelps found growing in the archipelago.

Maritime Tussock Grass formation

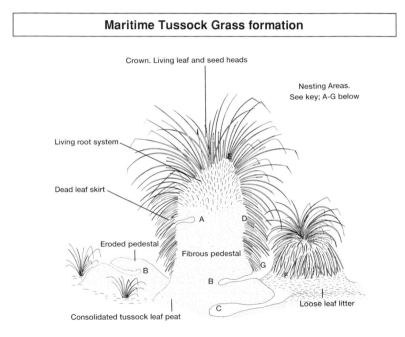

Fig. 72 Tussock Grass formation with nesting habitats of some bird species
A Grey-backed Storm Petrel
B Diving Petrel and Thin-billed Prion
C Sooty Shearwater, White-chinned Petrel and Magellan Penguin
D Cobb's Wren and Grass Wren
E Falkland Thrush, Siskin and Striated Caracara
F Black-bellied Storm Petrel
G Turkey Vulture, Short-eared Owl, Kelp Goose and Flightless Steamer Duck

Tussock Grass *Poa (Parodiochloa) flabellata* **Pl. 14**

A unique plant, forming the islands' most important terrestrial ecological niche as both a nesting and feeding habitat for many species of bird; as a valuable shelter for some species of seal; and as a very important niche for various forms of invertebrate fauna. The plant forms a tussock-like growth, with a fibrous pedestal base from which a mass of green leaf is produced. Individual leaves may grow 6 ft 4 in (2 m) in length, forming a canopy above the pedestal. Large plants are about 9 ft 6 in (3 m) in height, with exceptional growth reaching 13 ft (4 m). Young plants growing under optimum conditions develop a mass of leaf relatively quickly, plants reaching a height of 4 ft 9 in (1·5 m) in eight to ten years, but with little or no pedestal formation. The development of the latter is very slow, plants with pedestals of a metre high are probably 200 or more years old. In a survey of tussock stocks (Strange, 1987) the author estimated the total remaining area of this grass in the Falkland Islands as 10,272 acres (4159 ha). The estimated area of tussock which originally grew in the archipelago prior to settlement is 54,788 acres (22,181 ha).

Sword Grass or **Cornflag** *Carex trifida* **Pl. 14**

A large robust sedge which grows in association with tussock, usually confined to perimeter areas of the latter. Grows to a height of between 1 ft 7 in (0·5 m) to 3 ft 2 in (1 m). Stems distinctly triangular. Leaves in new growth glaucous green, older outer leaves often deep orange-yellow at tips, turning deep brown and becoming fibrous. Seed spikes reddish-brown or purplish. A rare species, although stands still exist on some outer tussock islands. Early descriptions of this sedge suggest it was probably quite common before the introduction of stock (see *History of depredation*).

Wild Celery *Apium australe* **Pl. 15**

Wild form of celery often found growing in association with tussock. Where the plant grows within the shelter of tussock it can attain a height of 3 ft 2 in (1 m), in exposed situations generally only 4–12 in (10–30 cm) high. Prefers damp situations in coastal regions. A perennial herb, with erect, branched stems of a light green colour. Base of stems often purplish. Flowers white in compound umbels. Stems and root are edible with a typical celery flavour, although slightly bitter.

Tussock island heath formation

This association or plant community is typical of the smaller, offshore islands, where the maritime Tussock Grass formation is interrupted, often by a small central plain of plants typical of some oceanic heath formation. However, these associations generally lack dwarf shrubs, ferns and White Grass. Depending on the elevation, precipitation and other factors, the following species may be dominant or co-dominant. The association may often integrate with the Tussock Grass formation wherever the perimeter of the latter is open or sparse.

Native Woodrush   *Luzula alopecurus*   **Pl. 15**

A small, grass-like, perennial herb with a short rootstock. Densely clothed with leaves 1–4 in (3–10 cm) long, which have dense marginal hairs resembling silvery-white wisps of cotton wool. Leaf colour varies from light green to a rusty-red. Inflorescence usually ovoid, with 1–4 grass-like bracts, the whole being covered with cotton wool-like hairs similar to those on leaves. Stem of flower usually exceeds leaves and can grow up to 12 in (30 cm). Common species, widely distributed amongst oceanic heath and rocky areas. On some tussock island heath it can be dominant. In this more sheltered environment flower stems commonly attain 8 in (20 cm).

Yellow Daisy   *Senecio littoralis*   **Pl. 15**

About 10 in (25 cm) high, erect. Stems usually woody and much branched at base. Leaves without stalks, narrow and pointed, about 1·5 in (4 cm) long, without hairs. Stems and leaves bright shining green. Flower heads solitary, about 1 in (3 cm) in diameter and bright yellow. This endemic species is one of the more showy perennial herbs, flowering November/December. Fairly common in both coastal and inland areas and can be common in tussock island heath formations and open Tussock Grass areas.

Mountain Blue Grass   *Poa alopecurus*   **Pl. 15**

A densely tufted, very erect perennial grass which grows up to 12 in (30 cm) high. Leaves narrow and usually a blueish grey-green with a purplish sheath. Panicle cylindrical to obovoid to oblong-lanceolate, yellowish-brown, tinged purple. May be dominant on some tussock island heath formations, more especially those situated in drier regions to the west of West Falkland. A native species which has probably disappeared from many areas due to over-grazing.

Blue Couch-grass   *Agropyron magellanicum*   **Pl. 15**

Rather loosely tufted with creeping rhyzomes. Deep powder-blue leaves 4–16 in (10–40 cm) long and fairly wide. Spike rigid, often curved and fairly long, 2·75–7·5 in (7–19 cm). Usually found by sea. May form pure stands on some tussock islands, often growing very prostrate, covering ground like a mat. May be locally common, but probably much reduced since the introduction of stock.

Creeping Pratia   *Pratia repens*

A prostrate, glabrous, perennial herb. The shiny, dark green leaves may be

Fig. 73   Creeping Pratia

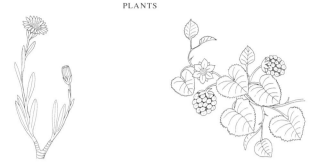

Fig. 74 Marsh Daisy and Wild Strawberry

rounded or ovate to oblong-ovate, with waved edges. Leaves are long-stalked and stems are long, up to 10 in (25 cm), and rooted at nodes. Flowers about 0·4 in (1 cm) and very conspicuous, with a bright lilac corolla and white inside. Corolla and calyx have five unequal petals and lobes, giving the impression that the flower has lost one of each. In exposed situations, or where it is subjected to grazing, creeps very close to the ground. In the sheltered environment of tussock island heath and preferred moist situations the plant often forms mats 2 in (5 cm) deep.

Marsh Daisy *Aster vahlii*

A perennial herb of the family Composita, 4–6 in (10–15 cm) high, usually erect and branched near base. Stems and leaves smooth, densely leafy in basal half, becoming less so towards the flower head above. Leaves narrowly ovate, widening below, pointed and sheaving at the base. Ray-florets a pale purple to rose, sometimes white with yellow disc. Flowers November and December. Grows in damp places amongst White Grass grassland and coastal heath. Is particularly common on some tussock island heath formations where the ground is perpetually wet or damp. Probably less common today than formerly, due to the gradual devegetation and subsequent drying-out of many areas.

Wild Strawberry *Rubus geoides*

Perennial herb with slender, creeping, somewhat woody stems growing to 24 in (60 cm) or more. Stems branched, rooting at nodes. Deep green to yellowish-green leaves on slender stalks, either on main stems or on short lateral branches. Leaves small, about 0·75 in (2 cm) in diameter, oblong to orbicular-ovate, with irregularly toothed edges and hairy on veins on under side. Flowers solitary, white on creamy-white with fine petals (similar to strawberry), formed very close to the ground. Fruit similar to that of a raspberry, about 0·5 in (1·5 cm) in diameter.

Flowers between November and January with fruit ripening late December/February. Locally common in moist, well drained areas of heath. On some tussock island heath it may form pure mats over old tussock hummocks. Probably much reduced on mainlands since the introduction of stock. Edible and although locally referred to as 'Wild Strawberry' the species belongs to the genus Rubus, a form of bramble.

Fen and bog formation

This formation might be better described as low-moor. Here the water table approaches the surface, or may, after heavy rainfalls (usually in winter time) come above and lie on the surface as clear water. The more typical bog, of the type generally associated with those of the northern hemisphere, is not found in the Falklands. In the islands 'bog' is generally a reference to areas of a deep plastic peat topped with a layer of tolerably firm vegetation. Occasionally, small areas of Sphagnum-covered mire, covering a few square metres, are found in depressions or erupting on the shoulders of slopes. Such areas are often distinct, appearing as vivid green or yellowish-green patches against the predominant buffs and browns of other vegetation in the landscape.

Brown Swamp Rush *Rostkovia magellanica*   Pl. 15

Rush-like plant with flowering stems, erect, terete (circular in cross section), bearing solitary terminal flower. Leaves 12–14 in (30–35 cm) high, usually exceeding flowering stems, sharply pointed, narrow, with conspicuous channel. Stems and leaves dark green or brownish-green with a yellowish-brown sheath. Flower subtended by one long bract. Perianth leaves not all equal, narrow and pointed. Grows in wet areas of grassland, often dominant. Can be confused with Tall Rush *Marsippospermum grandiflorum*, although latter has a single laminate leaf per stem and short bracts which do not exceed the perianth and lacks the conspicuous leaf channel. Both form dense stands, preferring moist but well drained soils, often in association with dwarf shrub heath and ferns. Both afford nesting cover for a number of birds.

Fig. 75   Spike Rush and Native Rush

Spike Rush   *Eleocharis melanostachys*

Rush-like perennial herb with a rhizome for creeping, which can form dense stands of stems. Stems terete, usually brown and reddish at base. Grows up to 18 in (45 cm). Sheaths obtuse to subacute, green to yellowish-brown, leafless. Spikelet cylindrical 0·25–0·75 in (0·6–1·7 cm), a dark reddish or brownish-purple, solitary and born on tip of stem. Found growing in shallows of ponds and streams. May form dense stands or mats producing nesting habitat for Rollands Grebe.

Native Rush   *Juncus scheuzerioides*

Perennial herb with long spreading rhizome bearing tufts of leaves. Leaf blade very narrow and grows to about 5·5 in (14 cm), usually exceeding flowering stems. Inflorescence 2–6 flowered, terminal, the outer bract usually larger than inflorescence. Leaves often a deep rich green. Inflorescence reddish-brown. Seed capsule cylindrical-ovoid with a dark shiny brown beak. Very abundant, found in moister areas, often in wet sandy ground at the margins of ponds and streams. Appears in tussock island heath formations having a high water table.

Marsh Marigold   *Caltha sagittata*   **Pl. 15**

Herbaceous plant, with annual stems arising from a perennial rootstock. Stem a creeping or erect rootstock, often thick and fleshy, with thick, fibrous roots. Shiny green leaves ovate to ovate-triangular with long stems. Flowers a pale greenish-white or yellowish, about 1·5 in (4 cm) diameter. Flower stalk varies in length 0·75–8 in (2–20 cm). Fruit a head made up of three or more follicles. Flowers in November and December. Plants may vary greatly in size according to where growing. On the margins of coastal ponds, where it benefits from moisture and from droppings of coastal birds, can form dense mats of growth up to 12 in (30 cm) high.

Sundew   *Drosera uniflora*   **Pl. 15**

Perennial insectivorous herb with leaves covered with small red, gland-tipped, motile hairs which entrap and digest insects. Leaves are small (0·25 in, 0·5 cm in diameter), rounded and long stalked and spread horizontally from a short stock. Plant may be only 0·5 in (1 cm) in diameter. Flower stalks erect, about 0·5 in (1 cm), bearing a single white flower which is conspicuous for the size of the plant. Seed capsule ovoid and smooth. In summer, hairs glisten from a dew-like secretion used to attract insects, hence its common name. Locally common in damp peaty areas, often growing in association with *Astelia* and on the perimeters of Sphagnum bogs.

Astelia pumila

Perennial herbs with male and female flowers forming on different plants. Forms hard, compact carpets which may cover several square metres. Often dominant or co-dominant with Sundew. Leaves narrow to triangular-lanceolate, sharply pointed, rigid and thick with a fringe of coarse hairs on margins and midrib below. Dark shiny green on upper surface, dull below. November/January has 1–3 creamy white flowers on short erect stalk, subtended by greenish-silvery bract. Very common, usually over deep wet peat, where, in winter, the water table may rise to surface levels. Also grows on hills, often to higher elevations.

Littoral zone

For the purpose of this guide the littoral zone is defined as that region of the sea coast lying from the normal high tidemark, extending inland to include areas influenced directly by the sea – areas subjected to sea spray and very occasional flooding, and coast formations built by the action of the sea such as raised storm beaches, shingle spits and beach dunes. This zone may often be dominated by tussock, especially on offshore islands, however, because of its unique form tussock is treated separately under *Maritime Tussock Grass formations*.

Sea Cabbage *Senecio candicans*   Pl. 15
Perennial herb growing to 3 ft 2 in (1 m) high. Very distinctive species with large ovate leaves of a silvery-white colour and a soft woolly surface. Inflorescence or flower heads radiate in clusters, each head on a woolly stalk. Yellow flowers usually appear in late December and seed heads form in late January. In winter, leaves may lose some of their silver-white appearance and turn a light green. Grows in almost pure sand immediately above the tide line. Often forms pure stands.

Spiky Grass *Poa robusta*   Pl. 15
A perennial grass forming stems which lie flat along the ground. Its leaves are very rigid and end in a stiff sharp point. Leaf blade usually rolled inwards, strigose on upper surface. Leaves usually a light blueish-green in new growth, gradually turning to light fawn. Panicle spike-like, usually dense, cylindrical, purplish-green turning yellowish. Grows in exposed coastal situations, often on very thin sandy soils overlying a rocky substrata. Forms pure mats of dense stems and leaves up to 12 in (30 cm) high. Often spongy to walk on and very prickly.

Fig. 76   Astelia pumila

Fig. 77 Native Crassula and Falkland Thrift (Sea Pink)

Native Crassula *Crassula moschata*

Small, succulent herb forming extensive mats. Stems prostrate, rooting at nodes, with erect or ascending leafy branches, green or reddish-purple. Leaves thick and fleshy, ovate-oblong, each pair united at base. Green, but often purplish at base. Grows to about 4 in (10 cm) high, but in exposed positions often prostrate. Flowers form in axils of upper leaves, very small, usually white tinged pinky-red. Common, often growing between or on rocks just above high water mark, where it may be subjected to seaspray. Frequently colonises old nesting sites of gulls and terns where it thrives in accumulations of fine shell grit.

Falkland Thrift or Sea Pink *Armeria macloviana*

A maritime perennial herb with leaves forming a basal rosette from a stout, woody, rootstock. Leaves in tufts, grass-like, about 2–4 in (5–10 cm) in length and very narrow. Dark green with a lighter central vein. Flowers in heads, surrounded by bracts and placed terminally at the end of a long, leafless stalk, about 6 in (15 cm). Rose-pink to mauvish-pink, often fading. Grows close to the sea in sandy areas amongst rocks.

Bush formation

There are only two native species large enough to qualify as bush formations, Native Boxwood and Fachine. However, there are a number of introduced forms, many of these having become valuable nesting habitats for a number of species. Probably the most significant is Gorse *Ulex europaea*, introduced at the time of early settlement and used as a form of fencing for stock. In some areas, especially about settlements, Gorse grows to a height of 5 ft–6 ft 6 in (1·5–2 m), single bushes spreading to some 32 ft (10 m) or more. Forms of *Cupressus macrocarpa*, some species of *Pinus* and a *Veronica* sp. are all introduced and well established in the Islands.

Native Boxwood *Hebe elliptica*   **Pl. 14**

Evergreen shrub growing to 9 ft 6 in (3 m) and up to 16 ft (5 m) in diameter. Woody stems at base, up to 6 in (15 cm) in diameter. Leaves elliptical to elliptic-oblong, apposite in pairs, the pairs alternating with each other. Shiny, light to dark green. Flowers crowded together at top of new growth. Corolla white, sometimes streaked with blue, anthers purple. Widely distributed to settlement areas, both on West Falkland and East Falkland. In its native habitat it is restricted to West Falkland and in particular to a selected group of offshore islands on the west. Grows in coastal areas, often in rocky situations close to the shoreline. May form large stands where it becomes dominant. In a few areas it is co-dominant with Tussock Grass. Probably far more common before introduction of stock. Forms a valuable nesting habitat for Siskins.

Fachine *Chiliotrichum diffusum*   **Pl. 15**

Evergreen shrub growing up to 6 ft 6 in (2 m) in established and ungrazed situations, but frequently 8–12 in (20–30 cm) high. Usually dense, erect growth with many branchlets. Young growth covered with dense grey-white hairs, underside of leaves similar. Top of leaves dark shiny green. Leaves alternate narrow. Flower heads about 0·75–1·25 in (2–3 cm) in diameter with long stalks. White with a yellow disc. Grows in sheltered, moist valleys, often beside streams. May form extensive stands, appearing as a grey-green on the landscape. Locally common but much reduced since the introduction of stock.

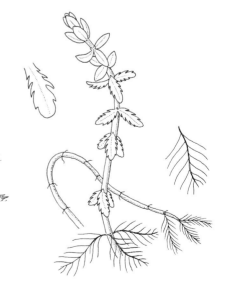

Fig. 78 Tall Rush and Native Water Milfoil

Fresh water vegetation

Although ponds are common to most areas, many appear to be sterile, supporting little or no animal life and devoid of any form of vegetation. In general, ponds associated with coastal greens and those fed by streams are more fertile, often supporting aquatic vegetation.

Native Water-milfoil *Myriophyllum elatinoides*

Perennial, aquatic or semi-aquatic herbs. Stems 4–20 in (10–50) cm or more, rooting at the lower nodes. Leaves formed on stems in a whorl. Submerged leaves pinnatisect, while leaves above water surface are oblong to elliptical or ovate, often reddish. Flower spike 1·25 in (3 cm) also reddish. Forms dense mats in shallow freshwater ponds and in slow-flowing streams or by-waters of some rivers. Often found growing in mud and sand when ponds dry out in summer. An important grazing plant for the Black-necked Swan, the Grebe and probably for some species of duck.

Tall Rush *Scirpus californicus*

A tall, stout rush-like perennial herb. Develops a robust, creeping rhizome. Stems, erect and triangular, reaching a height of 9 ft 6 in (3 m). New growth a dark green, changing to light brown. Stems have very spongy texture inside with numerous air canals. Branched inflorescence reddish-brown in colour. Very distinct species by virtue of its height, being the largest of the rush-like plants found in the islands. Forms very dense stands in muddy shallows of ponds and lagoons. A rare species, but where it does exist it provides a nesting habitat for grebe and Night Herons.

Oceanic heath formation

Most of the Falkland Islands are covered by some facies of the plant communities under this formation. Most of the communities integrate producing a very complex variety of facies, there are, however, a number of more striking associations. Flying over the main islands, or viewing the landscape from some hilltop, many of the different plant communities and associations are evident by their colour alone. The dominant colour, a light buffish-yellow, arises from White Grass. Even during the summer it never appears green, the growing point normally being covered by a mass of dead leaf. White Grass is the most widespread of all types of vegetation on both level and undulating areas of 'camp' or countryside below 328 ft (100 m). Contrasting with these meadows are irregular patches of dark brown – these are generally formed by Diddle-dee heath, a dwarf shrub which grows on comparatively dry, well-drained areas, usually hard dry peat. Diddle-dee heath, with associated dwarf shrubs such as Christmas Bush and Mountain Berry, is the most common association after White Grass.

In some moister areas of the heath, patches of dark green usually denote the mat-like growth of *Astelia*. *Blechnum* fern may be dominant or co-dominant, especially on higher slopes below the quartzite ridges, and cover large areas of the hillsides, often distinct by its dark browny-green colour. Of the large number of species which appear in the Oceanic Heath formation, a few of the common and more interesting forms are described below.

Diddle-dee or Red Crowberry *Empetrum rubrum* Pl. 15

Small, evergreen, heath-like shrub. Stems 4–20 in (10–50 cm) in length. Much branched, procumbent to ascending. Leaves not stalked, very crowded, oblong to oblong-ovate and hairy with turned back margins. Lower leaves often reddish and upper leaves dark green. Stems in large plants often twisted, deeply grooved, reddish-brown. Male and female flowers on different plants. Sepals yellow to orange often with red tips. Petals in female flowers dark brownish-red, in male flowers crimson. Anthers and (long) filaments crimson. Stigma dark purple. Flowers in October. Fruits often in dense clusters, globose, red to maroon. Dominant species, very common on drier, well-drained soils at nearly all altitudes. Berry edible, often used to make a preserve. Has a sweet but rather bitter tang. An important feed for Upland Geese and some seed-eating passerines.

Teaberry or Malvina Berry *Myrteola nummularia* Pl. 15

A common species in most dwarf shrub heath, especially in damper regions. Dwarf evergreen shrub with woody, straggling stems up to 16 in (40 cm) which lie prostrate, often intertwining to form extensive patches. Leaves tough shining green, elliptical to rotund. Stalks short or absent. Flowers small, insignificant and solitary, usually towards end of branches. White or creamish-white. Berry, up to 0·25 in (0·8 cm) in diameter, usually a delicate pink with red highlights, underside of berry usually white. Edible, sweet with a mild scented flavour, often collected in autumn and used for culinary purposes. Also grazed by Upland Geese and by seed-eating species such as Black-throated Finches. Probably an important winter food, as the berries hang into mid winter. The common name of 'Teaberry' originates from the late 1700s, when sealers and whalers used the leaves of the plant as a substitute for tea.

Gaultheria *Gaultheria microphylla* Pl. 15

Small evergreen shrub with stems about 8 in (20 cm) long. Much branched, prostrate to ascending or erect. Leaves ovate to elliptic-oblong with thick and toothed margins. Flowers solitary on a recurved stalk. Calyx-lobes purplish, corolla white or pinkish. Flowers November/January. Fruit, globose to pear-shaped, white or pink. Found in dwarf shrub heath, but not common. May be known also as Mountain Berry and might be confused with this plant.

Mountain Berry *Pernettya pumila* Pl. 15

Small evergreen shrub with stems up to 24 in (60 cm). Much branched, usually prostrate or ascending but rarely erect. Leaves alternate, not stalked, ovate to elliptic-ovate, entire or toothed. Shiny green, terminal leaves sometimes reddish.

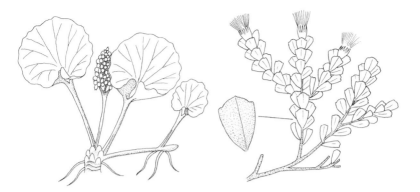

Fig. 79 Pig Vine and Christmas Bush showing enlarged leaf form

Flowers solitary on stalk recurved towards apex. Calyx green to purple, corolla white or sometimes pinkish. Fruit a berry, globose, whitish with a bluish to purplish tinge. Berries may be confused with those of Teaberry. An abundant species found in dwarf shrub heath.

Christmas Bush *Baccharis magellanica*

Dwarf evergreen shrub with male and female flowers on separate plants. Stems up to 10 in (25 cm). Usually grows prostrate often in cover of Diddle-dee heath or White Grass meadows. Stems much branched, slightly rough to touch, sticky when young. Leaves without stalks may vary in size and be entire or toothed, wedge-shaped, light green. Flower heads unstalked, solitary and terminal. Dense head-like inflorescence, yellowish-white, larger on female plants, with many long, slender hairs giving the flower a distinct brush-like appearance. Flowers in late December/January. Very abundant in both dwarf shrub heath and in White Grass meadow.

Pig Vine *Gunnera magellanica*

Perennial herb with male and female flowers on separate plants. Stems prostrate, branched and fleshy, rooting at nodes, up to 12 in (30 cm) in length. Leaves and stolons produced at apex of stem and branches. Leaves kidney-shaped up to 3 in (8 cm) in diameter with regular, rounded teeth to their edges. Smooth on upper surface, hairy on underside, leaf stalks also hairy. Leaves often grow close to ground but in sheltered and damp situations may grow to 8 in (20 cm) or more in height. Deep green with reddish stalks. Male flowers have stalks and spike is longer than leaves. Female spikes are short and flowers have no stalks. Fruit a drupe, forming a cluster, brilliant scarlet and quite distinct.Very common, found in all communities, but very luxuriant in damp, sheltered, coastal situations. Fruit eaten by some birds.

Fig. 80   Pale Maiden and Almond Flower

Scurvy Grass or **Vinaigrette**   *Oxalis enneaphylla*   **Pl. 15**

Perennial herbs, with fleshy stock producing a bulb-like rhizome. Stems about 4 in (10 cm) long, leaf and flower stalks about 10 in (25 cm), usually smooth and slender, pale green to reddish-pink. Leaflets orbicular in outline, between 4 and 20 radiate from apex of stalks. Leaves a light glaucous-green. Flower stalks have two leaf-like bracts. Flowers showy with five white, pink or pale pinky-mauve obovate petals, and about 1·75 in in diameter (4 cm). Sepals small and pale green. Flowers November/January. Widespread in dwarf shrub heath near coasts. Often grows through or between cover of Diddle-dee. May be prolific in stands of Spiky Grass. Varies greatly in size depending on situation. Edible. The stalks of leaves and flowers have antiscorbutic properties and were thus used by early mariners to prevent scurvy, hence its common name.

Native Pansy   *Viola maculata*   **Pl. 14**

Perennial herb, stems usually short. Leaves have long stalk, are ovate to ovate-lanceolate and grow up to 1·75 in (4 cm) long. Edges of leaves waved, sparsely hairy. Flower stalk long, about 4 in (10 cm), slender, slightly hairy and bears a pair of stipules. Flowers yellow with fine petals. Flowers in December. Usually grows on dry coastal slopes amongst Diddle-dee heath.

Pale Maiden   *Sisyrinchium filifolium*

Perennial herb with rhizome. Leaves very narrow and pointed, rather rigid and sheathed at base. Leafless stalk usually exceeds height of leaves. Flowers grow in a terminal cluster of between two and eight on very slender stems exserted from a spathe. They are pendulous and nodding. Petals white with green or purplish veins. Seed capsule globose, orange-brown, opening into three valves. Abundant

Fig. 81   Vanilla Daisy and Lady's Slipper

and very distinct in the spring (November) when their delicate, bell-like flowers stand out against a background of Diddle-dee heath. The rare *S. chilense* is much smaller with one to two flowers which are yellow with brownish veins. Flower stems are more erect, only occasionally nodding slightly.

Almond Flower   *Enargea marginata*
Prostrate perennial. Stems rather woody at base. Shoots are herbaceous. Stems may spread several feet, lower stems often blanched, or reddish, rooting at nodes. Leaves oblong or elliptical, almost almond-shaped, tapering to a fine point. Light glossy green to glaucous green on top, lighter below. Margins of leaves thickened and tough, cymbiform. Flowers white, solitary and bell-shaped, born on short slender stalks in axils of terminal leaves and facing downwards over upper leaf surface. Very fragrant with scent of almonds. Flowers November/December. Berry globose and a glossy dark purple. A common species, often creeping under cover of Diddle-dee and in rock crevices of 'stone runs'.

Vanilla Daisy   *Leuceria suaveolens*
Perennial herb. Stems when flowering 4–12·5 in (10–32cm), covered with dense, white, woolly hairs. Leaves erect, arising from root or stem, oblong to oblong-oblanceolate, deeply indented almost to the mid-vein and the segments have rounded tips. Underside of leaves covered with woolly hairs, less so on upper surface, but giving leaves a light greeny-grey appearance. Flower head terminal about 1·75 in (4 cm) in diameter, white with scent of vanilla. Flowers in December and January. An endemic species growing in sheltered situations often between clumps of Diddle-dee heath or *Blechnum* fern.

Lady's Slipper *Calceolaria fothergillii*

Perennial herb. Very hairy, with ovate-oblong or obovate leaves about 0·75 in (2 cm) long on short stalk. Flowers solitary, on long hairy stalks about 4 in (10 cm) high, very erect. Five sepals, resembling leaves. Corolla, upper lip shorter than sepals and yellow. Lower lip much longer, forming a 'slipper', usually yellow with red streaks inside and a broad red line around edge of lip. May be almost entirely red or entirely yellow with small red spots. Flowers December and January. Seed capsule ovoid-conical, brown, often remaining on dry stems late into the season. Locally common on some well-drained coastal slopes, amongst Diddle-dee heath. The much rarer *C. biflora* has a much shorter stem bearing a rosette of leaves. Flower stalk grows to 5·5 in (14 cm), erect, sparsely hairy with 2–5 flowers on short terminal stalks. Flowers yellow. Coastal regions, but rare.

White Orchid *Codonorchis lessonii*

Small orchid about 6 in (15 cm) in height. Has tuberous rhizome. Stem smooth with 3–4 leaves forming a whorl about the middle of the stem's height. Leaves, broadly ovate with apex more or less rounded; stalks short, deep green in colour. Single flower born on apex of stem about 1·25 in (3 cm) across, white with greenish mid-veins, purplish towards the base of segments. Inner segments of flower have purplish blotches. Seed capsule cylindrical to cylindrical-ellipsoid, dark purplish-brown. Flowers November to January. Usually found growing amongst dwarf heath and fern on moist but well-drained soils.

Fig. 82 White Orchid and Dusty Miller Primrose

Fig. 83   Small Fern and Fuegian Tall Fern

Dusty Miller Primrose   *Primula magellanica*

Perennial herb about 6·75 in (17 cm) high. Stem underground, bearing at ground level a group of basal leaves, spoon-shaped or ovate, narrowing gradually into stalk about 1·25 in (3 cm) long. Margins of leaves scalloped, pale green above, white and mealy on underside. Flower stalk erect and long, standing well above leaves. Stalk light green, often with white mealy coating. Flowers form a globose head born at terminal of stem. White, tinged with pale lilac and a yellow centre. Flowers during October and November. Locally common in dwarf shrub heath. Some of the finest examples are found on well drained slopes on Split Island, West Falkland, where they grow between Mountain Blue Grass.

White Grass   *Cortaderia pilosa*   **Pl. 14**

Very common, forming low dense tussocks up to about 12 in (30 cm). Leaves usually convolute, tapering to fine point. Tussocks somewhat deflexed and hemispherical. Flower spikelets large, somewhat compressed, with long, white, silky hairs. As its common name suggests, generally has a whiteish, light buff appearance. Most common, and in vegetative terms most important and dominant species in the islands. Forms very extensive 'meadows' on the main islands, but is noticeably absent from smaller offshore islands.

Cinnamon Grass   *Hierochloë redolens*   **Pl. 14**

A large grass, forming clumps with somewhat pendulous growth. Grows to a height of about 24–28 in (60–70 cm). Leaves wide and flat but edges of leaves towards apex often rolled inwards. Upper leaf surface glaucous green and ribbed, underside shiny green. Leaves often turn a deep reddish colour towards apex. Panicle 2·5–3·5 in (6 to 9 cm), lanceolate-cylindrical, pendulous and nodding, brownish-purple. Fairly common, forming dense stands in some areas. Prefers damp situations. Probably very common before introduction of stock. In summer, when new growth is forming, has scent of cinnamon. Important habitat for some ground-nesting species.

Small Fern *Blechnum penna-marina*

Small fern with slender rhizome, spreading to form extensive and sometimes dense mats up to 6 in (15 cm) deep. Stems naked, fronds hard and tough, narrowly lanceolate, deeply indented to form leaflets with a wide base and rounded apex. Barren fronds about 4 in (10 cm) long. Fertile fronds larger with smaller, narrower leaflets placed further apart on stems. In early summer, fronds are light green or reddish, gradually changing to a dark glossy green. Very common, often dominant both in coastal heath and in tussock island dwarf heath formations.

Fuegian Tall Fern *Blechnum magellanicum*

Rhizome erect, very stout and woody often forming a 'trunk' over 12 in (30 cm) high and covered with bases of old leaf stalks. Leaves pinnate, sterile leaves ascending to 5 ft (1·5 m) in height. Stalk one quarter to one third of total length of leaf, densely covered in stiff, dark brown, hair-like scales. Fertile leaves erect, equalling or rather shorter than sterile ones, leaflets narrower and, when mature, completely covered with sori. In early summer, young fronds come up bright golden-red, orange-yellow or bright red, gradually deepening to dark green. Common in dwarf shrub heath. May form 'beds' on hillsides.

Feldmark formation

Above 1968 ft (600 m) the dwarf shrub heath generally gives way to formations dominated by cushion plants, those more typical of Alpine Heath. Such regions are also characterised by larger areas of exposed, often thin, stony soils. Several plants may be found growing in these situations, although only two appear to be confined to the higher elevations.

Balsam Bog *Bolax gummifera*

Perennial herb forming very dense, hard cushions, usually hemispherical. Cushions may grow over 3 ft 2 in (1 m) high and 6 ft 4 in (2 m) in diameter. Exterior of cushion composed of stems densely covered with leaves. Leaves alternate, three-lobed, closely overlapping like roof tiles. Centre of cushion composed of decaying leaves into which roots penetrate. Leaves green with light glaucous highlight. Flower a simple umbel, greenish-white. In summer the cushions exude droplets of a sticky white latex which changes to reddish-brown as it dries. Grows in rocky areas, often in feldmark, but extends to lower coastal dwarf shrub heath. On some offshore islands, especially in drier western regions, can be dominant, taking place of tussock island heath formations.

Cushion Plant *Azorella selago*

Perennial herb, forming dense cushions 4–24 in (10–60 cm) high and up to 3 ft 2 in (1 m) in diameter. Stems ascending to erect, branched and close-set, covered with remains of leaves. Leaves overlap closely and are broadly and shortly

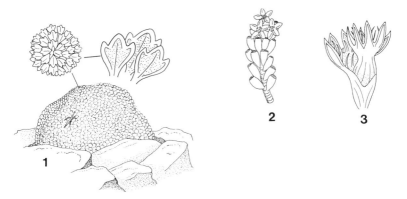

Fig. 84 Feldmark plants: 1 Balsam Bog showing dense cushion of plant and enlarged rosette and leaf; 2, Section of Fleshy Cushion Plant, flowers and leaves; and 3, Leaves of Cushion Plant

obovate in outline and dissected into three to five 'fork like' leaflets which are divided nearly to the base. Cushions often disintegrate inside, the living parts forming the outer crust. Umbels 2–3 flowered, yellowish-white. Locally common but only found at higher elevations in feldmark formations.

Fleshy Cushion Plant   *Valeriana sedifolia*

Cushion-forming perennial herb with male and female flowers on different plants. Plant forms dense cushions 6–24 in (15–60 cm) in diameter. Stems much branched, especially towards apex, and closely pressed. Leaves overlapping, cylindrical, thick and fleshy particularly at apex, smooth but hairy at base. Bright pale green, purple near base. Flowers 3–7 appearing at top of branches. Corolla 5 lobed, yellow. Flowers in December. Feldmark on highest elevations.

Marine algae: the sublittoral formation

For the purposes of this guide the sublittoral has been divided into three main zones. Each zone supports a number of different marine algae, of which the more important species are described. Offshore, in depths of 13–98 ft (4–30 m), is a zone supporting the giant kelp *Macrocystis pyrifera* and the tree kelp *Lessonia flavicans*, probably the two most common forms of marine algae in the islands. Between the extreme low water mark and extending offshore to waters about 9 ft 6 in – 12 ft 8 in (3–4 m) deep is a fringe zone. This is inhabited by two other large forms of kelp, two species of *Lessonia* and two species of *Durvillea*. Generally this zone lies in an area extending out from the lower shoreline to some 98 ft (30 m) deep. Kelps growing on the upper fringes of this belt are often exposed at low water. The third zone lies in the intertidal areas, the middle shore between average high and low water levels. This area supports some of the smaller marine algae which are exposed with the fall of each tide.

Giant Kelp or Basket Kelp   *Macrocystis pyrifera*   Pl. 16

A very common species, found in cool, coastal waters of the southern hemisphere and off Pacific North America. The most widespread and most common species of marine algae in the Falkland Islands. A large species, single strands growing to over 197 ft (60 m) in length. Forms a root system of tangled, much branched fibres, commonly found washed ashore. In their dry form they resemble clumps of intertwined wicker basket work, usually light brown in colour and measuring up to 3 ft 2 in (1 m) in diameter.

A growing root system attaches itself to stones and boulders on the sea bed. From the roots, stems arise which support fronds, each frond or 'leaf' stretching from pneumatocysts, small gas-filled bladders that keep the fronds afloat. Fronds are oblong-lanceolate, with finely toothed margins and a somewhat waved or wrinkled surface. New growth is a golden yellowish-brown, darkening in older fronds. Generally forms a wide belt of growth, one to two hundred metres wide in the offshore zone. In some regions beds may be very extensive, to 0·6 miles (1 km) or more. From a distance appears as a brown to golden-brown shadow on surface. In very calm conditions a natural excretion may give an oily, slick appearance to the water's surface. Forms a very important habitat for marine life on which a number of birds and mammals feed.

Tree Kelp   *Lessonia* sp.   Pl. 16

Three species of *Lessonia* are known to exist in the Falkland Islands; *L. flavicans*, *L. frutescens* and *L. nigrescens*. The distribution and status of the individual species is not clear, although it is probable that *L. flavicans* is the most common. In general, *Lessonia* is an abundant kelp found on most open coasts. Holdfast, or root system, is branched, ascending to many branched stems. Stems may often be free of leaves, standing semi-erect, like branches of a tree. Leaves lack pneumatocysts (air-sacs), are lanceolate to lanceolate-oblong, about 20 in (50 cm), entire or toothed and smooth. Also form in bunches. In *L. nigrescens* leaves are long and thin, with slightly serrated edges. The stipe or stems are dark to blackish and may reach some 9 ft 6 in (3 m) in length. *L. frustescens* has shorter, broader leaves and is a yellowish-brown colour. The stipe or stems of this species are very short causing the leaves to lie just above the substratum. *L. flavicans* is found in deeper water, usually associated with beds of *Macrocystis*. It is the only species which cannot be seen from the shoreline. Mature plants may reach several metres in height with trunk-like stems 4–6 in (10–15 cm) in diameter. The blades or leaves are generally long, 16 in (40 cm), and thin with serrated edges. Colour may vary from dark brown to a golden yellow. *L. flavicans* is more commonly observed as storm cast stems on shorelines. Beds of *Lessonia* are often composed of dense masses of stems and leaves forming in a fringe zone between the low water mark and commencement of offshore zone occupied by *Macrocystis*. An important habitat for many forms of marine life.

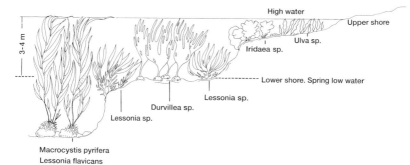

Fig. 85 Sublittoral zones with general growing position of marine algae species

Durvillea sp.   Pl. 16

A very large-fronded form of marine alga belonging to the order *Fucales*. Although kelp-like and generally referred to as a kelp, it is in fact a seaweed. Two species are known from the Falkland Islands: *D. antarctica*, a species with long, thin, rather flattened stem-like fronds, bright green to dark green in colour; and *D. caepestipes* with leaves that resemble huge irregularly shaped pieces of leather. This latter species may vary in colour from dark green to golden reddish-brown. Both forms have short thick stems which arise from an inverted saucer-shaped disc which forms the holdfast or root. *D. caepestipes* commonly grows on rocky shores in the fringe zone of more sheltered waters. It is often partly exposed at very low water. *D. antarctica* more commonly grows at a slightly lower level. The status of these two forms is not yet clear, some authorities believing *D. caepaestipes* to be a morphological variation of *D. antarctica*.

Iridaea sp.   Pl. 16

Grows in intertidal areas and below. Often forms dense patches, attaching to stones and rocks. Thin, short stem bears a number of individual leaves, roughly semi-circular in shape, 12 in (30 cm) by up to 16 in (40 cm) high. Leaves appear very irregular in outline due to crinkling and waving of frond. Basal regions of the younger lateral fronds appear very dark, purplish-brown, even black when dry. Outer parts of larger leaves appear light brown-green to golden-brown. When damp, dark areas appear iridescent. Plant has a very elastic nature but is easily torn. Beds grazed by Kelp Geese and occasionally Upland Geese. Edible, may be eaten raw or cooked by frying.

Sea Lettuce   *Ulva* sp.   Pl. 16

Grows in similar form to *Iridaea* but leaves more elongated, rather thin, and an almost transparent deep green colour and more fragile. Grows in intertidal areas, below and to about medium tide level. Appears variable in height, but generally

10–12 in (25–30 cm) up to 20 in (50 cm). Common, but generally found in less exposed positions. Grazed by Kelp Geese. Often appears as detached leaves on some sand beaches. Edible, can be eaten raw or cooked by frying.

Botanical Glossary

Axil   the angle between the leaf and the upper part of the stem.

Bracts   modified leaf with a single flower or inflorescence growing in leaf axil.

Calyx   whorl of leaves (sepal) forming outer case of a bud.

Corolla   whorl of leaves (petals) forming inner envelope of flower.

Convolute   rolled together longitudinally.

Cryptogams   plant having no proper flowers.

Cymbiform   boat-shaped, leaf with edges rolled inward.

Drupe   fleshy, one-seeded indehiscent (does not open to release seed) fruit, with seed enclosed in stony endocarp.

Elliptical   shape of ellipse, widest at middle and more than twice as long as wide.

Ellipsoid   of a solid object elliptical in section or outline.

Floret   one of small flowers making up a composite flower.

Follicle   a dry dehiscent fruit opening on one side.

Glabrous   without hairs.

Glaucous   blueish green colour.

Globose   spherical, globular form.

Holdfast   usually disc-shaped ground attachment of kelp (*Durvillea sp*) or bunch of ramifying strong root-like processes forming attachment.

Lanceolate   lance-shaped.

Lobed   partly divided into number of segments.

Motile-hairs   hairs capable of motion (see sundew).

Nodes   place on stem at which leaves spring.

Obovoid   ovoid shape attached at narrow end.

Obtuse   of blunt form with angle greater than 90°.

Orbicular   rounded in outline.

Ovate   egg-shaped attached by the wider end.

Ovoid   superficially egg-shaped, oval with one end more pointed.

Panicle   branched inflorescence.

Perianth   sepals and petals considered together forming floral envelope.

Petiole   stalk of a leaf.

Pinnate   when simple leaflets are arranged on each side of a common petiole.

Pinnatisect   from pinnate but with leaflet divisions reaching midrib.

Pneumatocysts   air sacs on stems and leaves of giant kelp.

Procumbent   growing along the ground.

Rhizome   underground stem.

Rootstock   tissue forming base of roots.

Sessile   without a stalk.

Sheath   basal part of the leaf enclosing a stem.

Sori   plural for sorus, group of sporangia on frond of a fern.

Spathe   large bract or pair of bracts enveloping flower head.

Spikelet   cluster of many sessile flowers arranged closely on common axis as in grasses.

Stand   reference to standing growth of tussock grass.

Stipules   pair of leaf-like appendages at base of petiole.

Stock   tissue at the junction of the root and stem.

Stolons   an overground creeping stem rooted at nodes.

Strigose   with sharp stiff opressed hairs and bristles.

Subacute   slightly or not quite sharply pointed.

Sublittoral   marine region lying off the shore.

Subtend   to have a bud or flower growing in axil.

Terete   circular in cross-section.

Umbels   flat or convex inflorescence umbrella-like.

Selected Bibliography

BAKER, A. N.   Whales and Dolphins of New Zealand and Australia (Victoria University Press, 1983)

"DISCOVERY" REPORTS   Vol. XVI, Coast Fishes (1937).

FRASER, N.   Giant Fishes Whales and Dolphins (1937, 1948)

HARRISON, P.   Seabirds (Croom Helm, 1983).

HAYMAN, P., MARCHANT, J. and PRATER, T.   Shorebirds (Croom Helm, 1986)

LEATHERWOOD, S. and REEVES, R.   The Sierra Club Handbook of Whales and Dolphins (1983).

MADGE, S. and BURN, H.   Wildfowl (Croom Helm, 1988)

MOORE, D. M.   Vascular Flora of the Falkland Islands (British Antarctic Survey Scientific Report No. 60, 1967).

MURPHY, Dr. C.   Oceanic Birds of South America. Vols. I and II (1936).

PERNETTY, D.   Histoire d'un Voyage aux Isles Malouines fait en 1763 et 1764 (1770)

SKOTTSBERG, C.   A Botanical Survey of the Falkland Islands (1907–09).

STRANGE, I. J.   The Falkland Islands (David and Charles, 1972, 1981, 1983)
The Bird Man (Gordon & Cremonesi, 1977)
Penguin World (Dodd, Mead USA, 1981)
The Falklands: South Atlantic Islands (Dodd, Mead USA, 1985)
The Falkland Islands and Their Natural History (David & Charles, 1987)
Breeding Ecology of the Rockhopper Penguin (*Eudyptes crestatus*) in the Falkland Islands (Le Gerfaut, 1982)
The Thin-Billed Prion, *Pachyptila belcheri*, at New Island, Falkland Islands (Le Gerfaut, 1980)
Sealion Survey in the Falklands (Oryx, November 1979)
Tussock Grass Survey in the Falkland Islands (Falkland Islands Government/ Falkland Islands Foundation report, July 1987)
The Striated Caracara (National Geographic Society; in preparation)
Conservation and Environmental Assessment Report 1989
Sea Lion Survey in the Falkland Islands 1990.

VALLENTIN, E. F.   The Flowering Plants of the Falkland Islands (1921).

WOODS, R.   The Birds of the Falkland Islands (Anthony Nelson, 1975, 1982, 1988).

INDEX

This index lists species and a selection of subjects from the introduction, and all main accounts in the identification sections. **Bold** type indicates main entries and colour plates (pl.); numbers in *italics* refer to pages with figures or photographs.